Obadiah through
Malachi

Westminster Bible Companion

Series Editors
Patrick D. Miller
David L. Bartlett

Obadiah
through Malachi

WILLIAM P. BROWN

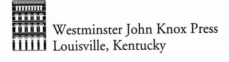
Westminster John Knox Press
Louisville, Kentucky

Book design by Publishers' WorkGroup
Cover design by Drew Stevens

First edition
Published by Westminster John Knox Press
Louisville, Kentucky

This book is printed on acid-free paper that meets the American National Standards Institute Z39.48 standard. ∞

PRINTED IN THE UNITED STATES OF AMERICA

96 97 98 99 00 01 02 03 04 05 — 10 9 8 7 6 5 4 3 2 1

Library of Congress Cataloging-in-Publication Data

Brown, William P., date.
    Obadiah through Malachi / William P. Brown, — 1st ed.
        p.   cm — (Westminster Bible companion)
    Includes bibliographical references.
    ISBN 0-664-25520-5 (alk. paper)
        1. Bible.   O.T. Minor Prophets—Commentaries.   I. Bible.   O.T.
    Minor Prophets.   English.   New Revised Standard.   Selections.
    1996.   II. Title.   III. Series.
    BS1560.B75   1996
    224'.9077—dc20   96-17773

Contents

Contents

Series Foreword

This series of study guides to the Bible is offered to the church and more specifically to the laity. In daily devotions, in church school classes, and in listening to the preached word, individual Christians turn to the Bible for a sustaining word, a challenging word, and a sense of direction. The word that scripture brings may be highly personal as one deals with the demands and surprises, the joys and sorrows, of daily life. It also may have broader dimensions as people wrestle with moral and theological issues that involve us all. In every congregation and denomination, controversies arise that send ministry and laity alike back to the Word of God to find direction for dealing with difficult matters that confront us.

A significant number of lay women and men in the church also find themselves called to the service of teaching. Most of the time they will be teaching the Bible. In many churches, the primary sustained attention to the Bible and the discovery of its riches for our lives have come from the ongoing teaching of the Bible by persons who have not engaged in formal theological education. They have been willing, and often eager, to study the Bible in order to help others drink from its living water.

This volume is part of a series of books, the Westminster Bible Companion, intended to help the laity of the church read the Bible more clearly and intelligently. Whether such reading is for personal direction or for the teaching of others, the reader cannot avoid the difficulties of trying to understand these words from long ago. The scriptures are clear and clearly available to everyone as they call us to faith in the God who is revealed in Jesus Christ and as they offer to every human being the word of salvation. No companion volumes are necessary in order to hear such words truly. Yet every reader of scripture who pauses to ponder and think further about any text has questions that are not immediately answerable simply by reading the text of scripture. Such questions may be about historical and geographical details or about words that are obscure or so loaded with meaning that one cannot tell at a glance what is at stake. They may be about the fundamental meaning of a passage or about what connection a particular text might have to our contemporary world. Or a teacher preparing for a church school class may simply want to know: What should I say about this biblical passage when I have to teach it next Sunday? It is our hope that these volumes, written by teachers and pastors with long experience studying and teaching the Bible in the church, will help members of the church who want and need to study the Bible with their questions.

The New Revised Standard Version of the Bible is the basis for the interpretive comments that each author provides. The NRSV text is presented at the beginning of the discussion so that the reader may have at hand in a single volume both the scripture passage and the exposition of its meaning. In some instances, where inclusion of the entire passage is not necessary for understanding either the text or the interpreter's discussion, the presentation of the NRSV text may be abbreviated. Usually, the whole of the biblical text is given.

We hope this series will serve the community of faith, opening the Word of God to all the people, so that they may be sustained and guided by it.

Introduction

It must be admitted up front that this particular group of biblical books does not inspire immediate relevance to the modern church member as do, say, Genesis through Deuteronomy or Matthew through John. Indeed for much of my career as an interpreter of the Bible, I deliberately avoided this mishmash of minor prophets. Recite this list of prophets and, granted, a couple of them may come to mind like Jonah and Micah, but who has recently heard a sermon from Obadiah or Haggai or Nahum? On the whole, these prophets of the canonical margins always seemed to me to pale in significance before those more central books of the Bible that told of God's dramatic deliverance of the Hebrew slaves or of God's creating the cosmos or of Christ's life and ministry. These were not just minor prophets by comparison; they were *tiny* prophets! What, then, were these obscure figures doing in the Bible anyway? That question nagged me for quite some time until I was given, no doubt providentially, the opportunity to write about them. So began my journey into the unfamiliar.

I learned on that journey that great things do indeed come in small packages. Reading these books was like being there when the prophet first proclaimed and agonized over God's words. Taken together, these nine prophets cover roughly two centuries' worth of the torturous history of God's people, from the impending threat of Assyria in the eighth century through the pain of the Babylonian exile in the sixth to the hopeful age of restoration in the late sixth and early fifth centuries. It was a history of painful wrenchings and surprising opportunities for God's chosen people, and the prophets were not immune to any of it. Far from being impassive, head-in-the-clouds spectators, these prophets were intimately bound up with the travails and needs of their community. These historical figures were as much the products of their age as they were God's own emissaries. Their words were words on target in times of crisis and complacency. Neither empty platitudes nor vague, timeless truths, the prophets' words were arrows shot from God's quiver (see Isa. 49:2).

What I also found surprising was that the human side of these prophets clearly shone forth. Overlooking the proud city of Nineveh, Jonah pouts under a bush once he realizes that God's mercy far outreaches divine judgment. Habakkuk shakes his fist at God over the rampant injustice he finds in Jerusalem. Nahum smacks his lips over Assyria's imminent destruction. However, when it came to irrevocable judgment against their own people, the prophets did not gloat, though they easily could have. They did not gleefully run around with placards proclaiming the end was near. Micah sums it up best: "For this I will lament and wail; I will go barefoot and naked" (Mic. 1:8; cf. Isa. 20:1–6). The prophets were bound up with the fate of their people, even in judgment. Solidarity was their vocation.

Yet that was not all there was to their calling. Diverse as they were, these prophets were God's earthly messengers, entrusted with the delivery of God's word. Each had a message to proclaim about God's ardent determination to redeem and save a people who had given up all resolve. Micah's first utterance is a commanding summons that calls his people to account: "Hear, you peoples . . . listen, O earth," the court of God is now in session. Yet there were those who had to be forcibly arraigned, while others had to be convinced that God was up to the task. "The Lord will not do good, nor will he do harm," Zephaniah's complacent audience presumed (Zeph. 1:12). To them God was, figuratively speaking, dead and gone, that is to say, indifferent to the ways of his people. Zephaniah, however, proved otherwise when he heralded the refining fire of God's passion (1:18; 3:8). Treating God's resolve as an empty promise, Nahum's audience had given up all hope for God's power to rescue them from Assyria's mighty grip. Yet through his words, Nahum brought his audience to see for themselves the defeated king of Assyria (Nah. 3:18–19). Calling God to account, Habakkuk bitterly complained that God was up to no good. Nevertheless, this prophet was struck with rapturous awe over God's beneficent plans for his people (Hab. 3:2). For Jonah, on the other hand, God's grace came as a scandal. This God to which the prophets point has a habit of circumventing human expectations, of wringing hope out of despair and refining our raw pride into humble openness.

Each in his own way, these prophets disclosed God as both judge and savior who directs the course of history in surprising ways. Even the most sweeping of judgments (for example, Mic. 3:2; Zeph. 1:2–3) has its saving aims. Judgment and salvation, these prophets proclaim, are the flip sides of God's zealous love for the children of Zion (Zeph. 3:8; Zech. 8:2). Such fierce regard can prompt even God to have a change of mind on occasion (Jon. 3:10), opting for mercy over judgment. Yet for that very reason God is proclaimed as never-changing (Mal. 3:6). Passionate in sovereignty and sovereign in love, God is, the prophets attest, utterly incomparable: "Who is a God like you, pardoning iniquity and passing over the transgression of the remnant of your possession? He does not retain his anger forever, because he delights in showing clemency" (Mic. 7:18; cf. Hos. 11:9).

For each prophet it was God's credibility in the world that was ultimately at stake, as it still is today. Where is the God of justice and mercy? What is God up to these days? What are we, in turn, to do? These neglected prophets invite us to come and see.

Obadiah

Introduction

The prophecy of Obadiah issues harsh judgment against an erstwhile oppressor of God's people. Having a distinctively narrow focus, the book of Obadiah addresses a particular set of events in Israel's history. Yet comprising only 21 verses, the shortest book of the Old Testament broaches the larger issues of judgment and salvation, of justice and restoration with a vision of history's consummation. Obadiah's enduring ethical message can be summed up in the terse statement in verse 15: "As you have done, it shall be done to you." This proverbial statement serves as the rationale for and basis of God's judgment.

Nothing much is known about the prophet himself. His name carries the meaning "servant of the Lord," an appropriate name for any prophet of God. The historical particularity of his message suggests a time soon after Judah's exile by the Babylonians (586–538 B.C.). Obadiah's prophecy of judgment targets one particular people, namely Edom, located in southern Palestine, east of the Arabah (the valley between the Dead Sea and the Red Sea). This desert nation had a love/hate relationship with Israel throughout their respective turbulent histories. Indeed, the book of Genesis traces the tension back to a very early time in history with the sibling rivalry between Jacob and Esau (see "brother Jacob" in Obad. 10; cf. Mal. 1:2–4). Whereas Jacob later came to be known as Israel (Gen. 32:28), Esau became the founder of Edom. Evidently, the strained relations between Israel and Edom came to a head at the time of Israel's exile by Babylon in 586 B.C., for Obadiah accuses Edom of betrayal and injury "on the day of [Judah's] misfortune" (v. 11–14). It is from this vivid memory of Edom's atrocities against God's people that Obadiah issues his judgment (cf. Psalm 137:7). The prophet announces judgment, however, not to add salt to Judah's wounds or stir up nationalistic fervor against a neighbor, but to let God and God alone bring about restoration and justice to a people whose past cannot be forgotten but can be vindicated and redeemed. Obadiah is all about throwing one's moral outrage upon the shoulders of God.

The structure of the book divides neatly into two parts: Verses 1–14 deal specifically with judgment against Edom; verses 15–21 deal with the results of God's judgment as they relate to Israel's restoration. The theme of judgment against the other nations is nothing new in the prophetic corpus, and it is frequently found in prophetic books that also speak of judgment leveled against Israel—God's own people (see Isaiah 13—23; Jeremiah 46—51; Ezekiel 26—32). In Obadiah's case, God's judgment against the other nations is yet to be fulfilled, now that Israel has suffered its own judgment at their hands (Obad. 15–16).

THE TITLE
Obadiah 1a

1a The vision of Obadiah.

This title, which is unusually terse, tells us only that the book is essentially a *vision* of the prophet. Visions are not uncommon among the prophets, as we read in the titles of other prophetic books (2 Chron. 32:32; Isa. 1:1; Nah. 1:1; cf. Mic. 1:1). The prophetic vision clearly meant more than simply a vision in the night (cf. Zech. 1:7–8). It included all manner of perception, including hearing (Isa. 1:1). In Obadiah, the title refers to the powerfully evocative language with which the prophet issues his judgment against Edom. Consequently, the prophet's message is to be heard and read imaginatively, for Obadiah's words together paint a powerfully compelling picture that draws the reader into a fuller understanding of God's majestic sovereignty over the world.

THE CRASH OF EDOM'S HUBRIS
Obadiah 1b–10

> 1b **Thus says the Lord GOD concerning Edom:**
> **We have heard a report from the LORD,**
> **and a messenger has been sent among the nations:**
> **"Rise up! Let us rise against it for battle!"**
> 2 **I will surely make you least among the nations;**
> **you shall be utterly despised.**
> 3 **Your proud heart has deceived you,**

you that live in the clefts of the rock,
　whose dwelling is in the heights.
You say in your heart,
　"Who will bring me down to the ground?"
4 Though you soar aloft like the eagle,
　though your nest is set among the stars,
　from there I will bring you down,
　　　　　　　　　says the LORD.
5 If thieves came to you,
　if plunderers by night
　—how you have been destroyed!—
　would they not steal only what they wanted?
If grape-gatherers came to you,
　would they not leave gleanings?
6 How Esau has been pillaged,
　his treasures searched out!
7 All your allies have deceived you,
　they have driven you to the border;
your confederates have prevailed against you;
　those who ate your bread have set a trap for you—
　there is no understanding of it.
8 On that day, says the LORD,
　I will destroy the wise out of Edom,
　and understanding out of Mount Esau.
9 Your warriors shall be shattered, O Teman,
　so that everyone from Mount Esau will be cut off.
10 For the slaughter and violence done to your brother Jacob,
　shame shall cover you,
　and you shall be cut off forever.

Obadiah's speech against Edom begins in typical prophetic fashion: "Thus says the Lord." The prophet's words are not his own; he is simply the messenger. Direct speech from God, however, does not actually occur until verses 2–18. The first verse recounts the speech of the nations. They have received a report that puts them on notice, a summons to battle. Yet the call is not a summons to dominate or control the nation of Edom but to rectify a heinous crime committed in the past. Like the Israelite tribes mustering themselves to punish Benjamin over the atrocity described in Judges 19—20, or Saul's call to the tribes to defend the helpless border town of Jabesh-gilead from the ruthless Ammonites (1 Sam. 10:27b–11:11), Obadiah's call to battle addresses a recent situation of unspeakable abuse. Unlike these previous summons to battle, the prophet's summons is cast in the international arena, perhaps indicating a covenant of cooperation among the nations to check and punish the wrongs of any one nation for abusing a neighbor (cf. Amos 1:9). In any case, the judgment announced by the prophet regarding the abuse of one country against another has explosive international repercussions.

The actual crime that brought about such judgment from the lips of Obadiah is not yet described, but Edom's self-image, which evidently led to this crime, is profiled in the following verses. This oppressive nation is prideful and arrogant; its head is as high as the clouds, as it were. Indeed, Edom was well known for its mountainous geography (see "Mount Esau" in vv. 8–9). Habitations carved out of cliffs were common. The prophet connects this feature of Edom's urban planning, which figuratively reached the stars (v. 4), with the nation's inflated self-image. Even from such lofty heights of hubris, God will bring them back down just the same (Amos 9:1–2). Using the example of Edom, the prophet incisively identifies the trap any nation is liable to fall into, namely, the snare of nationalistic arrogance. From the dawn of history to the present, nationalism has led nations to commit unspeakable acts of violence against humanity. This collective sin is precisely what leads Edom to commit the unpardonable crime that it did, according to the prophet.

Judgment, indeed, has already begun to be carried out against Edom (vv. 5–10). The country has been ravaged far beyond what thieves would have done in robbing a home or what grape gatherers would have done during the harvest (see the parallel in Jeremiah 49:9). At least they would have left something behind. Edom ("Esau"), however, has been pillaged completely (cf. v. 13). Former allies have turned against Edom (v. 7). Why? Because Edom had treated a close brother with "slaughter and violence" (v. 10). As a result, God declares the end of wisdom to a nation renowned for its wisdom throughout the ancient Orient (v. 8; Jer. 49:7). Even its sages have succumbed to the mind-numbing callousness of nationalistic pride. If anyone should have known better, it should have been the wise. God's judgment against the wise implies their acceptance of the atrocities the nation committed against God's own people.

In short, the prophet exposes a damning irony in his indictment against this foreign nation. Despite its wisdom, Edom succumbed to prideful ignorance, sequestering itself—as it were—in an ivory tower and bolting the doors, thereby cutting itself off from all reality. The prophet takes satisfaction in pointing out that Edom was so blinded by its own bloated wisdom that it did not even recognize deceit at its very doorstep, much less in its heart (vv. 3, 7). Wisdom bereft of its self-critical edge is a dangerous tool in the hands of the arrogant. Indeed, it is the first to go for any nation that seeks to subjugate others in the name of "truth" and "purity." One cannot forget the role of the intellectual elite, including much of the church, in supporting the Nazi agenda, which led to unspeakable abuse of Jews and Gypsies. Here, wisdom was blinded, sacrificed, and ultimately propped up in rationalizing service of a nationalism hell-bent on domination. Even consecrated ignorance is still ignorance.

CRIMES AGAINST A BROTHER
Obadiah 11–14

> [11] On the day that you stood aside,
>   on the day strangers carried off his wealth,
> and foreigners entered his gates
>   and cast lots for Jerusalem,
>   you too were like one of them.
> [12] But you should not have gloated over your brother
>   on the day of his misfortune;
> you should not have rejoiced over the people of Judah
>   on the day of their ruin;
> you should not have boasted
>   on the day of distress.
> [13] You should not have entered the gate of my people
>   on the day of their calamity;
> you should not have joined in the gloating over Judah's disaster
>   on the day of his calamity;
> you should not have looted his goods
>   on the day of his calamity.
> [14] You should not have stood at the crossings
>   to cut off his fugitives; you should not have handed over his
>   survivors
>   on the day of distress.

As for the specific crimes committed by Edom, the litany of evidence begins in verse 11. Brother Edom is charged with the crime of complicity on that terrible day in August 586 B.C., when Judah was ravaged by the armies of Babylonia and Jerusalem's temple destroyed (2 Kings 25:1–21). Obadiah does not speak against the strangers and foreigners who plundered Jerusalem. Indeed, his silence toward them is striking. Rather, the prophet's vehemence is focused on a brother who should have known better. Edom is no stranger. The rights and obligations of kinship have been flagrantly violated, and the moral outrage of hurt and betrayal runs deep.

Through the mouth of the prophet, God accuses Esau of not only standing by as Jerusalem was destroyed but having a hand in it. The people of Edom "were like one of [the foreigners]." That is where the hurt is most excruciating. Oblivious to kinship ties, Edom has treacherously crossed that well-defined boundary between being "one of us" to "one of them." Full of the language of betrayal, the prophet vividly recalls how Edom gloated and boasted over his brother's (Judah's) misfortune (vv. 12–13). Brother Edom not only helped loot Judah (cf. v. 6), but perhaps worst of all showed no compassion on the fugitives fleeing for their lives from the destructive might of the Babylonian army (v. 14). By cutting off and handing them over to the enemy, Edom violated all semblance of international propriety on that day of distress. Obadiah's point is that international standards of behavior are one thing; *familial* standards are quite another. Edom, in short, has betrayed a brother. Israel's outrage is no less valid than the cry of Abel's blood over Cain's murder of his brother (Gen. 4:8–16).

ISRAEL'S FINAL TRIUMPH
Obadiah 15–21

15 For the day of the LORD is near against all the nations.
As you have done, it shall be done to you;
   your deeds shall return on your own head.
16 For as you have drunk on my holy mountain,
   all the nations around you shall drink;
they shall drink and gulp down,
   and shall be as though they had never been.
17 But on Mount Zion there shall be those that escape,
   and it shall be holy;
and the house of Jacob shall
      take possession of those who dispossessed them.
18 The house of Jacob shall be a fire,
   the house of Joseph a flame,
   and the house of Esau stubble;
they shall burn them and consume them,
   and there shall be no survivor of the house of Esau;
                  for the LORD has spoken.
19 Those of the Negeb shall possess Mount Esau,
   and those of the Shephelah the land of the Philistines;

they shall possess the land of Ephraim and the land of Samaria,
    and Benjamin shall possess Gilead.
20 The exiles of the Israelites who are in Halah
    shall possess Phoenicia as far as Zarephath;
and the exiles of Jerusalem who are in Sepharad
    shall possess the towns of the Negeb.
21 Those who have been saved shall go up to Mount Zion
    to rule Mount Esau;
and the kingdom shall be the LORD's.

The prophet declares a final reckoning of Israel's grievance against a brother. The opening announcement of the "day of the Lord" (cf. v. 8) marks a complete turn of events, a day of reckoning that fulfills the pronouncement in verse 15b: "As you have done, it shall be done to you." Equivalent to the modern adage "what goes around, comes around," this proverbial judgment declares that Edom will finally taste its own medicine. Treachery will in the end destroy those who perpetrate it. Indeed, the prophet not only addresses Edom but all the nations that have feasted upon the demise of God's people. God fights on Israel's behalf. As Israel was punished by the exile, forced to drink God's wrath (Psalm 75:8; Isa. 51:17–23; Jer. 25:15–17), now all the nations shall do likewise with their victory toasts turned into vile drinking feasts of God's wrath (v. 16), sort of like fine wine turned into cod-liver oil or ipecac.

Obadiah alludes to the desecration of God's holy mountain Zion, upon which the temple of Jerusalem once stood before the Babylonians tore it down. Now Mount Zion will once again be consecrated. It shall be a holy refuge for those fleeing for their lives. Unlike Edom, who killed or handed over refugees fleeing from Jerusalem's destruction (v. 14), Zion shall protect even those fleeing from enemy lands! The house of Israel ("Jacob") will be the gathering place of the dispossessed. The holy fire of Jacob will consume the stubble that is Edom, leaving no survivors.

The results of God's judgment against the nations, and against Edom in particular, amount to a glorious restoration of the land of Israel (vv. 19–21). Judah will possess Edom and Philistia. The Negeb refers to the southern desert of Judah next to Edom; the Shephelah refers to the lowlands of Judah adjacent to the plain of Philistia. The extension of Israel's domain will also move northward, encompassing the land that was once part of the northern kingdom, Ephraim and Samaria. The small tribe of Benjamin will take possession of the Transjordanian region between the Sea of Galilee and the Dead Sea, "Gilead" (v. 19). Even the exiles—the Israelites exiled by Assyria to Halah (somewhere in northern Mesopotamia)

and those of Jerusalem in Sepharad (location unknown)—will return to
possess the lands of their foes. The prophet ends with the climactic image
of the inhabitants of Mount Zion (Jerusalem), God's holy abode, ruling
Mount Esau (Edom). Like the meek inheriting the earth (Matt. 5:5), Israel will come to possess the land of its oppressor. The victim will now be
victor.

The prophet is quick to point out that this is no human kingdom at
work but God's kingdom (v. 21). God's sovereign rule relativizes all
earthly powers, and any nation that denies God's absolute reign succumbs
to nationalistic self-delusion. God's kingdom is unlike any earthly one,
Obadiah reminds us, for like a two-edged sword it cuts to the very roots
of collective madness and violence. Under God's reign, "the bows of the
mighty are broken, but the feeble gird on strength" (1 Sam. 2:4). Similarly, Mary, the mother of Jesus, praises God upon receiving the news of
Jesus' birth with words that vividly describe the in-breaking reign of God:

> He has shown strength with his arm;
>   he has scattered the proud in
>   the thoughts of their hearts.
> He has brought down the powerful
>   from their thrones,
>   and lifted up the lowly;
> he has filled the hungry with good things,
>   and sent the rich away empty.
> He has helped his servant Israel,
>   in remembrance of his mercy.
>   (Luke 1:51–54)

In Christ, God's reign overcomes and transforms all powers of resistance.
In Christ we are more than conquerors, knowing that no power on earth
or elsewhere can separate us from God's love (Rom. 8:37–39).

Jonah

Introduction

Mention Jonah and most people will say "whale." Nevertheless, if one had to choose an image that best typifies the book, it would not be the "large fish" that swallowed the prophet (1:17; 2:1, 10) but the bush that withered away and prompted the prophet's anger (see 4:6–10). The story of Jonah is about a lone prophet's refusal to acknowledge God's forgiving love for a repentant, foreign people. The book chronicles the prophet's unavoidable journey to fulfill a mission that in the end brings good news to an enemy people but leaves him outraged and demoralized. In short, Jonah is about the scandal of God's mercy.

The prophet is named only once outside the book in the Old Testament, namely, in 2 Kings 14:25. He is also featured in two of the gospels (Matt. 12:39–41; 16:4 and Luke 11:29–32). "Jonah ben Amittai" was a prophet under the great King Jeroboam II (786–746 B.C.), whose reign marked the zenith of Israel's power on the international scene.

Yet the book of Jonah is not so much concerned with giving us a history as it is with teaching us about the wideness of God's mercy and the narrowness of human judgment. Indeed some scholars have called the story of Jonah a satire in which the whole prophetic enterprise is parodied: Jonah announces doom, but God cancels the judgment after Nineveh's repentance. If the book is indeed a satire, perhaps it could be retitled, "A Funny Thing Happened on the Way to Nineveh." Whether or not it is a prophetic parody, the book introduces a profoundly self-critical element into Old Testament prophetic literature. Here is a prophet of judgment who actually miscalculated, indeed resisted, God's merciful forbearance. Jonah's story is our story and is to be remembered whenever we prejudge and limit God's compassion for people, particularly strangers.

If viewed as a drama, the story of Jonah essentially can be divided into two parts or acts: In 1:1–2:10 Jonah is a man in flight who ends up where he began; in 3:1–4:11 the story line begins where 1:1 began, namely, with God's command to go once again to Nineveh.

JONAH'S CALL
Jonah 1:1–2

> 1:1 Now the word of the LORD came to Jonah son of Amittai, saying[2] "Go at once to Nineveh, that great city, and cry out against it; for their wickedness has come up before me."

In typical prophetic style, the book opens with God's address to the prophet. Jonah is summoned by God for a mission: "Go . . . and cry out!" The reason is starkly stated: God has taken note of the wickedness of the Ninevites. The actual content of Jonah's "cry" is not divulged until we find the prophet actually in Nineveh (3:4). To get there, however, he takes a rather roundabout route.

Located on the eastern banks of the Tigris, Nineveh was one of the greatest cities of Mesopotamia. At its height under the Assyrian kings Sennacherib, Esarhaddon, and Ashurbanipal, the city had no rival throughout the ancient Orient. There was plenty of reason to hate Nineveh, since it was the capital of Israel's oppressor in the eighth and seventh centuries B.C. In the book of Nahum, this city's doom is dramatically foretold. And, in fact, the city did meet its demise in 612 B.C., when it fell to the combined armies of the Babylonians and Medes. But that is jumping too far ahead of our story. In Jonah's heyday, Nineveh's size and splendor were unmatched, as the prophet himself could no doubt attest (see 3:3).

JONAH'S RESPONSE: FLIGHT
Jonah 1:3

> 1:3 But Jonah set out to flee to Tarshish from the presence of the LORD. He went down to Joppa and found a ship going to Tarshish; so he paid his fare and went on board, to go with them to Tarshish, away from the presence of the LORD.

Jonah refuses to set himself toward Nineveh at God's behest. Unlike his prophetic predecessors who did "just as the Lord commanded" (for example, Exod. 7:6; 40:16), Jonah does precisely the opposite, making a beeline to Tarshish. Located probably in southern Spain (Isa. 23:1–12; Jer.

10:9; Ezek. 27:12, 25), Tarshish was renowned for its exports, which included gold, silver, ivory, monkeys, and peacocks (1 Kings 10:22). This exotic, remote city was located farther west than Nineveh lay east. From Joppa, off the Mediterranean coast, Jonah pays his fare and flees from God's presence. Yet as the story demonstrates, there is no escape from God. As the psalmist states eloquently,

> Where can I flee from your presence?
> If I ascend to heaven, you are there;
>   if I make my bed in Sheol, you are there.
> If I take the wings of the morning
>   and settle at the farthest limits of the sea,
> even there your hand shall lead me,
>   and your right hand shall hold me fast.
>   (Psalm 139:7–10)

For the psalmist, God's pervasive presence is a secure refuge; for Jonah, however, it is a curse from which to flee. As Jonah will soon find out, however, even in flight from God there is return to God within the expansive circle of grace.

JONAH'S MARITIME ADVENTURES
Jonah 1:4–16

1:4 **But the LORD hurled a great wind upon the sea, and such a mighty storm came upon the sea that the ship threatened to break up.** [5] **Then the mariners were afraid, and each cried to his god. They threw the cargo that was in the ship into the sea, to lighten it for them. Jonah, meanwhile, had gone down into the hold of the ship and had lain down, and was fast asleep.** [6] **The captain came and said to him, "What are you doing sound asleep? Get up, call on your god! Perhaps the god will spare us a thought so that we do not perish."**

[7] **The sailors said to one another, "Come, let us cast lots, so that we may know on whose account this calamity has come upon us." So they cast lots, and the lot fell on Jonah.** [8] **Then they said to him, "Tell us why this calamity has come upon us. What is your occupation? Where do you come from? What is your country? And of what people are you?"** [9] **"I am a Hebrew," he replied. "I worship the LORD, the God of heaven, who made the sea and the dry land."** [10] **Then the men were even more afraid, and said to him, "What is this that you have done!" For the men knew that he was fleeing from the presence of the LORD, because he had told them so.**

> [11] **Then they said to him, "What shall we do to you, that the sea may quiet down for us?" For the sea was growing more and more tempestuous. [12] He said to them, "Pick me up and throw me into the sea; then the sea will quiet down for you; for I know it is because of me that this great storm has come upon you." [13] Nevertheless the men rowed hard to bring the ship back to land, but they could not, for the sea grew more and more stormy against them. [14] Then they cried out to the LORD, "Please, O LORD, we pray, do not let us perish on account of this man's life. Do not make us guilty of innocent blood; for you, O LORD, have done as it pleased you." [15] So they picked Jonah up and threw him into the sea; and the sea ceased from its raging. [16] Then the men feared the LORD even more, and they offered a sacrifice to the LORD and made vows.**

Jonah is a prophet on the run from God. As such, he is a living contradiction. At the top of any prophet's job description was to be ever vigilant in conveying God's messages. This messenger, however, refuses to deliver. He sequesters himself in the dark hold of the ship headed to the farthest reaches of the known world to hide from the Hound of Heaven. In command of the wind and the sea, God brings about a great storm that threatens to destroy the ship. Amid the crash and thunder of waves and storm, the cacophony of desperate prayers only adds to the commotion without avail. Jonah, however, in his misguided resistance to God's call, is oblivious to it all; he must be jolted awake as each sailor cries to his own god for deliverance, and the prophet is beckoned to do likewise.

The crew then tries another tack. By casting lots (cf. Lev. 16:8; 1 Sam. 14:42), the sailors identify the source of their predicament, and Jonah is found to be the culprit! Once the determination is made, the prophet is faced with a barrage of questions. Jonah responds with a simple testimony: He is a Hebrew, and therein lies both his identity and his vocation. He is a worshiper of the Creator God. His answer is a confession of faith, and an appropriately ironic one at that. Jonah confesses that God is the creator of both land *and sea*. His escape route is thus no escape at all; there is no domain on earth or sea, below or above, that is not within God's sight. His own lips testify against his attempted flight.

The revelation sends shock waves among the crew. A prophet fleeing from the presence of the Lord was simply unheard of; the worst case of professional misconduct. Just as Jonah's conduct is inconceivable to the sailors, so is his proposal to correct the situation (1:12). The prophet admits that he himself is the cause of their trouble and proposes that he be thrown overboard as if the sea required his life to calm it. But this is no sacrifice to some angry sea god; this is rather a case of ejecting the cause, like unwanted cargo (1:5).

Jonah fully realizes that he has no alternative except to cast himself upon the mercy of the God who rules both land and sea. His time of resistance is over. The mariners, likewise, no matter how hard they resist Jonah's proposal, come to realize that they, too, have no other option. So with a desperate petition directed to the Lord, Jonah is thrown into the sea. No longer addressing a plurality of gods (1:5), the crew petitions the one, true God (1:14). Their prayer comprises two simple requests: to be spared their lives and to be absolved of guilt in what surely will result in Jonah's death. The sailors appeal to God's sovereign will: "[F]or you, O Lord, have done as it pleased you" (1:14).

The deed is done. With Jonah overboard, the sea is calmed. Perhaps more amazing is the fact that the crew now reveres God alone. No longer fearing the storm and crying to their gods, they now cry out to the Lord in reverence. Jonah was a missionary of God *in spite of* himself! This first episode in Jonah's adventures demonstrates *God's* initiative in leading people into conversion, into the circle of grace. Jonah was simply an unwitting instrument.

HELD HOSTAGE
IN THE BELLY OF A FISH
Jonah 1:17–2:10

1:17 **But the LORD provided a large fish to swallow up Jonah; and Jonah was in the belly of the fish three days and three nights.**
    2:1 **Then Jonah prayed to the LORD his God from the belly of the fish,**
     2 **saying,**
"I called to the LORD out of my distress,
    and he answered me;
out of the belly of Sheol I cried,
    and you heard my voice.
  3 **You cast me into the deep**
    into the heart of the seas,
    and the flood surrounded me;
all your waves and your billows
    passed over me.
  4 **Then I said, 'I am driven away**
    from your sight;
how shall I look again
    upon your holy temple?'

> **5 The waters closed in over me**
>   **the deep surrounded me;**
> **weeds were wrapped around my head**
> **6 at the roots of the mountains.**
> **I went down to the land**
>   **whose bars closed upon me forever;**
> **yet you brought up my life from the Pit,**
>   **O LORD my God.**
> **7 As my life was ebbing away,**
>   **I remembered the LORD;**
> **and my prayer came to you,**
>   **into your holy temple.**
> **8 Those who worship vain idols**
>   **forsake their true loyalty.**
> **9 But I with the voice of thanksgiving**
>   **will sacrifice to you;**
> **what I have vowed I will pay.**
>   **Deliverance belongs to the LORD!"**
> **10 Then the LORD spoke to the fish, and it spewed Jonah out upon the dry land.**

God does not abandon Jonah. In what appears first to be a horrible fate of death, Jonah is actually delivered from death. God provides (literally "appoints") a "large fish to swallow up the prophet." This is God's second intervention (cf. 1:4). There is a certain irony here, since the language of "swallowing up" most often implies death, the entrance into Sheol, that shadowy underworld to which all must go upon death, according to Hebrew thought (Num. 16:30; Prov. 1:12). Yet Jonah does not die; he is rather saved from certain drowning (see 2:3). Such deliverance for Jonah is, however, a mixed blessing, as becomes evident in his prayer.

The Gospel writer Matthew refers to Jonah's time of residence in the belly of the fish as the "sign of the prophet Jonah" (Matt. 12:39–41; cf. Luke 11:29–32). In like manner, Jesus refers to the "three days and three nights" in which the "Son of Man will be in the heart of the earth" (Matt. 12:40). This stereotypical phrase of time is not meant to give an exact period; hence, Jesus can apply it to himself as a sign of his own death and resurrection. By referring to Jonah, Jesus forges an indelible link between Jonah's descent into the sea and the belly of the fish with his own descent into the underworld in order that, as Paul states in Ephesians, "he might fill all things" (Eph. 4:10). The Apostles' Creed, too, states that before Jesus ascended into heaven, he "descended into hell." Like God's pervasive presence, Jesus' reign extends, upon his death, to the ends of the earth, filling all things above and below. Again, Psalm 139 comes to mind. The prophet Jonah experiences the refuge of God's reign in quite a graphic way. His own residence in the fish's belly is, as will be seen, his sojourn from despair to renewed life and vocation.

Whether a large fish—a whale is most likely what the author had in mind despite the modern scientific distinction between marine mammals and fish—can actually swallow and sustain a person for three days is not an issue our author sets out to prove. Indeed, the incident itself is reported very matter-of-factly. Jonah goes from the dark hold of the ship to the inner belly of the fish. In the former he was momentarily protected, even oblivious, to the upheaval occurring around him. In the belly, he is likewise protected from the raging waves that could crush him. Jonah, in short, is both delivered and held captive by God's grace.

The prayer that issues from the prophet's mouth is a song of lament. Like the laments found in the Psalter (for example, Psalms 13, 17, 22), Jonah's prayer moves from the desperate plea for deliverance to the triumphant note of thanksgiving. As part of the narrative, this psalm, steeped in irony as it is, marks an important step in Jonah's transformation. It is his coming of age in reclaiming his prophetic calling.

Jonah's prayer is a petition, testimony, confession, and thanksgiving prayer all wrapped into one. It begins with a horrific description of the distress in which he finds himself. Jonah prays this psalm in retrospect, as part of the past. To be sure, the prophet interprets things a bit differently from the narrative. Jonah perceives himself in the "belly of Sheol," in the watery depths of death (2:2). God is the one who has cast Jonah into the deep (2:3). The prophet can only interpret his present situation as the result of being "driven away" from God's sight (2:4).

Castigation, however, is the last thing on God's mind! Jonah yearns to worship at the temple again, the place of communion with God for the prophet. Transported by inspired imagination, Jonah remembers God and prays as if he were back at the temple (cf. 1 Kings 8:30, 48–50), as his life is "ebbing away" (2:7). Like a hostage who finds solace and strength in remembering home and loved ones, this prophet finds his comfort in recalling his life in intimate communion with God there in the holy temple. Remembrance turns into strength and hope when Jonah, recalling the mariners' vain pleas to calm the storm (1:5), forsakes the false worship of "vain idols" (2:8). Jonah finds the resolve to fulfill his vows to God in making proper sacrifice if and when he returns, delivered from death (cf. 1:16). Jonah ends on a dramatic note of thanksgiving; he is a changed man.

Instead of wallowing in the dark depths of despair, Jonah ends in proclamation, defiant in hope and grateful in promise; "Deliverance belongs to
the Lord!" he proclaims (2:9). It is his victory over despair. Jonah has come
full circle, and so has his fate. At the very moment the prophet utters his
thanksgiving, God commands the fish to vomit him onto the dry land, presumably on the very spot from which he embarked on his flight from
God's presence.

The timing is no accident: Thanksgiving is not only the *result* of God's
deliverance, it can, as in Jonah's case, *anticipate* deliverance as well. An authentic posture of thanksgiving toward God both recalls God's past acts
and looks forward in anticipation of God's future acts. For Christians,
praiseful thanksgiving holds together the grace of Christ, whose life and
death is in one sense the stuff of ancient history, and the prospect of eternal life, which Christ's resurrection effects for all believers (John 3:16).
Thanksgiving means living in the present while surrounded on both sides,
past and future, by God's grace.

JONAH IN NINEVEH
Jonah 3:1–10

3:1 The word of the LORD came to Jonah a second time, saying 2 "Get up,
go to Nineveh, that great city, and proclaim to it the message that I tell you."
3 So Jonah set out and went to Nineveh, according to the word of the LORD.
Now Nineveh was an exceedingly large city, a three days' walk across.
4 Jonah began to go into the city, going a day's walk. And he cried out, "Forty
days more, and Nineveh shall be overthrown!" 5 And the people of Nineveh
believed God; they proclaimed a fast, and everyone, great and small, put on
sackcloth.

6 When the news reached the king of Nineveh, he rose from his throne,
removed his robe, covered himself with sackcloth, and sat in ashes. 7 Then
he had a proclamation made in Nineveh: "By the decree of the king and his
nobles: No human being or animal, no herd or flock, shall taste anything.
They shall not feed, nor shall they drink water. 8 Human beings and animals
shall be covered with sackcloth, and they shall cry mightily to God. All shall
turn from their evil ways and from the violence that is in their hands. 9 Who
knows? God may relent and change his mind; he may turn from his fierce
anger, so that we do not perish."

10 When God saw what they did, how they turned from their evil ways,
God changed his mind about the calamity that he said he would bring upon
them; and he did not do it.

The story does not end with Jonah's deliverance. He still has a mission to accomplish, and it appears that he now relishes it. God's commission comes a second time (3:2; cf. 1:2), beginning the second act of this two-part drama. This time, however, Jonah confidently sets out to do "according to the word of the Lord" (3:3). He heads straight to that great city. God's command, curiously, is more open ended than the initial one in 1:2. In God's first call, Nineveh's wickedness is given explicit reference. Now, however, God simply tells Jonah to proclaim "the message that I will tell you" (3:2). Once in Nineveh, Jonah delivers what appears to be an unconditional judgment. There are no loopholes or strings attached. Nineveh "shall be overthrown" in forty days, no ifs, ands, or buts. The Hebrew verb "to overthrow" is, however, fraught with ambiguity here. It can mean to destroy, as in the case of Sodom and Gomorrah (Gen. 19:25); yet it can also mean to turn or change something (Exod. 7:17; 1 Sam. 10:6), as in changing the heart (Psalm 105:25). What Jonah does not yet realize is that his prophecy is a double entendre! Will Nineveh be destroyed or will it be *transformed?* That remains to be seen, although Jonah himself seems certain of the former.

Jonah's announcement of "judgment" elicits a drastic change of heart among the Ninevites: They believe God, proclaim a fast, and don sackcloth, the traditional rites of mourning (Gen. 37:34; 2 Sam. 3:31; Job 2:8). In perhaps a humorous jab at royal bureaucracy, the king is the last one to hear of this announcement and issues an edict that requires not only every citizen of Nineveh but every animal to fast and to be covered with sackcloth (vv. 7–9). Nineveh's repentance is total in the desperate hope that God will "repent" from destroying the city. The king's question in verse 9, "Who knows?" is almost prophetic. The prophet Amos, after having announced God's terrible judgment against Israel, commands the people to "hate evil and love good and establish justice in the gate; *it may be* that the Lord, the God of hosts, will be gracious to the remnant of Joseph" (Amos 5:15). Similarly, the prophet Zephaniah adjures his people to "seek righteousness, seek humility; *perhaps* you may be hidden on the day of the Lord's wrath" (Zeph. 2:3). In both cases, the prophet utters terrible judgments yet keeps alive a vestige of hope that such judgment will be averted or mitigated if the people change their ways. So also the Assyrian king: In the light of such terrible judgment, the king does not give up in holding out the possibility, however slight, that God will relent from punishing the city.

Indeed, the king is not disappointed. Having seen how the people changed their ways, God reverses the judgment (3:10). That God "changes his mind" is not an uncommon assertion in the Old Testament. Moses at one point, for example, implores God not to consume the people in wrath because of their recalcitrance: "Turn from your fierce wrath; change your mind and do not bring disaster on your people" (Exod. 32:12). In response to Moses' bold intercession, "the Lord changed his mind about the disaster that he planned to bring on his people" (Exod. 32:14). That God could have a change of heart by refusing to carry out what was originally planned did not pose any problems, theological or otherwise, for our biblical authors; rather, God's capacity to change and thereby refrain from punishment was something to celebrate! That God responds to human repentance and need, even if it involves reversing previous decisions, is a testimony of divine grace. It is as if God were searching for an excuse, any excuse, to reverse all pronouncements of judgment. When human beings confess and repent, God responds in grace. Constant in love, God is ever responsive, ever changing, in demonstrating constant and gracious forbearance, always ready to "relent from punishing" (Jonah 4:2; Exod. 34:6–7).

RESISTANCE IN REPENTANCE
Jonah 4:1–11

4:1 **But this was very displeasing to Jonah, and he became angry.** 2 **He prayed to the LORD and said, "O LORD! Is not this what I said while I was still in my own country? That is why I fled to Tarshish at the beginning; for I knew that you are a gracious God and merciful, slow to anger, and abounding in steadfast love, and ready to relent from punishing.** 3 **And now, O LORD, please take my life from me, for it is better for me to die than to live."** 4 **And the LORD said, "Is it right for you to be angry?"** 5 **Then Jonah went out of the city and sat down east of the city, and made a booth for himself there. He sat under it in the shade, waiting to see what would become of the city.**

6 **The LORD God appointed a bush, and made it come up over Jonah, to give shade over his head, to save him from his discomfort; so Jonah was very happy about the bush.** 7 **But when dawn came up the next day, God appointed a worm that attacked the bush, so that it withered.** 8 **When the sun rose, God prepared a sultry east wind, and the sun beat down on the head of Jonah so that he was faint and asked that he might die. He said, "It is better for me to die than to live."**

9 **But God said to Jonah, "Is it right for you to be angry about the bush?" And he said, "Yes, angry enough to die."** 10 **Then the LORD said, "You are concerned about the bush, for which you did not labor and which you did not grow; it came into being in a night and perished in a night.** 11 **And should**

I not be concerned about Nineveh, that great city, in which there are more than a hundred and twenty thousand persons who do not know their right hand from their left, and also many animals?"

What is overthrown, then, is not Nineveh, but God's own decision. Or, to put it another way, Nineveh is overthrown in repentance. Jonah, however, is not one to appreciate such theological irony. He is seething over the fact that God does not shoot straight and destroy the city as promised. He does not realize that "judgment" was indeed carried out but in a manner at odds with his own presumptions, for God does not conform to human expectations (cf. Hos. 11:8–9). The prophet's dispute with God at this point is revealing: Jonah discloses for the first time why he fled from God's presence. Jonah seems to know more about God than we would give him credit. Citing the divine confession given to Moses on Mount Sinai (Exod. 34:6–7), Jonah knows full well that God is gracious and merciful, "abounding in steadfast love" (4:2). Yet Jonah, God's servant and prophet, finds this compassion utterly scandalous.

God's good news for Nineveh is Jonah's bad news for his credibility, so the prophet reasons. One senses some underlying, psychological baggage in his logic. Could it be that Jonah was banking on the city's destruction in order to vindicate himself and his understanding of his prophetic office? Did Jonah make the mistake of tying his personal aspirations to the results of his vocational calling? If so, Jonah represents a rather warped view of prophetism, one that confuses work with self-worth, indeed, a self-worth fueled by hatred of one's enemy. Jonah's own sense of mission was entirely dependent upon the prospect of Nineveh's destruction. Without the city's destruction, Jonah saw himself as an outright failure. Ironically, Jonah's mission was entirely successful: His ministry effected the complete conversion of a people, much to his own dismay. What the prophet had not counted on was that his message turned out to be good news for the Ninevites; it meant new life for them. For Jonah, however, it was news to die for, in embarrassment and shame.

So Jonah stations himself overlooking the city and pouts, refusing to give up on the prospect of its destruction. And wait he must. In the meantime, God appoints a bush to provide the prophet shade. This is God's third intervention. Like the appointment of the fish in 1:17, the provision of the bush is meant to protect Jonah (4:6). As a result, the prophet is placated for the time being. Things take a turn for the worse the next day, however. God appoints a worm to kill the bush as well as a sirocco (an unbearably hot desert wind) that results in Jonah's discomfort (vv. 7–8). God is clearly testing Jonah to demonstrate a point. The prophet reacts in the same way as he reacted to the sparing of Nineveh. Regarding Nineveh's fate, Jonah was angry over God's mercy in preserving the city; now he misses the protective grace that preserved him, and he is angry enough to die (v. 3).

God repeats the question posed in 4:4: "Is it right for you to be angry?" The prophet refused to answer the first time; now he responds with a resounding yes. Yet God has the last say in pointing out Jonah's misplaced anger. Whereas the prophet was concerned about a mere bush that flourished and died in one night, God's goodness includes a whole city, 120,000 people and "many animals." Jonah has no right to protest. To the contrary, the appropriate response would have been awe and joy over God's merciful love, which extends far beyond any humanly imposed boundaries and embraces enemies and animals alike. More humane than any human, God cares for all of creation. Jonah did not bring the shade plant into being, yet he loved it. How much more, then, does the Creator love and care for creation! Strikingly absent in God's final word to Jonah is any mention of repentance. Rather, what is stressed is an unconditional love for people who don't know any better, who "do not know their right hand from their left." And don't forget the animals. The wideness in God's mercy is something to sing about, not curse!

We do not know whether Jonah was convinced. Did he eventually come to rejoice in the magnitude of God's love or did he continue to mope and nurse his anger? It's the same question that a certain parable poses: Did the elder brother of the prodigal son ever come around to welcome and celebrate the return of his brother who had carelessly squandered his portion of the family inheritance (Luke 15:29–32)? Both stories end without an answer, for it is up to the reader—you and me—to answer the question and provide our own ending.

Micah

Introduction

Micah is a small book with an enduring message that extends far beyond the historical circumstances in which the prophecies were originally given. Micah boldly states, for instance, that all worship is false unless it incorporates a zealous concern for social justice (see commentary on 6:6–8). Micah's message grows out of his all-encompassing view of God. For this prophet from Moresheth, God acts in innumerable ways as judge and deliverer. God is the God of both justice and mercy, of judgment and forgiveness, of conflict and peace. This comprehensive view of God is reflected in the remarkable variety of literature contained in the book. Far from being a single-issue work (cf. Obadiah and Nahum), this compact book is a theological compendium filled with announcements of punishment as well as salvation, prayers, instructions, a lament, and a psalm—all in only seven short chapters! As such, Micah's message is filled not so much with abstract, *timeless* truths as with *timely* truths for all seasons and settings, including our own.

Little is known about the prophet himself, although his name does appear one time in the book of Jeremiah (see 26:18, which quotes Mic. 3:12). In this passage, Micah's prophecy regarding the destruction of Zion is cited as a precedent for sparing Jeremiah's life following his inflammatory sermon at the temple (Jer. 7:1–15; 26:1–6). The author of this episode in Jeremiah's life situates Micah "in the days of Hezekiah," who ruled from 715 to 687 B.C. Micah is thus roughly contemporaneous with Isaiah, Hosea, and Amos.

The eighth century was an eventful, turbulent time, a period of tremendous upheaval in which powerful nations clashed and prophets boldly preached. Indeed, it is from this century that we receive for the first time the words of the prophets collected in book form, with Amos and Hosea being the earliest. The eighth century was a time of fervent prophecy for fervent times, and Micah's proclamations were no exception.

This prophet announced judgment against the northern kingdom Israel and lived to see its downfall at the hands of the mighty nation of Assyria (722 B.C.). Yet amid the ashes of destruction, Micah foresaw a glorious future in store for God's people, a future of wondrous restoration and peace (7:8–20). From judgment to salvation, devastation to restoration, the prophet discerned God to be present and active. It is no wonder, then, that Micah's very name means "who is like the Lord?" (see 7:18). Both the prophet's name and his message attest to the incomparable majesty of God, whose sovereign reign is everlasting.

THE TITLE
Micah 1:1

> 1:1 **The word of the LORD that came to Micah of Moresheth in the days of Kings Jotham, Ahaz, and Hezekiah of Judah, which he saw concerning Samaria and Jerusalem.**

The verse that opens the book serves as title for it. The most important words are the first five. Everything else in the title is subordinate to the unequivocal fact that the words of Micah are "the word of the Lord." Nevertheless, this introductory verse takes great pains to situate God's word in a particular historical setting. The word is received and transmitted by a particular individual with an identifiable background and period of activity. Micah hails from the town of Moresheth, most probably an abbreviated name for Moresheth-gath (modern Tell el-Judeideh), which is mentioned in 1:14, a town approximately twenty-five miles southwest of Jerusalem in Judah. More than a small village, this strategic border town overlooking the plain of Philistia was fortified under King Rehoboam in order to protect any western incursion against the capital city Jerusalem ("Gath" in 2 Chron. 11:8). It was also situated along an important trade route from Azekah to Lachish. This was no isolated, backwoods village.

According to the title, Micah was active during the reigns of the successive kings Jotham (742–735 B.C.), Ahaz (735–715 B.C.), and Hezekiah (715–687/6 B.C.), a maximum of fifty-six years and a minimum of twenty. As mentioned in the introduction, the latter half of the eighth century was a time of drastic change in the political configuration of the fertile crescent—the region from Mesopotamia to Palestine. The northern kingdom Israel ("Samaria") succumbed to the power of Assyria (2 Kings 17) and Judah was reduced to being a vassal state under Assyrian rule. Some two decades later, Hezekiah heroically, but at great cost, defended Jerusalem against the Assyrian army led by Sennacherib in 701 B.C.

The title also claims that this imparted word of God was *perceived* by the prophet. God's word is not only auditory but somehow visually oriented. Yet this is no ordinary seeing. Prophets are frequently described as "seeing" their received message (2 Chron. 32:32; Isa. 1:1; Obad. 1; Nah. 1:1). What the prophets "saw" were more than simply visions in the night (cf. Zech. 1:7–8). It is no accident that Micah's prophecies, like those of his contemporaries and successors, are filled with rich visual imagery that convey a reality in which God reigns supreme over history and nature (for example, 1:3–4). To be sure, any prophet imparted God's word through speech, written word, and an occasional gesture or sign, but it is the power of the poetic word that is primary, since it invariably involves all the senses of human perception. Like the psalmist's invitation "O taste and see that the Lord is good" (Psalm 34:8), the poetry of the prophets draws the hearer into the reality of God's transforming work in the world.

In a culture accustomed to visual (television) images and sound-bites, the power of the spoken, poetic word is lost in our day and age. For the prophets, however, it was such a word that could most directly change lives and impact the course of history. Similarly, the task of preaching is only possible with a recognition of the power of the word to change people's lives. Perhaps the sermon is the remaining vestige of the prophetic word today. That is why, for instance, Martin Luther King, Jr. delivered sermons and not political speeches. That is why ministers get up every Sunday morning, hoping that in their preparation what they have to say in the pulpit is, by God's spirit, an enlivening, life-changing word for their parishioners. If the power of the spoken word is lost, why would anyone take the time and trouble to preach, and why would anyone listen? Indeed, a word spoken in faith is nothing less than an echo of the living Word that undergirds all of life.

Lastly, the prophetic word is a word on target. The first verse of Micah states a twofold subject matter, Samaria and Jerusalem, the respective capitals of the northern and southern kingdoms. Under David, Jerusalem became the political and religious center of both the northern and southern tribes. Solomon's successor Rehoboam, however, caused a split in the united kingdom, resulting in a separate kingdom and capital among the northern tribes. Located forty miles north of Jerusalem, Samaria under King Omri became that capital, and the two kingdoms, Israel and Judah, henceforth existed side by side. By focusing on the religious and political centers of God's people, Micah does not concern himself with peripheral issues; his message strikes at the two hearts of the Israelite community with repercussions that are still felt today among modern readers.

JUDGMENT AGAINST SAMARIA
Micah 1:2–7

> 1:2 Hear, you peoples, all of you;
>   listen, O earth, and all that is in it;
> and let the Lord GOD be a witness against you,
>   the Lord from his holy temple.
> 3 For lo, the LORD is coming out of his place,
>   and will come down and tread upon the high places of the earth.
> 4 Then the mountains will melt under him
>   and the valleys will burst open,
> like wax near the fire,
>   like waters poured down a steep place.
> 5 All this is for the transgression of Jacob
>   and for the sins of the house of Israel.
> What is the transgression of Jacob?
>   Is it not Samaria?
> And what is the high place of Judah?
>   Is it not Jerusalem?
> 6 Therefore I will make Samaria a heap in the open country,
>   a place for planting vineyards.
> I will pour down her stones into the valley,
>   and uncover her foundations.
> 7 All her images shall be beaten to pieces,
>   all her wages shall be burned with fire,
>   and all her idols I will lay waste;
> for as the wages of a prostitute she gathered them,
>   and as the wages of a prostitute they shall again be used.

Micah's message begins with a summons to a judicial hearing. The language suggests the setting of a court held to indict and render judgment. One can almost hear the gavel knocking against the wood as the prophet declares, "Hear ye, hear ye!" Indeed, some scholars have called this part of Micah's message a "covenant lawsuit" brought by God against the people over the violation of the covenant made at Sinai, including the Ten Commandments (Exod. 20:1–17; Deut. 5:6–21). The shocker, however, is that all the peoples of the earth are addressed not as jurors or witnesses, but as *defendants* (1:2)! The whole earth stands accused, and God, as plaintiff, is ready to testify. Yet God is also like the judge who leaves the inner chamber and enters the open court to begin the proceedings. God comes out from "his holy temple," that is, from heaven (Isa. 63:15; 66:1–2), to render judgment. More than any earthly plaintiff or judge, the manifestation of God's awesome majesty prompts all of creation to tremble and dissolve (1:3–4; Psalms 68:3; 97:5); God stands over and against nature; nothing in and of creation can withstand God's presence on the move (cf. Hab. 3:3–13).

God's destination is Samaria, the capital of the northern kingdom Israel (see introduction). Verse 5 supplies the reason behind God's holding court: the "transgression of Jacob" (Israel), which is identified with Samaria. Whatever this crime is, it strikes at the very heart of the community of faith. Something is rotten at Israel's very core. In parallel fashion, the prophet also indicts Judah, whose "high place" is Jerusalem. Such language delivers a stinging condemnation, for Jerusalem is likened to an abominable Canaanite shrine. A "high place" was an open-air or roofed site where pagan religious rites were practiced. Jerusalem, the supposed center of true worship, is no different than its Canaanite neighbors. Indeed, Jerusalem is no different than Samaria. The two kingdoms are thus inextricably linked by their common sin. What had formerly united them were God's dynastic promise to David (2 Samuel 7) and the glorious temple of Jerusalem (1 King 6—8). Now frequently bitter enemies since the secession of the northern kingdom in 920 B.C., Israel and Judah are united, ironically, only in apostasy, Micah declares.

Passing aside for the moment any mention of judgment against Judah, Micah moves from indictment to doom in his announcement against Samaria (v. 6). Samaria will, in effect, no longer be the city it once was. Its fortified walls and monumental buildings will not only be razed but the soil will be plowed for planting vineyards (cf. Isa. 1:8). No trace will be left of its former urban glory. Likewise, all the trappings of Samaria's illicit splendor will be destroyed. Images and idols, the religious paraphernalia of apostate worship, are likened to the wages of a prostitute. For Micah, Samaria's idolatrous worship was as illicit as prostitution. The comparison may not be simply a figurative one. So fully was the worship of God identified with pagan practice that temple prostitution was commonplace (Hos. 4:10–15). Now, however, all the evidences of idolatrous worship are to be destroyed. The purpose, as well as the reason, of God's terrible judgment against Samaria is now made clear, namely to abolish all forms of idolatrous worship, worship that flagrantly violated the first and second commandments (Exod. 20:3–5).

THE PROPHET'S WAIL
OVER JUDAH'S WOUND
Micah 1:8–16

1:8 For this I will lament and wail;
      I will go barefoot and naked;
I will make lamentation like the jackals,
      and mourning like the ostriches.
9 For her wound is incurable.
      It has come to Judah;
it has reached to the gate of my people,
      to Jerusalem.
10 Tell it not in Gath,
      weep not at all;
in Beth-leaphrah
      roll yourselves in the dust.
11 Pass on your way,
      inhabitants of Shaphir,
      in nakedness and shame;
the inhabitants of Zaanan
      do not come forth;
Beth-ezel is wailing
      and shall remove its support from you.
12 For the inhabitants of Maroth
      wait anxiously for good,
yet disaster has come down from the LORD
      to the gate of Jerusalem.
13 Harness the steeds to the chariots,
      inhabitants of Lachish;
it was the beginning of sin to daughter Zion,
for in you were found
      the transgressions of Israel.
14 Therefore you shall give parting gifts
      to Moresheth-gath;
the houses of Achzib shall be a deception
      to the kings of Israel.
15 I will again bring a conqueror upon you,
      inhabitants of Mareshah;
the glory of Israel
      shall come to Adullam.
16 Make yourselves bald and cut off your hair
      for your pampered children;

make yourselves as bald as the eagle,
for they have gone from you into exile.

One might think that a southern prophet like Micah would smack his lips in glee over such an announcement of judgment against the north. Perhaps that is a justified stereotype of many self-declared prophets of today, but not so with Micah. No profits are to be reaped by this prophet! Far from rejoicing over the prospect of doom over Samaria, Micah laments and weeps. The prophet does not consider himself apart or even exempt from the people's transgressions. By striking at the heart of his people, the prophet pierces his own. Micah has identified himself with his people and their fate. Out of enduring love for his people, the prophet, like the inhabitants of Shaphir described in verse 11, shamefully walks the street naked and mourning on their behalf (see Isa. 20:1–6). The images of the jackal and the ostrich (v. 8) suggest that the prophet, like Job himself (Job 30:29), laments in a wasteland of despair. Micah, a southerner, realizes that the northern kingdom's sin and resulting judgment bodes only doom for his own people. The incurable wound has reached Judah, even to the very "gate of my people" (v. 9).

What follows in Micah's address is his own lament (vv. 10–16). Evident in the original Hebrew language, the list of cities in this section is set within a distinctive poetic pattern. It is a dirge or lament for the dead (cf. 1 Sam. 1:19–27, especially v. 20 with Mic. 1:10). Verbal puns are frequent. All towns southwest of Jerusalem, which can be identified with some certainty, fall in proximity to the prophet's hometown, Moresheth-gath (v. 14). Micah portrays these cities as good as dead. Exiled and bewailed, they are the objects of his lament. Although many of the towns listed here remain unidentifiable, it is suggested by many scholars that they all comprise a part of the destructive march of the Assyrian army under Sennacherib to the gates of Jerusalem in 701 B.C. (For another listing of cities used to illustrate the march of an invading army, see Isaiah 10:27–32.) Sennacherib himself proudly portrayed the defeat of Lachish (1:13) on a wall of his palace. He boasts of having shut up king Hezekiah of Jerusalem like "a bird in a cage." In addition, the Assyrian king claims to have captured forty-six strong cities, including countless villages, as well as deported over two hundred thousand of the Judean population. Indeed, as verses 9 and 12 make horrifyingly clear, disaster has reached the very gate of Jerusalem. Before such an impending swath of destruction, the only thing left to do is observe the mourning rites for one's own death (v. 16).

In all this, Micah dramatically demonstrates the contagion of sin and judgment. The sin that erupts from the center has irreparable repercussions for even the farthest boundaries of the community of faith. As sin explodes outward from within, God's judgment implodes upon it, from the outside in. No one is exempt from God's judgment, not even the prophet, who in extreme vulnerability walks naked in the street, anticipating the fate of all, as well as his own.

DISINHERITING THE INHERITORS
Micah 2:1–5

> 2:1 Alas for those who devise wickedness
>   and evil deeds on their beds!
> When the morning dawns, they perform it,
>   because it is in their power.
> [2] They covet fields, and seize them;
>   houses, and take them away;
> they oppress householder and house,
>   people and their inheritance.
> [3] Therefore thus says the LORD:
> Now, I am devising against this family an evil
>   from which you cannot remove your necks;
> and you shall not walk haughtily,
>   for it will be an evil time.
> [4] On that day they shall take up a
>   taunt song against you,
>   and wail with bitter lamentation,
> and say, "We are utterly ruined;
>   the LORD alters the inheritance of my people;
> how he removes it from me!
>   Among our captors he parcels out our fields."
> [5] Therefore you will have no one
>   to cast the line by lot
>   in the assembly of the LORD.

Micah moves from judgment to accusation against his own people. The first verse begins a so-called woe-oracle, a prophetic indictment of guilt (for example, Isa. 5:8–24; 10:1–4; Amos 5:7; 5:18–20; 6:1–3; Hab. 2:12–14, 15–17). The prophet targets the rich who seize property from the defenseless in order to expand their estates. Micah characterizes them as "bedside" oppressors (2:1, cf. Psalm 36:5; Prov. 6:10). Micah probably has the same class of people in mind as Isaiah: "Ah, you who join house to house, who add field to field, until there is room for no one but you" (Isa.

5:8). They formulate their plans by night and implement them at leisure by day. They wield uncontested power.

Micah's reference to the dawn of morning is striking. Usually the break of dawn marks the restoration of order by ushering in divine deliverance (Gen. 1:3; Job 38:12–15; Psalm 46:5). In stark contrast, however, those who devise wickedness implement their devious plans in the bright light of day. In so doing, they act in total discord with God's will. Like devouring predators, they ruthlessly seize property from the defenseless. They rob the people of their inheritance with impunity.

The land was the life and blood of God's people. God brought the tribes of Israel into the promised land, their inheritance of grace. The land was a gift from God to be developed and passed on from generation to generation. The inviolability of such inheritance is what underlies, for example, Naboth's refusal to sell his property to King Ahab (1 Kings 21:2–3). Land was the God-given means by which families and communities survived and prospered. To lose one's land was to lose one's independence and identity. The power of a few, Micah proclaims, is despoiling what establishes and sustains the very identity of God's people. Indeed, it has come down to one "family" (2:3) destroying the God-given inheritance of all other families. Micah's indictment should not sound strange to our modern ears. Almost without exception in third world countries, the land is controlled by a powerful few, leaving impoverished families to eke out their existence on unsuitable land as wage laborers. Even in the United States, farmers are forced to sell their land to ever-growing corporations, and the gulf between the rich and the poor only widens. The prophet's words ring just as true today as they did in his time.

God, however, will not let them get away with it. The prophet calls forth judgment against "this family;" an "evil time" from which there is no escape (2:3). Such evil is lodged squarely in the eyes of the beholder. It is evil to those who suffer judgment, but to God as well as to the victimized, it is just-deserts. God's partiality toward the dispossessed deprives the dispossessors of their ill-gotten possessions. They will suffer the very fate that they inflicted on others. Like Micah himself, they will wail and lament (cf. 1:8). Yet unlike the prophet's lament in 1:8, which was directed to all of God's people, the wailing of the wicked is hopelessly self-centered (2:4). It is a complaint mired in the rhetoric of selfish grievance and misguided irony: victimizers making an appeal as victims, not unlike the crazy son who killed his parents and then threw himself upon the mercy of the court for being an orphan.

Their complaint accuses God of removing their "inheritance," their property gained through theft in the name of economic progress. A rose, however, is not a rose by any other name. Unrepentant to the end, the outrage of the wicked blinds them from seeing that their misfortune is the work of God's justice, and that their punishment is directly correlated with their guilt. By dispossessing others, they have in the end dispossessed themselves. Consequently, they will no longer have standing in the assembly of the Lord to (re)acquire property (2:5). As the tribes of Israel once received their inheritance by lot (Josh. 14—21), those who have attempted to redraw the property lines for profit will be excluded when their land is redistributed by the sacred assembly.

RESISTANCE TO
MICAH'S PROPHECY
Micah 2:6–11

> 2:6 "Do not preach"—thus they preach—
> "one should not preach for such things;
> disgrace will not overtake us."
> [7] Should this be said, O house of Jacob?
> Is the Lord's patience exhausted?
> Are these his doings?
> Do not my words do good
> to one who walks uprightly?
> [8] But you rise up against my people as an enemy;
> you strip the robe from the peaceful,
> from those who pass by trustingly
> with no thought of war.
> [9] The women of my people you drive out
> from their pleasant houses;
> from their young children you take away
> my glory forever.
> [10] Arise and go;
> for this is no place to rest,
> because of uncleanness that destroys
> with a grievous destruction.
> [11] If someone were to go about uttering empty falsehoods,
> saying, "I will preach to you of wine and strong drink,"
> such a one would be the preacher for this people!

Naturally, such bold words are considered inflammatory and dangerous. This section begins and ends on the issue of Micah's credibility as a prophet. Micah's integrity is placed into question at the outset. Like Amaziah's attempt to silence Amos (Amos 7:12–13), Micah's detractors order him to cease such negative preaching. And, as with Amos before him and Jeremiah after him (see Jeremiah 28), the issue is one of God's judgment. Micah's detractors make the counterclaim that "disgrace will not overtake us" (2:6). They cannot fathom the fact that they are in the wrong for having placed their community into jeopardy. Their glib defense elicits a barrage of rhetorical questions from the prophet, which ends with a vindication of his prophetic office. Micah claims that even the words of judgment are edifying to the righteous, for they know that even in punishment, God is glorified (see the end of v. 9). He also declares that those who see no reason for judgment, on the other hand, set themselves up as enemies of the people (v. 8). The real enemies are not the Assyrian armies or any other outside force but those within the community who profit at its expense. Those who cannot fathom judgment fail to understand even the most basic tenets of justice and fair play. Consequently, they act with impunity. Micah accuses them of covertly conducting war from within, irreparably overturning the *shalom* or peaceful well-being that God desires for the community. "Cursed are the peacemakers" is their motto.

In his scathing indictment, Micah returns to describing their unpardonable acts: seizing land that is not theirs, evicting the most vulnerable, namely women and children (2:9; see 2:2). Micah's contemporary, Isaiah, anticipates the day when such estate owners have displaced all the inhabitants and therefore must live alone in utter isolation—a fitting punishment (Isa. 5:8–9). Micah, on the other hand, adjures them to leave the land (2:10). This land, the land set apart by God for Israel, is no place for them to reside and rest (cf. 2:1a), for their ways defile the land with destruction. Inseparably tied to the divine gift of land, "rest" was the goal of settling the promised land in the first place (Deut. 12:9–10; Psalm 95:11).

The prophet's words could not be more blistering. By unjustly appropriating the property of others, such as taking land in pledge and forcing a foreclosure at the slightest failure in payment, they have given up all rights of membership in the community. As they have evicted the women and children, so they, too, must be expelled.

The prophet concludes his discourse by describing the kind of preacher these enemies of the people prefer, namely one who lies and babbles on about wine and beer. Since the oppressors have become callously numb to the reality of suffering that is of their own creation, they prefer prophets who will intoxicate them to the point of oblivion. Micah, in contrast to these false prophets, finds his calling in opening the eyes of his audience so that they may see the destructive consequences of their behavior. His indictment is meant to break the code of silence that suppresses the cries of those who suffer the brunt of these land-grabbers.

More broadly, prophets like Micah confront us with the incontrovertible fact that we are all intertwined in a web of relations. Like the wings of a butterfly in Australia that affect the weather patterns in Canada (so scientists claim), what we say and do can have unforeseen consequences outside of our own limited fields of vision. Prophets help cast off our blinders and break down our dividing walls of ignorance, while revealing the ties that bind us all together. To shield ourselves from those who suffer, prophets and apostles alike have said, is to shield ourselves from God. The Church is not a cloister; it is an open refuge and welcoming sanctuary. As Paul states succinctly, "If one member suffers, all suffer together" (1 Cor. 12:26).

HEALING THE WOUND THAT DIVIDES
Micah 2:12–13

> 2:12 **I will surely gather all of you, O Jacob,**
>   **I will gather the survivors of Israel;**
> **I will set them together**
>   **like sheep in a fold,**
> **like a flock in its pasture;**
>   **it will resound with people.**
> [13] **The one who breaks out will go up before them;**
>   **they will break through and pass the gate,**
>   **going out by it.**
> **Their king will pass on before them,**
>   **the LORD at their head.**

This chapter ends on a remarkably positive note, one that demonstrates that judgment does not exhaust the font of salvation. Many scholars date these two concluding verses to the time of the Babylonian exile (587–539 B.C.), the time in which many were permanently separated from their land and deported a century and a half after Micah's prophecies. Whether announced by the prophet or a later editor, God's promise of salvation is shown to be the end and goal of judgment. What was dividing and destroying the community now gives way to reconciliation. Those who were evicted from home and land are restored. Judgment turns to salvation.

Like a shepherd, God will gather the dispersed people. Not one will be lost; all will be gathered together (Luke 15:4–7; John 10:11–18).

This irenic image suggests a picture of undisturbed rest and restoration (cf. 2:10). The final verse depicts how this all will come about. The Lord as shepherd-king will lead the flock on a new exodus, breaking through the walls of hostility and oppression, back to the gate of Jerusalem, where Israel's sin and judgment once held sway (see 1:9, 12). The city of holiness has come full circle, from a community ravaged by sin and conflict to a city restored in salvation. Such is the expressed intent of our Judge and Savior who leads us all on the journey of faith as a community united in faith.

JUSTICE CORRUPTED
Micah 3:1–4

3:1 **And I said:**
Listen, you heads of Jacob
and rulers of the house of Israel!
Should you not know justice?—
2 **you who hate the good and love the evil,**
who tear the skin off my people,
and the flesh off their bones;
3 **who eat the flesh of my people,**
flay their skin off them,
break their bones in pieces,
and chop them up like meat in a kettle,
like flesh in a caldron.

4 **Then they will cry to the LORD,**
but he will not answer them;
he will hide his face from them at that time,
because they have acted wickedly.

There comes a point sometimes in which the interpreter of biblical verse must admit a loss of words to elucidate a particular passage, for fear that such words will only dilute the power of what is conveyed in scripture. Here is just such a case. No words can clarify, much less further, what is so graphically expressed in this text, namely the devouring of God's people by Jerusalem's public leaders. Micah likens those who turn justice on its head to cannibals. Undermining justice wreaks unspeakable violence upon people. Ask a Guatemalan peasant, an El Salvadorean refugee, a

Palestinian Christian, or a black South African, and you will find whole-hearted agreement. Whereas justice provides the only solid foundation for peace and prosperity, injustice can quickly and irreparably undermine it, leaving only the rotting carcasses of its victims among the ruins (cf. v. 10).

Micah's address moves beyond indictment to judgment in verse 4. The prophet asserts that it is only a matter of time before the oppressors find themselves in the caldron, and when they do, God will turn away from them. Those that abandon all concern for the needy will themselves be abandoned.

Prophecy Perverted
Micah 3:5–8

> 3:5 Thus says the LORD concerning the prophets
>   who lead my people astray,
> who cry, "Peace"
>   when they have something to eat,
> but declare war against those
>   who put nothing into their mouths.
> 6 Therefore it shall be night to you, without vision,
>   and darkness to you, without revelation.
> The sun shall go down upon the prophets,
>   and the day shall be black over them;
> 7 the seers shall be disgraced,
>   and the diviners put to shame;
> they shall all cover their lips;
>   for there is no answer from God.
> 8 But as for me, I am filled with power,
>   with the spirit of the LORD,
>   and with justice and might,
> to declare to Jacob his transgression
>   and to Israel his sin.

Having called forth judgment on the public leaders of God's people, Micah next targets his fellow prophets. However, they are colleagues by name alone. They mislead the people, talking a false peace while secretly waging war. Far from being genuine peacemakers, they are mercenaries who tell the people what they want to hear for their own gain while cursing those who give them nothing. Prophecy is twisted for self-gain. Thus darkness shall overcome them. Bereft of vision and answer from God, the false prophets will no longer be able to practice their vocation (v. 6). Destroying the very integrity of their office, they have tailored their words to the whims and desires of those whom they serve. They are prophets by commission, not of God but of their self-serving hearts (cf. v. 11). They have sold the word and consequently lost it. Pay them for services rendered and you will be blessed; but if your check is still in the mail, they will quickly pronounce your doom. The shame of silence is in store for them, as well as for the abominable diviners, who purport to discern God's will through natural signs (v. 7; see commentary on 5:12). There is no greater shame than a prophet without an answer or, for that matter, a preacher without a message. To be sure, the perversion of the ministerial office still runs rampant today.

For Micah, however, the prophetic ministry is more than a profession. Ministry is not a business; it is a life led in service to God regardless of the cost. Empowered by God's spirit, the prophet lives by and speaks of justice, and it is in the name of that justice that the prophet declares Israel's ("Jacob's") sin (3:8). He can do no other. Micah's words, in contrast to the timid, ever-shifting words of his colleagues, gush forth as if from the very heart of God.

THE CITY TURNED
A FIELD OF BLOOD
Micah 3:9–12

3:9 **Hear this, you rulers of the house of Jacob,**
    and chiefs of the house of Israel,
who abhor justice
    and pervert all equity,
10 **who build Zion with blood**
    and Jerusalem with wrong!
11 **Its rulers give judgment for a bribe,**
    its priests teach for a price,
    its prophets give oracles for money;
yet they lean upon the LORD and say,
    "Surely the LORD is with us!
    No harm shall come upon us."
12 **Therefore because of you**
    Zion shall be plowed as a field;
Jerusalem shall become a heap of ruins,
    and the mountain of the house a wooded height.

As in 3:1, Micah targets the rulers of Israel. Renowned for perverting justice, these officials undermine the very structures that support the community. In so doing, they lay waste to Jerusalem ("Zion"). A city built by the blood of its people is no city; it is a cemetery to be plowed over as a field (vv. 10, 12). Zion has only itself to blame for its ignominious end. The rulers, the priests, and the prophets all pervert their honorable vocations only to line their pockets and yet audaciously claim God to be on their side. But their very words reveal that they expect God to ignore their crimes (v. 11b). Driven by profits and bribes, these professionals have undercut all standards of equity, not to mention integrity, of office. Devoid of justice, Jerusalem like Samaria (1:6) will lie in ruins. With the temple razed ("the mountain of the house"), only a forested mound will remain (v. 12).

Such a terrible judgment was never fulfilled during Micah's lifetime. The prophet's message, however, was by no means lost. Over a century later, Micah's prophecy was cited in connection with the disturbing message of Jeremiah (Jer. 26:18–19; see introduction). Like Micah, Jeremiah too condemned Jerusalem and the temple (Jeremiah 7 and 26) with a judgment that was fulfilled in 587 B.C. On that infamous day the Babylonian army breached the city's walls, burned the temple to the ground, and exiled much of the population. The blood that was shed on that day, Micah would no doubt claim, was simply the inevitable outgrowth of generations of sin and abuse. Israel has sunk into its own pit (cf. Psalm 9:15).

THE PEACE
THAT SURPASSES ALL STRIFE
Micah 4:1–5

4:1 **In days to come**
   the mountain of the LORD's house
shall be established as the highest of the mountains,
   and shall be raised up above the hills.
Peoples shall stream to it,
2 **and many nations shall come and say:**
"Come, let us go up to the mountain of the LORD,
   to the house of the God of Jacob;
that he may teach us his ways
   and that we may walk in his paths."
For out of Zion shall go forth instruction,
   and the word of the LORD from Jerusalem.

³ He shall judge between many peoples,
   and shall arbitrate between strong nations far away;
they shall beat their swords into plowshares,
   and their spears into pruning hooks;
nation shall not lift up sword against nation,
   neither shall they learn war any more;
⁴ but they shall all sit under their
      own vines and under their own fig trees,
   and no one shall make them afraid;
   for the mouth of the LORD of hosts has spoken.

⁵ For all the peoples walk,
   each in the name of its god,
but we will walk in the name of the LORD our God
   forever and ever.

Zion's destruction, foretold in 3:12, is shown only to be a prelude in the prophet's announcement of what will happen in the "latter days," that is, in the consummation of history. Closely paralleled in Isaiah 2:2–4, this well-known passage tells of the glorious restoration of Jerusalem's temple, "the mountain of the Lord's house," and the end to warfare. The temple will surpass its former glory to become the highest of the mountains. One need only look at the topography of Jerusalem and its environs to note that the prophecy is yet to be fulfilled. In addition to the height of Zion's glory, there is also the political dimension. The multitude of nations will stream to Jerusalem to receive direct instruction from God (see Psalm 122:1, 4; Zech. 8:20–23). Jerusalem will become the center for learning God's ways. The image of the path is a suggestive one (4:2). A path suggests a particular direction in life, a course of conduct (see 6:8). Elsewhere, God's paths are defined as the paths of righteousness, justice, and equity (Psalm 23:3; Prov. 2:9). To walk these paths, the nations must act in obedience to the ordained stipulations of communal conduct set forth in God's covenant with Israel (for example, Exodus 20—23; Deuteronomy). These are not lonely paths for solitary individuals, for how is a path formed if not through the passage of many feet? God's paths are the paths of the community of faith as it discerns and obeys God's will for itself in the world. Implied in Micah's prophecy is that Israel, God's chosen community, is the trailblazer in helping set the path the other nations must follow (see 4:5), for it is from Zion that instruction (torah), God's very word, comes forth (4:3).

From Jerusalem the nations will study war no more (4:3b). From Zion God will judge the nations, even those most remote. A nation's strength will no longer depend on its weapons of destruction. The education of the nations will involve the renunciation of war, with all instruments of war converted into agricultural tools (cf. Psalms 46:9; 76:3; cf. Joel 3:10). A nation's strength will stem from its abundant produce, not from its destructive potential. If the rationale for war is self-protection and fear, as is often claimed, then it is undercut once and for all by the pronouncement of security in verse 4. Everyone of every nation shall sit securely amid luxuriant vines and fig trees, unafraid and undisturbed. In light of Micah's sweeping prophecy, war is, at best, an absurd and tragic preoccupation of the unlearned and, at worst, an abomination of God's holy purpose in history.

Micah's sweeping condemnation of war has appropriately become the motto and rationale for a host of groups and movements, from activist pacifists to conflict management programs. It is a message that underlies all attempts, no matter how feeble or unsuccessful, to find alternatives to potentially divisive confrontations. Micah's vision is one that is rooted in a vision of a common humanity in a world, created and nurtured by God, a reality that overcomes the clash of sabres and the divisive exchange of words. A pastor friend of mine once related the time he tried to convince his session to take a certain action in the community. He carefully laid out the theological arguments and employed the best of his persuasive powers, only to find out that all the elders, in the end, voted against him. I asked him whether he was disappointed, to which he said, "Sure I was; they're still all wrong, but I was proud of them for listening and holding forth discussion, and I realized more than ever before, I loved each and every one of them." The pastor and his session, whether they knew it or not, anticipated Micah's vision of harmony, one based upon mutual respect and common purpose without the necessity of agreement. Indeed, every attempt toward peace is a reflection of God's coming kingdom, a glimpse of the fulfillment of history.

Verse 5 is the present response to Micah's vision of the future, a pronouncement on the part of God's people in response to that vision of peace and unity throughout all the peoples of the earth (vv. 1–4). At the news of history's consummation, Israel finds new resolve to be the first to walk "in the name of the Lord," while all the other nations still acknowledge only their own gods. The light of the glorious future that is in store for all the peoples of the earth, a new reality in which "every knee shall bow, every tongue shall swear" to God (Isa. 45:23; cf. Rom. 14:11; Phil. 2:10), strengthens the conviction of God's own people to commit themselves to the Lord. Centuries later, the community of faith still exists in the realm of the "not yet," in a world yet unredeemed, eagerly awaiting the time in which there will be a new heaven and a new earth for all the inhabitants of God's creation (Revelation 21).

This glorious vision of universal acknowledgement of God in no way dilutes but rather strengthens the resolve of the Church to share the *particular* message of its Lord to the world. For Christians, Jesus being "lifted up" to heaven in his ascension (Acts 1:9), like Zion lifted up above the hills (Mic. 4:1), has inaugurated a new age in which God has been "reconciling the world to himself" (2 Cor. 5:19). Indeed, the book of Revelation identifies the new temple not with any building but with the Lord and the Lamb, to whom all the people will bring the "glory and honor of the nations" (Rev. 21:22). As Jesus began his ministry with the words "the kingdom of God has come near; repent, and believe in the good news" (Mark 1:14), Jesus' ascension brings God's kingdom of justice and peace into the hearts of believers, who await the final consummation when Jesus will return in glory.

ZION'S RESTORATION: FROM JUDGMENT TO TRIUMPH
Micah 4:6–13

> 4:6 In that day, says the LORD,
>   I will assemble the lame
> and gather those who have been driven away,
>   and those whom I have afflicted.
> 7 The lame I will make the remnant,
>   and those who were cast off, a strong nation;
> and the LORD will reign over them in Mount Zion
>   now and forevermore.
>
> 8 And you, O tower of the flock,
>   hill of daughter Zion,
> to you it shall come,
>   the former dominion shall come,
>   the sovereignty of daughter Jerusalem.
>
> 9 Now why do you cry aloud?
>   Is there no king in you?
> Has your counselor perished,
>   that pangs have seized you like a woman in labor?

> ¹⁰ Writhe and groan, O daughter Zion,
>   like a woman in labor;
> for now you shall go forth from the city
>   and camp in the open country;
>   you shall go to Babylon.
> There you shall be rescued,
>   there the LORD will redeem you
>   from the hands of your enemies.
>
> ¹¹ Now many nations
>   are assembled against you,
> saying, "Let her be profaned,
>   and let our eyes gaze upon Zion."
> ¹² But they do not know
>   the thoughts of the LORD;
> they do not understand his plan,
>   that he has gathered them as sheaves to the threshing floor.
> ¹³ Arise and thresh,
>   O daughter Zion,
> for I will make your horn iron
>   and your hoofs bronze;
> you shall beat in pieces many peoples,
>   and shall devote their gain to the LORD,
>   their wealth to the Lord of the whole earth.

The following series of promises explicate the vision of peace and security so powerfully conveyed in verses 1–4. As in 2:12, God intends to gather together the people like a good shepherd. Here, the outcast and the afflicted are singled out for special attention (4:6). The prophet's message comes on the other side of judgment; it tells of a time in which judgment has run its course, giving way to restoration. With judgment fulfilled, God now comes to renew the ties that bind. The lame, in particular, are designated the special remnant of a mighty nation (4:7). Those who mercilessly wielded power to destroy others are no longer around to pervert justice and destroy the community (3:9). The weakest, on the other hand, have endured and now, like Jacob whose hip was dislocated at the banks of the river Jabbok (Gen. 32:25–31), receive God's special blessing. Divine irony has reached its zenith: The outcast now constitute the birth of a new nation with the Lord reigning from the heights of Zion. In such irony the fullest measure of grace is extended: To the meek is given the inheritance of the earth (Matt. 5:5).

With the bulwark of God's dominion founded upon the powerless (see

Psalm 8:2; 1 Cor. 1:25), "daughter Zion" will be restored to its former glory (Mic. 4:8). The feminine image is a common expression of endearment used by the prophets to personify a city, frequently Jerusalem (for example, Isa. 1:8; 37:22; Jer. 4:31; Lam. 1:6; 2:13; Zeph. 3:14). It implies an enduring relationship between the people and God, one that evokes the pain as well as the pride and joy that only a parent can feel regarding his or her children. Such is the case in verses 9–13. The prophet leads "daughter Zion" through the travail of judgment into the glory of her restoration. Zion's guilt is nowhere in doubt, as the prophet has so powerfully presented in the previous chapter. Consequently, the people are without their wise king. In agony like a woman in labor, they are uprooted from their home and deported to Babylon. The prophet has in mind that dark age in Israel's history in which the Babylonian empire destroyed Zion, tore down the city's temple, and deported much of the people (587 B.C.).

However, that is not the end of the story. God comes to the rescue to redeem Israel in a foreign land (v. 10). Although an act of grace, redemption is in part an acknowledged duty. Redemption implies a recognized obligation based upon kinship ties. Long ago God became committed to a particular people by delivering them from the house of bondage and establishing a formal covenant with them at Sinai so that God could claim them and they could claim God as their own. That familial bond endured through much testing and hardship and now provides the basis for Israel's redemption by God.

Such redemption, however, is violently contested by the nations (vv. 11–12). The rise of Zion represents a threat to their rule over the land. Zion's humiliation is their pronounced goal as they assemble and surround God's city, poised to act on their lust for power (see Psalm 2:1–3). Little do they know, however, that their conspiracy to crush daughter Zion is part of God's plan to vindicate her and to consecrate her wealth. The assembling nations are unaware that they are being gathered up like cut grain for the threshing floor (4:11–12; see Isa. 21:10; Jer. 51:33; Hos. 13:3). Daughter Zion is empowered to thresh and vanquish her enemies and devote their wealth to God (4:13). That is to say, Zion's dominion, which represents God's dominion over the earth, is not carried out to the drum beat of imperial self-expansion. Whatever gain results from the defeat of the nations is not for self-enrichment but rather for God's glory. The spoils of the conquered are not to be possessed but devoted to God. Zion's triumph is God's victory. This is a war to end all wars.

THE FUTURE RULER
FROM BETHLEHEM
Micah 5:1–6

> 5:1 Now you are walled around with a wall;
>   siege is laid against us;
> with a rod they strike the ruler of Israel
>   upon the cheek.
> 2 But you, O Bethlehem of Ephrathah,
>   who are one of the little clans of Judah,
> from you shall come forth for me
>   one who is to rule in Israel,
> whose origin is from of old,
>   from ancient days.
> 3 Therefore he shall give them up until the time
>   when she who is in labor has brought forth;
> then the rest of his kindred shall return
>   to the people of Israel.
> 4 And he shall stand and feed his flock in the strength of the LORD,
>   in the majesty of the name of the LORD his God.
> And they shall live secure, for now he shall be great
>   to the ends of the earth;
> 5 and he shall be the one of peace.
>
> If the Assyrians come into our land and tread upon our soil,
> we will raise against them seven shepherds,
>   and eight installed as rulers.
> 6 They shall rule the land of Assyria with the sword,
>   and the land of Nimrod with the drawn sword;
> they shall rescue us from the Assyrians
>   if they come into our land
>   or tread within our border.

As in 4:9–13, the prophet presents a gripping panorama of events that move from suffering to restoration, from calamity to peace. Whereas the absence of a king is lamented in 4:9, the king of Israel in 5:1 is under attack, struck upon the cheek. The city is under siege all around. The context suggests that the enemy is Assyria (vv. 5–6); hence, King Hezekiah is the best candidate for the unnamed king in verse 1 (see commentary on 1:8–16). Under a situation of extreme distress, Micah delivers a message of hope from God. Beginning in verse 2, God, through the mouth of the prophet, singles out one of the smallest clans of Judah, "Ephrathah." A small town located about six miles south of Jerusalem, Bethlehem in

Ephrathah is proclaimed the birthplace of the once and future king who will restore peace throughout Israel and beyond. Though cast in the indefinite future, the prophecy hearkens back to an ancient origin, rooted in an ancient promise (5:2). The prophet's promise recalls the tradition of David's rise to kingship. Anointed in Bethlehem (1 Sam. 16:1–13), David pacified the land and united the northern and southern tribes, selecting Jerusalem as the political and religious capital of the new nation. God granted David an everlasting dynasty and a temple to be built by his son (2 Samuel 7).

Standing in continuity with these ancient traditions, Micah announces that a new Davidic king will arise from similar origins to secure permanent and universal peace throughout the land. The current time of travail is simply prefatory for this new age, like labor necessary for birth (5:3). As the good shepherd, this future king will provide for his people in strength and majesty not his own but derived from the "Lord his God" (v. 4).

The last two verses in this section shift in tone and message (vv. 5b–6). Bethlehem is no longer addressed (v. 2); rather this small unit records the people's response of confidence to the certain prospect of deliverance from a crisis of siege (cf. v. 1). In concrete terms, the peaceful reign of God will involve the subjugation of Israel's archenemy, Assyria. From "the stump of Jesse" (Isa. 11:1) will come forth several shepherds or rulers to defend God's people against Assyrian onslaught (v. 6; the numerical progression of seven to eight signifies an indefinite number [cf. Prov. 30:18, 21, 29; Amos 1:3, 6]). Otherwise known as the land of Nimrod (Gen. 10:8–12), this warlike nation was a continual threat to be reckoned with throughout the ancient Near East. Like Egypt in the Exodus centuries earlier, Assyria was the archetypal enemy in Micah's day, a nation that not only studied war but excelled in the art of brutality (cf. 4:3). As a formidable obstacle to peace, Assyria's great might must give way to the bulwark of peace.

THE PURGE OF VICTORY
Micah 5:7–15

> 5:7 **Then the remnant of Jacob,**
> **surrounded by many peoples,**
> **shall be like dew from the LORD,**
> **like showers on the grass,**
> **which do not depend upon people**
> **or wait for any mortal.**

8 And among the nations the remnant of Jacob,
     surrounded by many peoples,
shall be like a lion among the animals of the forest,
     like a young lion among the flocks of sheep,
which, when it goes through, treads down
     and tears in pieces, with no one to deliver.
9 Your hand shall be lifted up over your adversaries,
     and all your enemies shall be cut off.

10 In that day, says the LORD,
     I will cut off your horses from among you
     and will destroy your chariots;
11 and I will cut off the cities of your land
     and throw down all your strongholds;
12 and I will cut off sorceries from your hand,
     and you shall have no more soothsayers;
13 and I will cut off your images
     and your pillars from among you,
and you shall bow down no more
     to the work of your hands;
14 and I will uproot your sacred poles from among you
     and destroy your towns.
15 And in anger and wrath I will execute vengeance
     on the nations that did not obey.

The future holds not only peace but also empowerment for the "remnant of Jacob." The few that are left after the devastation of divine judgment (1:6; 3:12), comprised of the lame and the outcast (4:7), will become as plentiful as the dew or rain upon the grass (see Zech. 8:6, 12). Though a fraction of Israel's former greatness, this remnant has every reason to hope. In 2 Samuel 23:3–4, the gleaming of the rain on the grassy land is a powerful metaphor of God's justice mediated through the king. For Micah, the remnant's existence, like fresh dew in the early morning, is divinely fashioned (see vv. 10–15). Though surrounded by the nations, this remnant, like Zion in the dramatic second Psalm, is invulnerable to human contrivance and force. Through God's strength, God's people are empowered. This is the God of small beginnings and tremendous results, as so amply demonstrated in the entire history of God's work with Israel. The future king of peace, for example, is chosen from the "little clans of Judah" (v. 2). Gideon, the smallest in his family, is chosen from the weakest clan in Manasseh to defeat the dreaded Midianites (Judg. 6:15). Abraham and Sarah, a lonely, vulnerable couple sojourning through foreign lands, are elected to bear the blessing of God to "all the families of the earth" (Gen. 12:3). Israel, the smallest of the nations, is to be raised up as a "light to the nations" (Isa. 49:6). Once vulnerable to the imperial whims of other nations, God's people will no longer have to fear. Their aggressors will be "cut off" (Mic. 5:9, 15).

Yet that will not be the only thing cut off. Purged not only of their enemies, God's people will be inwardly purged (5:10). Delivered from their enemies, Israel will also be delivered from itself. Like the petitioner in Psalms 139:19 and 24, vindicated Israel cannot claim to be blissfully immune from the wickedness that so characterized her enemies. All things and practices that have hindered God's relationship with the people will be searched out and eliminated. Here, punishment is purification. The first to go are the staples of military power in the ancient Orient: horse and chariot (see also Hag. 2:22; Zech. 9:10). The prophecy echoes the injunction against the king in Deuteronomy regarding the buildup of military arms: "[The king] must not acquire many horses for himself, or return the people to Egypt in order to acquire more horses, since the Lord has said to you, 'You must never return that way again'" (Deut. 17:16). It was there at the crossing of the Red Sea, on the way out of Egypt, that the horses and chariots of Pharaoh were overthrown (Exod. 15:1, 19, 21). Nevertheless, king Solomon was remembered for having amassed chariots and horses, marking the beginning of his downfall (1 Kings 10:26–29). Scripture is quite clear that military strength is a trap that inexorably leads to self-reliance and pride, thereby placing faithful reliance upon God in jeopardy. God's people are not to depend upon their own military strength, but upon the militant and zealous compassion of God. For identical reasons, even the fortresses will be eliminated (5:11).

Next to go are the sorcerers and soothsayers, those who practiced magic and attempted to discern God's will through natural signs or omens (5:12). Perfecting such practice to a veritable science, the ancient Mesopotamians, for example, actively solicited signs that could foretell the future. Diviners consulted the distinctive features of the internal organs of slaughtered animals, particularly the liver, gall bladder, and lungs. Other observable signs ranged from the flights of birds to the patterns of oil on water. Astrology would also fall under this "science" (Isa. 47:13). Such practices, however, in ancient Israel were considered abhorrent to God (Deut. 18:10–11; Lev. 19:26), for not only could they be manipulated by the practitioners but they also contradicted the very means by which God communicates with human beings, namely through the exclusive initiative of God through God's word.

Finally and most reprehensible are the paraphernalia of idolatrous worship: images, pillars, and sacred poles (vv. 13–14). Such religious symbols fashioned from various materials were employed to represent God as well as other gods. The first two commandments, however, make absolutely clear that images of God and worship of other deities were strictly forbidden (Exod. 20:2–5). Though surrounded by "many peoples," God's people are commanded not to adopt the pagan practices of the nations and thereby lose their distinctiveness in the world, their distinction as a divinely elected people. The situation is not much different today. Professing faith in Jesus Christ is a profession the world is, as of yet, incapable of making. And yet we are called to be engaged in transforming our world without adopting its ways. Simply put, God's people march to the beat of a different drummer whose simple yet distinctive rhythm does not vary as the world wildly flits from one rhythm to the next.

GOD'S CASE AGAINST ISRAEL
Micah 6:1–5

> 6:1 Hear what the LORD says:
> Rise, plead your case before the mountains,
> and let the hills hear your voice.
> ² Hear, you mountains, the controversy of the LORD,
> and you enduring foundations of the earth;
> for the LORD has a controversy with his people,
> and he will contend with Israel.
>
> ³ "O my people, what have I done to you?
> In what have I wearied you? Answer me!
> ⁴ For I brought you up from the land of Egypt,
> and redeemed you from the house of slavery;
> and I sent before you Moses, Aaron, and Miriam.
> ⁵ O my people, remember now what King Balak of Moab devised,
> what Balaam son of Beor answered him,
> and what happened from Shittim to Gilgal,
> that you may know the saving acts of the LORD."

Having glimpsed the promised land of Israel's glorious restoration (4:1–4, 6–8; 5:1–15), the prophet returns to the problems of the present. This section begins in striking manner with a lawsuit submitted by God against Israel, "a controversy with his people" (6:2). (For similar "case studies," see Psalm 50; Isaiah 1:1–6; Hosea 4:1–3). Like the striking of the gavel, the prophet introduces the Lord's case to the attention of His people (v. 1a).

The divine pronouncement that follows summons the people, as defendants, to state their case publicly (v. 1b). The mountains and the hills are enlisted as witnesses (v. 2), for they were there when God's covenant was first established with Israel (cf. Psalm 50:4; Isa. 1:2). Indeed, it was upon a mountain, Mount Sinai (or Horeb), in which out of cloud and fire the commandments were spoken to formalize God's relationship with the people (Deut. 4:11–13). It was upon two mountains that the blessing and curses of the people were uttered to ensure faithful loyalty to the covenant (Deut. 27:11; Josh. 8:33–35). Indeed, all of creation, both heaven and earth, bore witness to the forging of God's covenantal relationship with Israel (Deut. 4:26; 30:19; 31:28; Psalm 19). Nevertheless, God's people have breached the covenant, the very norms of faithful obedience and identity (see 6:9–16), and, as a result, violated creation itself. Consequently, God approaches the bench as plaintiff to address the mountains to hear the case ("controversy") against Israel. The cosmic court is now in session.

God presents the lawsuit with a poignancy almost unmatched in Scripture (vv. 3–5). With impassioned words, God does not condemn outright but implores Israel to state what God has done to them to provoke such criminal behavior. God seeks not irrevocable judgment but, first and foremost, dialogue and a common understanding. God's initial pronouncement is a profession of innocence. Recounting the events of the exodus and wilderness wanderings, God demonstrates steadfast love and loyalty to an ungrateful people. Redeemed from bondage and curse, God's people have enjoyed the privileges of election (cf. Jer. 2:2–13). God brought them out of Egypt, a ragtag band of slaves, and rescued them from the powerful King Balak, who employed Balaam, that renowned prophet and diviner, to curse them out of existence (Numbers 22—24). Nevertheless, God at no point lets Israel go, preserving them amid a hostile world bent on destroying them. Despite all of God's compassion, however, Israel's stiff-necked recalcitrance could not be overturned.

WHAT TO BRING BEFORE THE LORD?
Micah 6:6–8

> 6:6 "With what shall I come before the LORD,
>   and bow myself before God on high?

> Shall I come before him with burnt offerings,
>   with calves a year old?
> ⁷ Will the LORD be pleased with thousands of rams,
>   with ten thousands of rivers of oil?
> Shall I give my firstborn for my transgression,
>   the fruit of my body for the sin of my soul?"
> ⁸ He has told you, O mortal, what is good;
>   and what does the LORD require of you
> but to do justice, and to love kindness,
>   and to walk humbly with your God?

This most well-known passage conveys the people's response within the context of the lawsuit (6:1–5). Yet this unit also has a life of its own and is frequently claimed as providing the basis of true piety.

Unlike a modern court session, the defendant Israel poses a series of questions in order to receive a definitive answer. Each question essentially asks the same thing: What should I bring in worship to restore my relationship with God? (v. 6). A list of examples, dramatically escalating both in value and quantity, are offered: burnt offerings, a thousand ram offerings, ten thousand rivers of oil, and the firstborn. All, except for the last, are material gifts that have to do with ancient Israel's sacrificial system; gifts presented for the purpose of restoring one's relationship with God (6:7b). Such questions were frequently asked of the priest, whose role was to decide which sacrifices were appropriate for a given occasion. The last gift mentioned, however, is intended to astonish, for it reaches far beyond the bounds of acceptable sacrifice. The sacrifice of the firstborn child is extravagant to the point of abomination.

Although the Old Testament bears witness that the firstborn child was especially claimed by God, prohibition was made against actual sacrifice (Exod. 13:2, 13; 22:28; 34:20). Both the law and the prophets categorically condemned such practice (Deut. 18:10; Lev. 18:21; Isa. 57:5; Jer. 7:21; 19:5; Ezek. 16:20). However, the Bible does record a few reprehensible cases (Judg. 11:34; 2 Kings 3:27; 16:3; 21:6). On the other hand, there is the disturbing story of the binding of Isaac (Gen. 22:1–19), in which God's request to Abraham constitutes the supreme test of faith with a sacrifice to end all human sacrifices. In addition, foundational to the Christian faith are the Gospel accounts of the sacrifice of God's own Son, Jesus Christ, for the sins of the world, the sacrifice that ends all sacrifice. That the worshiper in verse 7 is willing even to sacrifice his firstborn to restore his broken relationship with God demonstrates extreme, albeit misguided, urgency.

To this multiple choice question comes an answer that is just as surprising as the proposal to offer up the firstborn. Micah reminds his audience that God has already given the answer through the words, presumably, of his prophetic and sagacious predecessors (for example, Psalm 37:2;
Prov. 11:27; 12:2; Isa. 1:17; 5:20; Amos 5:14–15). The answer strikes like
a swift knife to puncture everything presupposed in the question: Everything that was proposed by the defendant is simply unnecessary baggage.
"With what shall I come before God in worship?" "Only yourself" is the
answer, but a self of a certain character.

God's answer dramatically shifts the attention from cultic paraphernal-
lia to the contours of correct character, from the handling of external, sacrificial objects to the managing of one's life. The *what* about which the
worshiper asked is the good, defined as doing justice, loving kindness, and
walking humbly with God. What the worshiper is required to bring is a
transformed self, one who is committed to an unwavering life of justice
based on mercy ("kindness") and humble devotion to God. To walk
humbly is to follow wholeheartedly the sovereign God who acts in justice
and mercy. It is not a lonely path; rather, it is the path of the worshiping
community, both past and present. Micah's most famous words are con-
victing yet benedictive, an appropriate counterpart and partner to the
great Aaronic benediction in Numbers 6:24–26. In the church in which I
am active, our concluding benediction is frequently sung with these words
of Micah arranged loosely to the stirring tune of Pachabel's *Canon in D*.
It is an inspiring send-off back into the world! When the Church concludes its worship every Sunday, it disperses with the light of God's countenance in its heart (Num. 6:25–26) and the requirement of God's justice
in its hands (Mic. 6:8).

In the end, God's answer in verse 8 calls for a sacrifice to end all sacrifices, namely the sacrifice of the self in humble obedience to God. What
we bring, apart from a listening and obedient heart, is unnecessary baggage, useless props that can only burden and divert us from faithful obedience, at best, and, at worst, encourage us in blissfully assuming that
everything is hunky-dory between God and us. Such presumption is de-
ceptive, the prophet warns. On the one hand, true piety comes from the
heart and not from what we possess or do; and, on the other hand, true
piety is not a private affair, like a pleasant stroll on the beach with God at
one's side. What God requires is a life of engagement with others in the
quest for justice and mercy in a world that clamors for hatred with a
vengeance. A humble walk with God is demonstrated in a life of continual reexamination and self-questioning of one's motives and purposes in

life in service to God. Yet it is also a life that is not so self-critical as to quit the journey out of a sense of inadequacy. As much as we are required to commit ourselves to walk in justice and humility, God is committed in accompanying us. God calls us to present ourselves "as a living sacrifice, holy and acceptable to God" (Rom. 12:1).

FAILURES IN COVENANT LIVING
Micah 6:9–16

> 6:9 The voice of the LORD cries to the city
>   (it is sound wisdom to fear your name):
> Hear, O tribe and assembly of the city!
> 10 Can I forget the treasures of
>   wickedness in the house of the wicked,
>   and the scant measure that is accursed?
> 11 Can I tolerate wicked scales
>   and a bag of dishonest weights?
> 12 Your wealthy are full of violence;
>   your inhabitants speak lies,
>   with tongues of deceit in their mouths.
> 13 Therefore I have begun to strike you down,
>   making you desolate because of your sins.
> 14 You shall eat, but not be satisfied,
>   and there shall be a gnawing hunger within you;
> you shall put away, but not save,
>   and what you save, I will hand over to the sword.
> 15 You shall sow, but not reap;
>   you shall tread olives, but not anoint yourselves with oil;
>   you shall tread grapes, but not drink wine.
> 16 For you have kept the statutes of Omri
>   and all the works of the house of Ahab,
>   and you have followed their counsels.
> Therefore I will make you a
>   desolation, and your inhabitants an object of hissing;
>   so you shall bear the scorn of my people.

What Micah has put positively in the previous passage, he now casts negatively concerning the rights and duties of covenant living. As God spoke passionately about the history of Israel's salvation amid crisis (vv. 3–5), God now cries out to Jerusalem about the people's transgressions. As much as the history of Israel's election and blessing is vividly remembered

(6:3–5), God cannot forget Israel's flagrant failures (6:9–12). Business is conducted by deception with fraudulent weights and scales (Deut. 25:13–16; Prov. 20:10, 23; Hos. 12:8; Amos 8:5) to line the pockets of the rich, who are "full of violence." The violence of corporate takeovers and ruthless downsizing may not have been unknown to this prophet of the past. Hopelessly mired in deceit, speech itself has lost all credibility. Only "doublethink" reigns, to borrow a term from George Orwell's book, *1984*. In short, Israel has stored up "treasures of wickedness" as much as it has banked on and relied upon God's unmerited grace in times of trouble.

This time, however, God does not come in grace to deliver but in judgment to correct (vv. 13–15). God will and has delivered Israel from external threat, but refuses to deliver the people from themselves. Instead, they shall not even reap what they have sown (v. 15), a fate worse than prescribed in a popular adage! The insatiable drive of greed will in the end eat them alive with a "gnawing hunger" (v. 14). Whatever can be gained will slip through one's fingers like sand. An economy based on fraud and violence will, like any modern-day pyramid scheme, eventually collapse under its own crushing weight, and the prophet does not even need to proclaim that God is behind it all (v. 13). God's judgment is at the same time the inevitable and logical outcome to Israel's corrupted life. The text claims that the people, the inhabitants of Jerusalem, set their course toward self-desolation by following the wicked ways of Omri and son Ahab (v. 16a), those infamous kings of Samaria who reigned from 876 to 850 B.C. (1 Kings 16:25–26; 30–33). One is reminded of Ahab's ruthless takeover of Naboth's vineyard through conspiracy and outright murder, thereby bringing down the wrath of God through the prophet Elijah (1 Kings 21–22). Thus shall God's judgment fall upon a community that acts violently and unjustly. Thus shall disaster result from their own doing.

THE CONTAGION OF CORRUPTION
Micah 7:1–7

> 7:1 **Woe is me! For I have become like one who,**
>   **after the summer fruit has been gathered,**
>   **after the vintage has been gleaned,**
> **finds no cluster to eat;**
>   **there is no first-ripe fig for which I hunger.**
> 2 **The faithful have disappeared from the land,**
>   **and there is no one left who is upright;**
> **they all lie in wait for blood,**

and they hunt each other with nets.
³ Their hands are skilled to do evil;
   the official and the judge ask for a bribe,
and the powerful dictate what they desire;
   thus they pervert justice.
⁴ The best of them is like a brier,
   the most upright of them a thorn hedge.
The day of their sentinels, of their punishment, has come;
   now their confusion is at hand.
⁵ Put no trust in a friend,
   have no confidence in a loved one;
guard the doors of your mouth
   from her who lies in your embrace;
⁶ for the son treats the father with contempt,
   the daughter rises up against her mother,
the daughter-in-law against her mother-in-law;
   your enemies are members of your own household.
⁷ But as for me, I will look to the LORD,
   I will wait for the God of my salvation;
   my God will hear me.

There is something rotten in Judah, rotten to the core, laments the prophet. All the faithful have been swept away; only the violently wicked remain, an anti-remnant, as it were. Micah likens their disappearance to a harvest of summer fruit; not one good fig remains. The prophet Jeremiah some hundred years later, similarly likened those who were carried off in exile by the Babylonians to a basket of good figs. Those who remained were the bad figs, "so bad that they [could] not be eaten" (Jer. 24:3). Likewise, Micah complains of no "first-ripe fig" left in the land (v. 1). What is left are the bloodthirsty, who specialize in violence and perverting justice (cf. Prov. 1:10–19). Their ilk even includes the respected civil leaders (v. 3). Corruption, in short, runs rampant from the top down, so much so that the prophet is left in the ironic position of exhorting his audience to trust no one, even loved-ones (v. 5). "We have met the enemy, and it is us," the prophet seems to say, à la Pogo, the comic strip possum. With one generation pitted against the other, distrust and rebellion have taken root in every household (v. 6), with the fifth commandment of the Decalogue (the Ten Commandments) lying in shambles (Exod. 20:12). Akin to the most virulent of viruses, wickedness infects and destroys everything in its path. Jerusalem has become a "hot zone" of corruption.

Conflict between generations was and still is a perennial problem. At one point, Jesus uses Micah's message in 7:6 to illustrate the cost of discipleship

(Matt. 10:34–39). Households will inevitably be divided as certain members choose to follow Jesus over and above fulfilling family responsibilities.

For the prophet, however, anarchy in the home is far from his prophetic mission; it is the inevitable result of a community that has wholeheartedly perverted the just ways of God. The ways of the community and household are bound up together. What undermines the community also eats away at the very fabric that holds any family together. The cloistered walls of hearth and home offer no safe haven in a society bent on self-destruction. The prophet takes his stand apart from the contagion of chaos to wait upon the God of his salvation (v. 7). Micah is utterly convinced that God will respond in steadfast love to his desperate cries of petition. What there is to look forward to amid this whirlpool of torment remains to be seen, but perhaps it is no coincidence that the prophetic canon, indeed, the Old Testament canon, ends with a vision that is diametrically opposed to the familial chaos that surrounds the prophet: "Lo, I will send you the prophet Elijah before the great and terrible day of the Lord comes. He will turn the hearts of parents to their children and the hearts of children to their parents" (Mal. 4:5–6a; see Luke 1:17). Such family harmony prefigures the very goal and consummation of history.

MICAH'S PSALM OF HOPE
Micah 7:8–20

> 7:8 **Do not rejoice over me, O my enemy,**
> **when I fall, I shall rise;**
> **when I sit in darkness,**
> **the LORD will be a light to me.**
> 9 **I must bear the indignation of the LORD,**
> **because I have sinned against him,**
> **until he takes my side**
> **and executes judgment for me.**
> **He will bring me out to the light;**
> **I shall see his vindication.**
> 10 **Then my enemy will see,**
> **and shame will cover her who said to me,**
> **"Where is the LORD your God?"**
> **My eyes will see her downfall;**
> **now she will be trodden down**
> **like the mire of the streets.**

¹¹ A day for the building of your walls!
   In that day the boundary shall be far extended.
¹² In that day they will come to you
   from Assyria to Egypt,
and from Egypt to the River,
   from sea to sea and from mountain to mountain.
¹³ But the earth will be desolate
   because of its inhabitants,
   for the fruit of their doings.

¹⁴ Shepherd your people with your staff,
   the flock that belongs to you,
which lives alone in a forest
   in the midst of a garden land;
let them feed in Bashan and Gilead
   as in the days of old.
¹⁵ As in the days when you came out of the land of Egypt,
   show us marvelous things.
¹⁶ The nations shall see and be ashamed
   of all their might;
they shall lay their hands on their mouths;
   their ears shall be deaf;
¹⁷ they shall lick dust like a snake,
   like the crawling things of the earth;
they shall come trembling out of their fortresses;
   they shall turn in dread to the LORD our God,
   and they shall stand in fear of you.
¹⁸ Who is a God like you, pardoning iniquity
   and passing over the transgression
   of the remnant of your possession?
He does not retain his anger forever,
   because he delights in showing clemency.
¹⁹ He will again have compassion upon us;
   he will tread our iniquities under foot.
You will cast all our sins
   into the depths of the sea.
²⁰ You will show faithfulness to Jacob
   and unswerving loyalty to Abraham,
as you have sworn to our ancestors
   from the days of old.

As the conclusion to Micah's prophecies, this passage gives an impassioned voice to God's people who have suffered the indignity of judgment and shame, and look forward to their restoration. Micah is no doomsday prophet, isolated from the people whom he serves. Rather, he lives in solidarity with his people. He laments when they suffer (1:8) and rejoices in their restoration. It is only fitting, then, that the prophet's final words give voice to the people's deepest hopes. When Micah speaks as an "I," he speaks on behalf of God's people.

Judgment is not the final word. Although God's people have fallen, they shall also rise again. Indeed, to stumble and fall on the path of righteousness is no unpardonably shameful fate, "for though [the righteous] fall seven times, they will rise again; but the wicked are overthrown by calamity" (Prov. 24:16). Israel has endured the judgment and now awaits vindication, much to the dismay and shame of enemy Assyria (see 5:5–6), who reproachfully asked where the God of Israel was to allow Israel to be defeated (7:10). The insulting question insinuates that the Lord God was not up to the task of delivering Israel from the mighty grip of Assyria (see Psalms 42:3, 10; 79:10; Joel 2:17). Contrary to popular opinion, however, God is not only up to the task of vindicating Israel but will exceed all expectations to punish those who afflicted God's people.

With its territory vastly expanded, Israel will exceed its former glory, commanding submissive respect from even those two great superpowers of the ancient Near East—Assyria and Egypt. From Egypt to the Euphrates ("the River"), the nations shall come to learn God's ways from Zion (4:2). As the good and powerful shepherd, God will lead the flock into the choicest of lands: the fertile plateau of Bashan and the highland region of Gilead, both northeast of the Jordan river. As the mighty power of Egypt was vanquished when God delivered a struggling band of slaves from bondage, so all the nations shall see and fear the majestic power of God at work when Israel is restored (vv. 16–17). Having repeatedly and ruthlessly trampled over God's people, the nations will be reduced to "crawling things," groveling before God and God's people. Their accursed fate resembles that of the wily serpent in the garden who was condemned to a life of lowly existence: "Upon your belly you shall go and dust you shall eat all the days of your life" (Gen. 3:14).

For Micah, the vindication of God's people at the expense of the worldly principalities and powers attests, in the end, to the incomparable wideness in God's mercy. This final passage is the prophet's recasting of God's sublime confession given to Moses at the renewal of the covenant in Exodus 34:6–7 on the mountain of Sinai. Such solemn and compassionate words can only inspire deep and reverential awe (Exod. 34:8). As much as God is willing to renew the covenant with the Israelites on Sinai,

God will "pass over" transgression and "delight" in forgiveness (Mic. 7:18). The anger of judgment is only a passing phase. Divine wrath stems from God's uncompromising resolve to fight against evil and sin. Yet the well of God's anger is not inexhaustible. What ultimately endures is God's mercy. In the end, sin will be cast "into the depths of the sea," forever out of sight. Micah finds clear precedent of God's inexhaustible grace in Israel's ancestral history, the time of the patriarchs and matriarchs. With Abraham and Sarah, God swore loyalty to a sojourning couple in a foreign land (for example, Gen. 12:1–3; 15:5, 18–21; 17:1–8), promising them progeny and prosperity. Wherever they journeyed, God accompanied them in blessing. As with Jacob's (Israel's) ancestors, Micah claims, so will God continue such faithfulness to his descendants. And we, as the "children of the promise," are also counted as descendants (Rom. 9:8).

Nahum

Introduction

Nahum is a book that, to put it bluntly, revels in judgment. Yet it is not designed to terrorize its readers. Much to the contrary, Nahum extols divine judgment against a foreign city (Nineveh, the capital of Assyria) as the means by which God's people are to be delivered. In short, Nahum is a celebration of the certainty of judgment. Understandably, many readers have criticized the book as vengeful and, therefore, morally suspect. By contrast, the book of Jonah, whose focus is also upon divine judgment against the same foreign city, quite clearly stresses God's compassion for a penitent people.

For Nahum, however, repentance is no longer an option when judgment is set and ready to be executed. Yet the prophet realizes that God's plan is more far reaching than the execution of judgment against a particular people. Nahum finds God to be a refuge in times of doubt and crisis (1:7). The prophet addresses a people who harbored doubts as to whether God was at all able to carry through in liberating Judah from the oppressive yoke of that dreaded enemy Assyria. Nahum reminds us today that without judgment, mercy comes cheap; without accountability, compassion lacks passion.

Although the opening verse of the book does not indicate the time in which the prophet was active, it is clear in his message that Nahum was active some years prior to the actual fall of Nineveh, the capital of the Assyrian empire (612 B.C.). Assyria, over a century earlier, had destroyed the northern kingdom, Israel (722 B.C.) and reduced Judah to vassaldom. But in Nahum's time the winds of change were blowing. The prophet realized all too well that he was living on the edge of history; the tables were turning on the power brokers of the land. Assyria, Judah's oppressor, was headed toward collapse, to be displaced by newly emerging powers of the ancient Near East—the Medes and the Babylonians.

THE TITLE
Nahum 1:1

> 1:1 **An oracle concerning Nineveh. The book of the vision of Nahum of Elkosh.**

This twofold title identifies what follows as an oracle and a vision. An oracle denotes a particular kind of prophetic message, usually of a judgmental nature. The subject matter of Nahum's oracle is Nineveh, the capital of Assyria since the reign of Sennacherib (705–681 B.C.). For over a century Assyria was able to rule the fertile crescent—from the region of Mesopotamia to Palestine (see introduction). The title also makes clear that the prophet stands fully behind this book. Described as a vision, Nahum's message is replete with powerful images and metaphors that evoke an overpowering sense of the majesty of God at work in history. The prophet's message clearly overshadows his identity. His background remains obscure. Not even his hometown of Elkosh can be identified with certainty.

REFUGE IN JUDGMENT
Nahum 1:2–8

> 1:2 **A jealous and avenging God is the LORD,**
>   **the LORD is avenging and wrathful;**
> **the LORD takes vengeance on his adversaries,**
>   **and rages against his enemies.**
> 3 **The LORD is slow to anger but great in power,**
>   **and the LORD will by no means clear the guilty.**
>
>   **His way is in whirlwind and storm,**
>   **and the clouds are the dust of his feet.**
> 4 **He rebukes the sea and makes it dry,**
>   **and he dries up all the rivers;**
> **Bashan and Carmel wither,**
>   **and the bloom of Lebanon fades.**
> 5 **The mountains quake before him,**
>   **and the hills melt;**
> **the earth heaves before him,**
>   **the world and all who live in it.**
> 6 **Who can stand before his indignation?**
>   **Who can endure the heat of his anger?**
> **His wrath is poured out like fire,**
>   **and by him the rocks are broken in pieces.**

7 **The LORD is good,**
   a stronghold in a day of trouble;
he protects those who take refuge in him,
8   **even in a rushing flood.**
He will make a full end of his adversaries,
   and will pursue his enemies into darkness.

The book begins in praise of God as the one who directs the course of history and demands righteousness among the peoples (1:3). Jealousy, vengeance, wrath, and rage are all divine traits set within the overarching context of God's slowness to anger and unmatched power (1:3). Indeed, forbearance and mercy are the truly enduring marks of God in the Old Testament (Exod. 34:6–7), and it is within these characteristics that God's wrath and rage must be set. These qualities are not emotive whims; each is firmly rooted in God's resolve to follow through in judgment. Nahum's audience evidently doubted whether God was up to the task of executing judgment and changing the current state of injustice. If God refrains from judgment, it is out of merciful forbearance, not out of weakness. God is the Lord of history and justice, the prophet reminds his hearers. God does not back down when it comes to implementing justice and establishing order in the world. Consequently, God does not allow human injustice to have the final say. In short, God is a jealous God who demands whole-hearted faithfulness and categorically rejects evil (see Exod. 20:5–6). Without judgment, love is impotent.

Having testified to God's power (1:2–3a), the prophet then recounts the dramatic ways in which such power can manifest itself (1:3b–5). Images of storm, drought, and earthquake paint a graphic picture of God's unsurpassable power (cf. Habakkuk 3). This is no god to be identified with nature. Rather God stands over and against creation to judge and refashion it. God is the source of *both* fertility and drought, not one or the other. The fertile plateau of Bashan, the lush mountains of Carmel, and the majestic cedar fields of Lebanon are all dependent on the source of all life.

The prophet describes God burning with rage (1:6). However this is no vengeful God, breathing destruction for destruction's sake. Rather, Nahum is quick to point out that "the Lord is good" (1:7). Judgment issues from the well of goodness; thus, God will not let injustice prevail. With all of nature at God's behest, no one can withstand God's fierce power. Nothing can frustrate the divine purpose; every wall of resistance tumbles before God, who is the only true refuge (1:7; see Psalms 46:1, 7, 11; 59:16; 94:22; 142:5). God's protection is impregnable (Psalm 46:1) and it is squarely rooted in the assurance of God's judgment.

This may sound paradoxical, but Nahum would no doubt add to the title of the popular hymn "There's a Wideness in God's Mercy" the line "There's a refuge in God's judgment." It is the kind of protection that was at work when the Israelite slaves were shielded from the final plague against Egypt (Exod. 11:1–12:32). Though a loud cry of lament was heard throughout Egypt, not even a dog growled against the Israelites as they prepared to make their exodus (Exod. 11:6–7)! To take refuge in God is to acknowledge absolute reliance upon the Lord of history, particularly amid chaos and crisis. Security that is self-generated is, by contrast, finite and fleeting, like a house built on sinking sand.

DELIVERANCE IN JUDGMENT
Nahum 1:9–15

> 1:9 Why do you plot against the LORD?
>   He will make an end;
>   no adversary will rise up twice.
> 10 Like thorns they are entangled,
>   like drunkards they are drunk;
>   they are consumed like dry straw.
> 11 From you one has gone out
>   who plots evil against the LORD,
>   who counsels wickedness.
> 12 Thus says the LORD,
> "Though they are at full strength and many,
>   they will be cut off and pass away.
> Though I have afflicted you,
>   I will afflict you no more.
> 13 And now I will break off his yoke from you
>   and snap the bonds that bind you."
>
> 14 The LORD has commanded concerning you:
>   "Your name shall be perpetuated no longer;
> from the house of your gods I will cut off
>   the carved image and the cast image.
> I will make your grave, for you are worthless."
>
> 15 Look! On the mountains the feet of one
>   who bring good tidings,
>   who proclaims peace!
> Celebrate your festivals, O Judah,
>   fulfill your vows,

for never again shall the wicked invade you;
  they are utterly cut off.

This extended passage alternates between words of judgment and words of assurance. Continuing the thought of verses 7–8, the prophet begins this passage by specifically addressing those who are to suffer judgment, namely adversaries who have afflicted God's people (1:9). As the source of wickedness, Israel's enemies entangle themselves with their own evil devices. Made drunk by their own drink, they consume themselves. The prophet, as God's messenger, then turns to his own people in consolation and assures them of their impending deliverance (vv. 12–13). Yet God's judgment seems to fly in the face of reality. The enemies of God's people appear invincible (v. 12). Assyria, Israel's archenemy, was still enjoying the zenith of its might in the prophet's day. Nevertheless, the fate of this dreaded nation is sealed, the prophet announces.

Like the rise and fall of mighty nations throughout history (for example, Babylonia, Rome, Nazi Germany, the Soviet Union), the might of Assyria too shall pass. God had used this great and terrible nation to afflict Israel in judgment (Isa. 10:5–19). Consequently, Assyria destroyed the northern kingdom Israel about a century before Nahum's time (722 B.C.). But once was enough. God will now break the yoke of this idolatrous nation and liberate the people of Judah. This mighty nation will be so bereft of its gods and means of support that no one will be left to dig its grave except God (v. 14). God's judgment means Judah's liberation, for only in the execution of justice will lasting peace take place (v. 15). The messenger of peace announces the victory of justice (see Isa. 52:7). It is a time to rejoice. The prophet commands a restoration of the joyous festivals (2 Kings 23:21–25). Indeed, as historical fulfillment, under king Josiah the greatest passover feast since the period of the judges was conducted. God's people were once again able to taste freedom, as their ancestors did under Moses.

THE FALL OF NINEVEH
Nahum 2:1–13

2:1 **A shatterer has come up against you.**
  Guard the ramparts;
    watch the road;
  gird your loins;
    collect all your strength.

2 (For the LORD is restoring the majesty of Jacob,
    as well as the majesty of Israel,
though ravagers have ravaged them
    and ruined their branches.)

3 The shields of his warriors are red;
    his soldiers are clothed in crimson.
The metal on the chariots flashes
    on the day when he musters them;
    the chargers prance.
4 The chariots race madly through the streets,
    they rush to and fro through the squares;
their appearance is like torches,
    they dart like lightning.
5 He calls his officers;
    they stumble as they come forward;
they hasten to the wall,
    and the mantelet is set up.
6 The river gates are opened,
    the palace trembles.
7 It is decreed that the city be exiled,
    its slave women led away,
moaning like doves
    and beating their breasts.
8 Nineveh is like a pool
    whose waters run away.
"Halt! Halt!"—
    but no one turns back.
9 "Plunder the silver,
    plunder the gold!
There is no end of treasure!
    An abundance of every precious thing!"
10 Devastation, desolation, and destruction!
    Hearts faint and knees tremble,
all loins quake,
    all faces grow pale!
11 What became of the lions' den,
    the cave of the young lions,
where the lion goes,
    and the lion's cubs, with no one to disturb them?
12 The lion has torn enough for his whelps
    and strangled prey for his lionesses;
he has filled his caves with prey
    and his dens with torn flesh.

13 **See, I am against you, says the LORD of hosts, and I will burn your char-iots in smoke, and the sword shall devour your young lions; I will cut off your prey from the earth, and the voice of your messengers shall be heard no more.**

In this extensive collection of speeches, the prophet directs his attention to Nineveh itself. His address begins on an ironic note. The prophet warns the city of an impending military confrontation and beckons the inhabi-tants to prepare for the onslaught. But it all functions as a taunt. Behind the prophet's warning is the image of the divine warrior about to lay siege against the city. Why is God attacking the city? Because the Lord is about to restore Israel (the "pride of Jacob"), which has been ravaged by plun-derers (v. 2). Jacob's restoration can only occur upon the destruction of Assyria, much like the liberation of the Hebrew slaves came about at the expense of Egypt's might. Nahum is a realist enough to know that we are all caught up in a tangled web of power. However configured or distrib-uted, power is invariably used to demoralize and abuse others. That is an inescapable fact of the sinful tragedy of the human condition. The liber-ation of a people will always upset the balance of power.

The prophet launches into a riveting description of God's army set to attack Nineveh (v. 3). It is as if Nahum personally takes us, the readers, into the heat of battle. The language suggests an invincible army, suffi-ciently equipped to tackle any job, from their crimson outfits to their gleaming, lightning-fast chariots. The army successfully breaches the wall with "the mantelet"—a mobile siege tower used by besieging armies to shield the troops manning the battering rams (vv. 5–6). The prophet then announces the consequences of Nineveh's defeat: The city is exiled and its wealth is plundered. Nineveh was known for its sophisticated system of dams, gates, and channels that controlled the flow of water into the city. The opening of the river gates suggests a flood inundating the city, reach-ing even to the palace (v. 6), then draining away, leaving only devastation (v. 8). As Assyria once vanquished and exiled the peoples of the fertile cres-cent—from the region of Mesopotamia to Palestine—it now suffers the same fate. All this mighty nation can do now is cower in fear.

The prophet ends his taunt by invoking a familiar symbol of Assyrian might—the lion. Archaeologists have discovered the figure of the lion fea-tured widely in Assyrian reliefs. Indeed, this "king of beasts," at the top of the food chain, was a natural symbol for Assyrian kingship. Now the lion, whose very survival depended on violently overcoming its prey, is killed by the sword (vv. 11–13). The young lions (the Assyrian army?) are also defeated. Nahum summarizes his taunt by delivering God's declaration of

war in verse 13. God has thrown down the gauntlet and is ready to com-
mence battle. God intends to destroy the city's army and weapons as well
as cut off its messengers, whose business was to strike terror in the hearts
of the king's subjects and deliver the conditions of surrender among the
foreign nations (for an example, see 2 Kings 18:17–37). In short, Nineveh's glory days are over, and the dawning of a new era of freedom for
God's people is underway.

ORACLE AGAINST NINEVEH
Nahum 3:1–17

> 3:1 **Ah! City of bloodshed,**
> **utterly deceitful, full of booty—**
> **no end to the plunder!**
> 2 **The crack of whip and rumble of wheel,**
> **galloping horse and bounding chariot!**
> 3 **Horsemen charging,**
> **flashing sword and glittering spear,**
> **piles of dead,**
> **heaps of corpses,**
> **dead bodies without end—**
> **they stumble over the bodies!**
> 4 **Because of the countless debaucheries of the prostitute,**
> **gracefully alluring, mistress of sorcery,**
> **who enslaves nations through her debaucheries,**
> **and peoples through her sorcery,**
> 5 **I am against you,**
> **says the LORD of hosts,**
> **and will lift up your skirts over your face;**
> **and I will let nations look on your nakedness**
> **and kingdoms on your shame.**
> 6 **I will throw filth at you**
> **and treat you with contempt,**
> **and make you a spectacle.**
> 7 **Then all who see you will shrink from you and say,**
> **"Nineveh is devastated; who will bemoan her?"**
> **Where shall I seek comforters for you?**
>
> 8 **Are you better than Thebes**
> **that sat by the Nile,**
> **with water around her,**

her rampart a sea,
   water her wall?
9 Ethiopia was her strength,
   Egypt too, and that without limit;
   Put and the Libyans were her helpers.

10 Yet she became an exile,
   she went into captivity;
even her infants were dashed in pieces,
   at the head of every street;
lots were cast for her nobles,
   all her dignitaries were bound in fetters.
11 You also will be drunken,
   you will go into hiding;
you will seek
   a refuge from the enemy.
12 All your fortresses are like fig trees
   with first-ripe figs—
if shaken they fall
   into the mouth of the eater.
13 Look at your troops:
   they are women in your midst.
The gates of your land
   are wide open to your foes;
   fire has devoured the bars of your gates.

14 Draw water for the siege,
   strengthen your forts;
trample the clay,
   tread the mortar,
   take hold of the brick mold!
15 There the fire will devour you,
   the sword will cut you off.
   It will devour you like the locust.

Multiply yourselves like the locust,
   multiply like the grasshopper!
16 You increased your merchants
   more than the stars of the heavens.
   The locust sheds its skin and flies away.
17 Your guards are like grasshoppers,
   your scribes like swarms of locusts
settling on the fences
   on a cold day—

when the sun rises, they fly away;
no one knows where they have gone.

Nahum's language in this passage drives deeper into the heat of battle. The prophet piles words upon words that describe the commotion and ensuing panic of military confrontation. His words are so vivid that one can almost hear the staccato crack of the whip, see the blinding flashes of wielded sword, and view towering heaps of blood-drenched corpses. The prophet paints a horrific "you-are-there" scenario. The power of prophetic poetry lies in its capacity to announce the future as if it were underway before our very eyes, bringing the listener or reader into a wholly different world; a world under sudden and cataclysmic transformation that must first be torn down before it can be built up. Nahum takes us into battle against Nineveh, a battle in which the Lord's chosen army decimates the city that once prospered by destroying others. Why has God targeted this city (3:5; 2:13)? Nahum likens the city to a predatory prostitute who lures her lovers—the nations—into enslavement (cf. Prov. 7:1–27). Alluring promises of prosperity and protection turned out to be curses that entrapped the other nations like Judah in a demoralizing cycle of dependency and oppression. And so, in punishment fitting for a prostitute in biblical times (Jer. 13:22, 26; Ezek. 16:37–41; Hos. 2:3), God intends to strip Nineveh publicly before the nations, allowing them to gaze upon the city's nakedness. Nineveh will be exposed in humiliating defeat, stripped of its power and bereft of all manner of defense. The deceitful city will be put to shame, so much so that no one will be willing to comfort it.

Yet Nahum's audience remains unconvinced of Nineveh's demise. Assyria's imperial power seems unassailable, given its almost century-long rule over the land. To assure his people that God will indeed carry through in judgment, Nahum lifts up the example of the once invincible city of Thebes (No-amon in Hebrew), one of the greatest urban centers in Egyptian history (vv. 8–10). Located on the east bank of the upper Nile, Thebes was a well-fortified city equipped with great moats, similar perhaps to Nineveh's own defenses. Despite its legendary defenses, this great city was captured by the Assyrian king Ashurbanipal in 663 B.C., some twenty or thirty years before Nahum's prophecy. It was once thought that if ever any city was invincible, it was Thebes, which enjoyed unlimited support not only from Egypt but also from the neighboring nations Ethiopia, Put (location unknown), and Libya. Yet its defenses crumbled under Assyrian force. Unspeakable atrocities were committed against its people, who were imprisoned and exiled (v. 10).

Nineveh will suffer a comparable fate, the prophet proclaims. The violent victor will become the violated victim. The prophet parodies Nineveh's fortifications and military power (vv. 10–13). Appearances can be deceiving. The city's impregnable fortresses will fall like figs ripe for the plucking before the conqueror; its invincible gates will actually welcome the enemy; the guards will desert their positions like grasshoppers (v. 17). As in the taunt of 2:1, Nahum exhorts the city to prepare for the siege (v. 14). It is a challenge, however, for disaster. Even the vast multitude of Assyria's people cannot help in the defense of their capital. To the people of Judah, the Assyrian soldiers, officials, and merchants were like locusts; they were everywhere in the land. How then could Judah ever be free of them? That question was undoubtedly in the mind of the prophet's audience. The prophet counters using the same example of the locusts. Though locusts can wreak great destructive force on the land, they can just as easily vanish into thin air, as when they shed their skin or when the sun warms them on a cold day. They may be here today, but they will surely be gone tomorrow, never to be seen again.

NAHUM'S ADDRESS TO THE KING
Nahum 3:18–19

> 3:18 **Your shepherds are asleep,**
> **O king of Assyria;**
> **your nobles slumber.**
> **Your people are scattered on the mountains**
> **with no one to gather them.**
> ¹⁹ **There is no assuaging your hurt,**
> **your wound is mortal.**
> **All who hear the news about you**
> **clap their hands over you.**
> **For who has ever escaped**
> **your endless cruelty?**

With great rhetorical flourish the prophet has the audacity to address the (once) great and powerful Assyrian king. Like his prophetic predecessors (for example, Elijah, Nathan, Isaiah), Nahum confronts the king to his face! He addresses the king as if he were oblivious to the dissolution of his own kingdom. The irony is that the king of all people is the *last* person to know that his power has been pulled out from under him. The prophet pricks the bubble of royal denial. All the king's men ("shepherds" and "nobles") likewise slumber. Indeed, it is the slumber of death. They either have been killed or have scattered to the hills. The king now sits alone, mortally wounded and the object of scorn. To add insult to injury, the prophet informs the king that his defeat is joyfully celebrated by those he once victimized. The tables are now turned; the victims of endless cruelty are now liberated and restored. Nahum's address, indeed his book, ends with a question that indicts all those who thrive on oppressing others.

By bringing his audience up to the toppled throne of the king, Nahum provides a vivid and compelling picture of the certainty of God's judgment. It is not a picture that is designed to evoke pity for the defeated king, but rather to allay all doubts that God will follow through in judgment. The time of oppression by the principalities and powers of this world is over, Nahum could say. God reigns victorious in judging a world that thrives on lording power over others. Even the greatest kingdoms in history have had their shameful falls. God's kingdom, however, is of a different order; an order that will transform the world when the meek inherit it (Matt. 5:5). Only then will true and lasting peace reign.

Habakkuk

Introduction

The book of Habakkuk is unique among the prophetic books in that it begins with laments of protest directed against God and ends with an overwhelming vision of God's saving presence (3:13). Habakkuk is a prophet who, like Job, anguishes over the seeming injustice of God's ways and demands explanation concerning the course that history has taken at God's hand. Like Amos and Jeremiah, Habakkuk is a prophet who considers God big enough to handle complaints and probing questions. He exhibits a faith that dares God to be God.

Habakkuk was probably a resident of Jerusalem, perhaps even a prophet employed in the temple itself. Given the historical references in the first two chapters, Habakkuk's prophecies evidently began at the end of the seventh century during the reign of Jehoiakim, when the Neo-Babylonian empire had become the unrivaled superpower of the ancient Near East; that is, sometime between 609–605 B.C. Habakkuk's prophetic career extended to sometime after 597 B.C., when the Babylonian emperor Nebuchadrezzar captured Jerusalem for the first time. Taken together, Habakkuk's prophecies demonstrate that even amid the violent upheavals of history, judgment makes way for salvation.

THE TITLE
Habakkuk 1:1

> 1:1 **The oracle that the prophet Habakkuk saw.**

The first verse identifies the book and its author in unusually terse form. Unlike the titles of many other prophetic books, no information concerning the prophet's family or historical location is given. Even the prophet's name is nondescript. All that we know is that Habakkuk is a bona fide prophet who had an oracle or prophetic message to impart. The word for *oracle* in Hebrew can also mean *burden*, which may indicate the judgmental nature of the prophet's received message. Although the prophet's background and life are shrouded in obscurity, his message is not. Habakkuk *sees* his message; it is visually revealed to him. It is no coincidence, then, that God's answer to the prophet begins with a command to look (1:5), and it is not a pretty picture.

HABAKKUK'S FIRST PROTEST
Habakkuk 1:2–4

> 1:2 O LORD, how long shall I cry for help,
>   and you will not listen?
> Or cry to you "Violence!"
>   and you will not save?
> 3 Why do you make me see wrongdoing
>   and look at trouble?
> Destruction and violence are before me;
>   strife and contention arise.
> 4 So the law becomes slack
>   and justice never prevails.
> The wicked surround the righteous—
>   therefore judgment comes forth perverted.

The first words we read from the prophet are words of bitter protest directed toward God. There is no introductory "thus says the Lord," so typical of many biblical prophets. Rather, Habakkuk starts off with a bitter complaint. The prophet's question "How long, O Lord" introduces the language of lament (see Psalm 13). It is the language of utter anguish over a seemingly hopeless situation. Indeed, Habakkuk does not mince words in accusing God of rubbing his nose in the wrongdoings of the prophet's society (v. 3). The prophet finds himself mired in a hopeless situation of violence and injustice (see Job 19:7). The wicked prevail over the righteous, justice is perverted, and violence carries the day. Habakkuk sees his hometown, Jerusalem, on the verge of collapse. Peace and justice, the two pillars that hold any community together, are quickly crumbling. The prophet's predicament is perhaps not unlike what many today feel is happening with their cities: rampant violence and flagrant disregard for law and order. Like the prophet, we too can cry "How long, O Lord!" The question does not imply a lack of faith; to the contrary, it is a faith that is bold enough to charge God to take notice and be God. If, as Presbyterian minister and theologian Frederich Buechner, claims, "Doubt is the ants in the pants of faith," then protest is the ants in the pants of piety.

GOD'S RESPONSE
Habakkuk 1:5–11

1:5 Look at the nations, and see!
　　Be astonished! Be astounded!
For a work is being done in your days
　　that you would not believe if you were told.
6 For I am rousing the Chaldeans,
　　that fierce and impetuous nation,
who march through the breadth of the earth
　　to seize dwellings not their own.
7 Dread and fearsome are they;
　　their justice and dignity proceed from themselves.
8 Their horses are swifter than leopards,
　　more menacing than wolves at dusk;
　　their horses charge.
Their horsemen come from far away;
　　they fly like an eagle swift to devour.
9 They all come for violence,
　　with faces pressing forward;
　　they gather captives like sand.
10 At kings they scoff,
　　and of rulers they make sport.
They laugh at every fortress,
　　and heap up earth to take it.
11 Then they sweep by like the wind;
　　they transgress and become guilty;
　　their own might is their god!

Habakkuk need not wait long; God's answer comes quickly. The prophet is commanded to open his eyes and *see* the answer (see 1:1). Habakkuk is to look beyond his immediate environs and discern what is looming upon the international horizon. The prophet is forced to look at the larger picture, without rendering his problem insignificant. God in no way belittles the prophet's anguish, but wants him to realize that outside intervention is required. What the prophet finds is so astounding that mere words cannot convey it. It must be seen to be believed. Consequently, what follows in 1:6–11 is not so much a report as it is a visual montage of powerful images; a message that is to be beheld, not simply read or heard.

God's revelatory message to Habakkuk begins with reference to a foreign nation. The name "Chaldeans" refers to the Neo-Babylonian empire, which was founded by Nabopolassar (ca. 626–605 B.C.) and reached its zenith under the powerful Nebuchadrezzar (605–562 B.C.), who captured and destroyed Jerusalem, ending the southern kingdom of Judah in 587 B.C. (see 2 Kings 24:8–25:21). Babylonia quickly became the superpower of Mesopotamia near the end of the seventh century, conquering Assyria in 612 and routing the armies of Pharaoh Neco of Egypt at Carchemish in 605. The Babylonians were soon able to rule over Assyria, Syria, Palestine, and Egypt. And yet less than fifty years after the destruction of Jerusalem, this ancient superpower fell as quickly as it had risen, conquered without resistance in 539 B.C. by Cyrus II, king of Persia. Habakkuk is one of many biblical prophets who attribute the rise and fall of nations to God's plan. What that plan means for Israel will become clear soon enough.

God's revelation to Habakkuk begins with the meteoric rise of Babylonia. God raises up this "fierce and impetuous" nation to execute swift and terrible judgment. Its cavalry is compared to a variety of wild predators. The strength of the Babylonian forces is unmatched by human being or beast. All earthly sovereigns are a joke to this nation. Yet because of its fearsome might, this is no virtuous instrument of God. The nation of Babylonia heeds only its own brand of justice (v. 7). Indeed, violence is its only aim (v. 9). This warring nation is not immune to sin: It deifies its own strength (v. 11). Puffed up by self-glory, this nation has its own agenda, even though it unknowingly plays a part in God's agenda. So was also the case with Assyria, Babylonia's mighty predecessor, over a century earlier. In a striking case of history repeating itself, Assyria, the rod of God's anger, was sent to destroy the northern kingdom Israel, "a godless nation" (Isa. 10:5–6). Yet, like the Chaldeans, Assyria attributed success to its own strength and wisdom, thereby incurring divine judgment of its own (Isa. 10:13–19).

In short, God's sovereign work extends even to those who are utterly convinced they operate on their own. The vision that Habakkuk receives belies that mysterious blend of self-determination and divine appointment. Babylonia, a heathen nation, unknowingly figures into God's larger plan. In the end all things are related to God. The opening verse of Psalm 24, "The earth is the Lord's and all that is in it," dismantles all provincial barriers and preconceived ideas about what is truly possible for God.

God's power is limitless and inclusive; it can surprise and confound even the most pious, as it did for Habakkuk.

HABAKKUK'S SECOND PROTEST
Habakkuk 1:12–17

> 1:12 Are you not from of old,
>   O LORD my God, my Holy One?
> You shall not die.
> O LORD, you have marked them for judgment;
>   and you, O Rock, have established them for punishment.
> 13 Your eyes are too pure to behold evil,
>   and you cannot look on wrongdoing;
> why do you look on the treacherous,
>   and are silent when the wicked swallow
>   those more righteous than they?
> 14 You have made people like the fish of the sea,
>   like crawling things that have no ruler.
>
> 15 The enemy brings all of them up with a hook;
>   he drags them out with his net,
> he gathers them in his seine;
>   so he rejoices and exults.
> 16 Therefore he sacrifices to his net
>   and makes offerings to his seine;
> for by them his portion is lavish,
>   and his food is rich.
> 17 Is he then to keep on emptying his net,
>   and destroying nations without mercy?

Habakkuk is shocked. How can God be involved with such an evil people? How can God associate with this devil of a nation? The prophet's sharp response questions the very means by which God plans to resolve his first complaint (1:2–4). For Habakkuk, the answer he receives is not becoming of God and he tells why in this passage. The prophet begins with provisional praise to God, phrased as a leading question (v. 12). The God whom Habakkuk addresses is the same one whose intentions are everlasting, established from eternity. Even if the people perish, God remains everlasting and sovereign. "The grass withers, the flower fades; but the word of our God will stand forever" (Isa. 40:8).

As for God's plans, Habakkuk repeats what God has already said: The

Chaldeans are appointed to judge and to punish God's people (1:12). Yet the language has a double meaning, since the prophet's affirmation could easily mean that this enemy of Israel is appointed for its *own* judgment and punishment. Whose judgment does Habakkuk have in mind, Israel's or Babylonia's? Habakkuk's pronouncement in verse 12 is intentionally vague. When one reads on, however, it becomes quite clear that the prophet desires the latter. In his address to God, Habakkuk declares that God's nature is absolutely incompatible with evil; God's eyes are "too pure" (1:13). Habakkuk is not construing God as a divine Pollyanna; God's "spectacles" are by no means rose colored. Rather, what Habakkuk means to say is that to look upon something (v. 13) is to accept, even delight in it (see Psalm 84:9; Amos 5:22). Conversely, to refuse to look at something is to reject it outright. In short, the prophet accuses God of complicity with the treacherous and the wicked! As the one to ensure justice and order, God has abdicated the position of ruler over creation (cf. Judg. 8:23). Without rulership, only anarchy prevails (Judg. 21:25). Consequently, God treats human beings no better than lizards and fish (1:14), according to Habakkuk.

So also the enemy: Like a fisherman, the Chaldean nation ("the enemy") captures its prey with hooks and nets, the means by which it gains its wealth. Fearsome and powerful though this nation be, it is also stupid and religiously apostate, Habakkuk points out to God. This enemy is so engrossed in its triumphs that it mistakenly worships the means rather than the source of its success (1:16). Not knowing the true agent of its success, Babylonia deifies its own weapons of warfare. Habakkuk issues a stinging indictment by announcing that the gods of Babylonia are simply idolatrous projections of its weaponry and lust for power. In a nutshell, idolatry is the practice of giving absolute value to things of relative worth, and it is no different today. The things around which we structure our lives reveal what we truly worship: money, job, property, power, technology, and influence. Not acknowledging the true source of our blessings has disastrous consequences: We displace God with consuming neuroses that grasp for everything and yet are satisfied with nothing. By contrast, acknowledging God as Creator and Lord of all provides a life-affirming structure for our lives.

Habakkuk ends his lament with a question: Shall such an apostate nation continue to fulfill God's judgment? If so, this is judgment run amok. The prophet refuses to believe that God is behind this ruthless purveyor of violence. Is not God, who is by nature good and just, able to make moral discriminations? It is to these concerns that the prophet awaits an answer.

FAITHFUL WAITING
Habakkuk 2:1–4

> 2:1 I will stand at my watchpost,
>   and station myself on the rampart;
> I will keep watch to see what he will say to me,
>   and what he will answer concerning my complaint.
> 2 Then the LORD answered me and said:
> Write the vision;
>   make it plain on tablets,
>   so that a runner may read it.
> 3 For there is still a vision for the appointed time;
>   it speaks of the end, and does not lie.
> If it seems to tarry, wait for it;
>   it will surely come, it will not delay.
> 4 Look at the proud!
>   Their spirit is not right in them,
>   but the righteous live by their faith.

And so the prophet stands at his watchpost and rampart waiting with bated breath for a response to his "complaint" (v. 1; 1:12–17). Talking back to God is not unique to biblical figures. Abraham, Moses, Jeremiah, and Job all did not hesitate to complain to God. Indeed, the line between petition and complaint is a fine—if not blurred—one, for both kinds of prayer recognize that something is amiss that only divine agency can resolve. God wants us to lift up our needs and concerns in prayer, even if they have to be cast as complaints. God revels in the freedom of communication, even, or perhaps especially, when it becomes brutally and passionately honest. Jesus himself told the parable of the widow and the judge to illustrate the necessity of vigilant prayer (Luke 18:1–8). Habakkuk is not punished for his own reproach against God; rather, he is granted another response, one that requires this time a public arena (v. 2).

The reference to the runner in verse 2 is a puzzling one, but it probably refers to the way in which messages were written down on clay tablets and transported by messengers who ran to designated destinations. Runner-messengers were the pony express of the ancient Near East. In this case, God's message to Habakkuk is to arrange for public dissemination. Not a private, esoteric message, God's response must be broadcasted to the ends of Israel. Writing down prophecies was a way of confirming their import, especially when the prophesied event transpired (see Isa. 8:16–18; 30:8). God guarantees the efficacy of this vision, a vision that tells the truth about the final resolution of the prophet's concerns. Though human patience may dry up, the fulfillment of the vision will come in God's good timing, at the *right* time. God instructs Habakkuk to wait in faithfulness, confident in the end result. The prophet must live betwixt and between, in that interim between the vision and its fulfillment, between predicament and resolution.

Christians also live within such a temporal conundrum, between the cross and the consummation, when all things in the end will be reconciled to God, but not quite yet. It is the righteous who live by their faith knowing that despite all apparent evidence to the contrary, God's way will in the end prevail. Indeed, it already has in the life, death, and resurrection of Christ. And so we wait, not like "waiting for Godot," stumbling aimlessly about in the realm of the absurd, but with patient confidence in the total redemption ushered in by Christ (see Rom. 8:18–25; 1:17; Gal. 3:11; Heb. 10:36–39). The proud, on the other hand, do not have the spiritual wherewithal to look beyond themselves and wait. Thinking they have the power to bring about whatever they want, they cannot endure, so Habakkuk implies (see also 2:5), for they have really nothing to look forward to beyond themselves. By contrast, the righteous live in humility, fully recognizing that they themselves cannot bring about God's kingdom, as if presuming to build it brick by brick. The new heaven and the new earth are strictly God's prerogative. Nevertheless, that does not mean that we can not anticipate, if not prefigure, God's kingdom in the way we live out the Good News in our day-to-day lives. The righteous trust in the reliability of God's fulfilling the vision; the proud trust only in themselves.

JUDGMENT MAKES WAY
FOR DELIVERANCE
Habakkuk 2:5–20

> 2:5 Moreover, wealth is treacherous;
>   the arrogant do not endure.
> They open their throats wide as Sheol;
>   like Death they never have enough.
> They gather all nations for themselves,
>   and collect all peoples as their own.
> 6 Shall not everyone taunt such people and, with mocking riddles,
> say about them,
> "Alas for you who heap up what is not your own!"
>   How long will you load yourselves with goods taken in pledge?

7 Will not your own creditors suddenly rise,
  and those who make you tremble wake up?
  Then you will be booty for them.
8 Because you have plundered many nations,
  all that survive of the peoples shall plunder you—
because of human bloodshed, and violence to the earth,
  to cities and all who live in them.

9 "Alas for you who get evil gain for your houses,
  setting your nest on high
  to be safe from the reach of harm!"
10 You have devised shame for your house
  by cutting off many peoples;
  you have forfeited your life.
11 The very stones will cry out from the wall,
  and the plaster will respond from the woodwork.

12 "Alas for you who build a town by bloodshed,
  and found a city on iniquity!"
13 Is it not from the LORD of hosts
  that peoples labor only to feed the flames,
  and nations weary themselves for nothing?
14 But the earth will be filled
  with the knowledge of the glory of the LORD,
  as the waters cover the sea.

15 "Alas for you who make your neighbors drink,
  pouring out your wrath until they are drunk,
  in order to gaze on their nakedness!"
16 You will be sated with contempt instead of glory.
  Drink, you yourself, and stagger!
The cup in the LORD's right hand
  will come around to you,
  and shame will come upon your glory!
17 For the violence done to Lebanon will overwhelm you;
  the destruction of the animals will terrify you—
because of human bloodshed and violence to the earth,
  to cities and all who live in them.

18 What use is an idol
  once its maker has shaped it—
  a cast image, a teacher of lies?
For its maker trusts in what has been made,
  though the product is only an idol that cannot speak!

¹⁹ Alas for you who say to the wood, "Wake up!"
to silent stone, "Rouse yourself!"
Can it teach?
See, it is gold and silver plated,
and there is no breath in it at all.

²⁰ But the LORD is in his holy temple;
let all the earth keep silence before him!

God stated to Habakkuk that he will have to wait for the vision, even though it will not tarry. Indeed, in its placement in the book, the vision does not follow upon the heels of its announcement in 2:2–3; it is not to be found until 3:3–15. In the meantime, a series of indictments against that fierce and impetuous nation, Babylonia, are given by God through the prophet, marking it for judgment and punishment (see 1:12). Habakkuk first condemns this nation for the exorbitant and ill-gotten wealth it has gained by collecting "all peoples as their own" (v. 5). Gathering the peoples, however, is solely God's right (Isa. 11:12; 43:5; 54:7). Like death itself, the craving of this presumptuous nation is insatiable. In ancient Hebrew thought, Sheol denoted the realm of the dead, to which all people went upon death (see Psalm 139:8), not an afterlife *per se*, but a shadowy realm of subsistence. Death, of course, claims all, an apt metaphor to illustrate the insatiable appetite of this predatory nation, which thinks the whole world is theirs to devour.

The tables, however, will be turned against this arrogant people. The object of taunts, this nation will have to take its own medicine. They will fall by the very sword they wielded and become the booty of others (2:6–8). Thinking they were safe and immune to violence in their distant homes, they will face a punishment that will also come from within, from the very walls and woodwork of their homes (vv. 9–11). Conquering cities by bloodshed and rebuilding them will in the end benefit them nothing. God will sever the connection between exploitation and profit. Revenue gained from the blood and sweat of others will only feed the flames of judgment. A judgment that will burst the barriers of human presumption and make way for the "flood" of the knowledge of God's glory (2:14; cf. Isa. 11:9).

Knowledge of God implies *acknowledgment* of God, and when the nations come to acknowledge God, their exploitative ways will be exposed for what they are: heinous exercises in futility. No gain is to be had from the violent grasp of the powerful, unless it be self-destruction. The cup of suffering from which this nation forced others to drink will come around to be drunk (v. 16). Babylon, once the "golden cup in the Lord's hand" to punish the nations (Jer. 51:7), must now take its own medicine and be punished. Violence done against the other nations like Lebanon, and even to the animals, will be turned against the doer. Self-glory will be replaced by contempt and shame. How so? Because violence knows no boundaries. Incapable of restriction, it extends to all inhabitants of the earth (2:8, 17). From those who shed much blood, much blood will be shed. Modern history is no better example than ancient history. In the twentieth century alone, the first world war began with a single assassination in Sarajevo, Bosnia on June 28, 1914. When one looks at the more recent "balkanization" of Yugoslavia, it seems as if the world is ever poised to explode, like a canister of gas, in flames of violence with only a single spark.

The prophet ends his series of indictments with a reflection on the absurdity of idolatrous worship (2:18–20). To a lifeless figure of wood and stone, how could anyone, the prophet seems to ask, attach ultimate value and worth? Ornate gold and silver plating do not help; the idol is still as lifeless as the inanimate material from which it was fashioned. Like Elijah mocking the priests of Baal during the contest at Mount Carmel (1 Kings 18:27), Habakkuk depicts the artisan commanding his idols to rouse themselves to no avail. How absurd that an idol warrants the trust of anyone, let alone its maker! By contrast, God, the creator of all, requires total reverence and trust, relativizing all other allegiances and concerns. While idols require the futile badgering of their worshipers, God commands silence over all the earth. It is the kind of hushed silence that excitedly anticipates decisive action on the part of God. As Zechariah commands, "Be silent, all people, before the Lord; for he has roused himself from his holy dwelling" (Zech. 2:13). And, as the last chapter of Habakkuk discloses, God is about to act with irrevocable force.

HABAKKUK'S VISION:
THE RESCUE OF GOD'S PEOPLE
Habakkuk 3:1–15

3:1 A prayer of the prophet Habakkuk according to Shigionoth.
2 O LORD, I have heard of your renown,
   and I stand in awe, O LORD, of your work.
In our own time revive it;
   in our own time make it known;
   in wrath may you remember mercy.

3 God came from Teman,
   the Holy One from Mount Paran.
                                        Selah
His glory covered the heavens,
   and the earth was full of his praise.
4 The brightness was like the sun;
   rays came forth from his hand,
   where his power lay hidden.
5 Before him went pestilence,
   and plague followed close behind.
6 He stopped and shook the earth;
   he looked and made the nations tremble.
The eternal mountains were shattered;
   along his ancient pathways
   the everlasting hills sank low.
7 I saw the tents of Cushan under affliction;
   the tent-curtains of the land of Midian trembled.
8 Was your wrath against the rivers, O LORD?
   Or your anger against the rivers,
   or your rage against the sea,
when your drove your horses,
   your chariots to victory?
9 You brandished your naked bow,
   sated were the arrows of your command.
                                        Selah

   You split the earth with rivers.
10 The mountains saw you, and writhed;
   a torrent of water swept by;
the deep gave forth its voice,
   The sun raised high its hands;
11 the moon stood still in its exalted place,
   at the light of your arrows speeding by,
   at the gleam of your flashing spear.
12 In fury you trod the earth,
   in anger you trampled nations.
13 You came forth to save your people,
   to save your anointed.
You crushed the head of the wicked house,
   laying it bare from foundation to roof.
                                        Selah
14 You pierced with his own arrows the head of his warriors,
   who came like a whirlwind to scatter us,
   gloating as if ready to devour the poor who were in hiding.

¹⁵ **You trampled the sea with your horses,**
   churning the mighty waters.

The vision foretold in 2:2–3 finally comes to Habakkuk (3:3–15). As earlier commanded by God, we find that the prophet has faithfully recorded it, in the form of a prayer no less. The reference to *Shigionoth* in verse 1 denotes a kind of sung prayer that was used as part of the liturgy in temple worship (see 3:19 and Psalm 7:1). The prophet's prayer begins in praise of God, particularly in God's action in the past. The prophet is intimately familiar with the stories and traditions of God's action in history. Habakkuk is keenly aware, for example, of the Exodus story, in which God acted in strength to deliver a people long ago. That was the "old time Gospel story" for Habakkuk, and the prophet wants God to repeat it for his day (3:2). His request is no retreat into the past for nostalgia's sake. Rather, the past bears the promise of hope. Habakkuk petitions the one who holds the past, present, and future together to remember the past in order to shape the present and open up new possibilities for the future. Habakkuk ultimately appeals to God's very nature, trusting that the God who acted with passionate mercy to deliver a suffering people in the past is the same God of today. The prophet does not yearn for the good old days; he firmly believes that the best is yet to come. The vision that follows in verses 3–15 serves to vindicate this bold faith of Habakkuk. God is ready to come again to save.

The vision in 3:3–15 touches upon many ancient traditions about God. As in Deuteronomy 33:2–3, Judges 5:4–5, and Exodus 15:14–16, God is seen advancing from the south to Israel, across the southeastern highlands of Edom (Teman and Mount Paran). Mount Sinai is also frequently connected with God's march from the south (Deut. 33:2; Judg. 5:5). All of these traditions depict God's coming as an awe-filled, fearsome event. In Habakkuk's vision in particular God is accompanied by blinding light, plague and pestilence, earthquakes, and storm. Cushan and Midian, two southern peoples, tremble in fear and can only hope to scurry out of the way in time, lest they be trampled. Unimpeded, the divine warrior marches on, clearing the way to the final destination. Like lightning bolts, God's arrows and spears find their mark, destroying the "wicked house" of Babylon. This wicked nation is likened to the sea, the traditional symbol of chaos and resistance, which must be trampled and destroyed (for example, Psalms 77:17, 20; 104:7–9; Jer. 5:22; cf. Gen. 1:2).

All creation is in travail as God fights on behalf of Judah (3:13). Through all the conflict and the carnage, God's purpose does not waver.

In the heat of battle God comes to deliver and save. This is God's freedom march. As in the story of the Exodus, to save a people involves dismantling and reconfiguring the balance of power. There seems to be no other way around it, as history lamentably attests. Egyptians drown in the Red Sea, Assyria is overcome, Babylon is defeated; all those who came "like a whirlwind to scatter" God's people must themselves be defeated in order to make way for deliverance. Habakkuk's vision attests to the world's intractable resistance to God's plans; only defeat can bring about renewal. Yet the vision also attests that God refuses to stand above the fray and idly watch human injustice run amok. God crosses time and space to enter into the sinful messiness of human existence to save those who are most victimized by the world's ways (see 3:14). God comes down to wrestle with and defeat the principalities and powers that control us all. In Christ, we see even death itself conquered in the one who offered himself up in death—power defeated by powerlessness. Christ as both victim and victor testifies to the limitless extent to which God's saving power takes hold and transforms.

HABAKKUK'S RESPONSE: PROLEPTIC JOY
Habakkuk 3:16–19

> 3:16 I hear, and I tremble within;
>   my lips quiver at the sound.
> Rottenness enters into my bones,
>   and my steps tremble beneath me.
> I wait quietly for the day of calamity
>   to come upon the people who attack us.
> ¹⁷ Though the fig tree does not blossom,
>   and no fruit is on the vines;
> though the produce of the olive fails
>   and the fields yield no food;
> though the flock is cut off from the fold
>   and there is no herd in the stalls,
> ¹⁸ yet I will rejoice in the LORD;
>   I will exult in the God of my salvation.
> ¹⁹ GOD, the Lord, is my strength;
>   he makes my feet like the feet of a deer,
>   and makes me tread upon the heights.
>
> To the choirmaster: with stringed instruments.

Although Habakkuk's vision powerfully describes the deliverance of his people, the prophet does not react with self-righteous glee. To the contrary, the trembling that the nations suffer (3:7) is also felt by the prophet. The majestic and unmatchable power of God is appropriately met with fear and trembling. Indeed, no human being can withstand more than a glimpse of God and survive (Exod. 34:18–23). The vision renders the prophet speechless; there is nothing for him to do except to wait quietly for the day of God's coming.

And yet there is something more. Habakkuk, for the first time, can rejoice (3:18). He can rejoice over a deliverance that has not yet arrived, a deliverance that is still contradicted by what he sees around him. The land still languishes, ravaged by battle or drought due to the perversion of justice (1:4; see Hos. 4:1–3). The prophet refuses to be held hostage by the misery around him, for his laughter cannot be contained. It is a joy unbound. Habakkuk knows the true source of his strength, and it is not whatever can enable him to gain wealth or win battles (cf. 1:11, 16); it is the font of life itself. Moreover, the kind of strength that issues from the Creator is of a different order than the power that is lorded over others, the power of brute force. Once wearied by the crushing weight of human injustice, Habakkuk now leaps for joy, renewed and invigorated like the agile deer upon the mountains (Isa. 35:6; Song of Sol. 2:17; 8:14). It is an inner joy that cannot be defeated or stifled, for it stems from no human or material source.

Perhaps this is the most enduring part of Habakkuk's prophecy, one to which his life also attests. Such joy and renewed vigor for life can be reached only by plumbing the depths of our deepest pains and disillusionments and lifting them up in honest and intimate conversation with God.

Zephaniah

Introduction

The words of the prophet Zephaniah both plumb the depths of judgment and climb the heights of grace. In fact, the overall movement of the book is defined by judgment giving way to salvation. The book begins with the harsh reality of judgment against God's people, indeed, against the whole world. It is a well-deserved judgment whose warrant is found in the corrupt worship and injustice Zephaniah sees polluting the land. Yet Zephaniah's message does not end with doom. The prophet moves toward forgiveness and restoration, toward the vision of a transformed community in which the people will finally seek God in earnest. In short, Zephaniah's message moves from chastisement to comfort, from a people judged to a people restored. Consequently, it is imperative to read the book from beginning to end before focusing on any one text. Zephaniah's message bears a certain logic of development with a climactic resolution at the end. To focus on any one text without accounting for how it fits into the larger picture does not do justice to the dramatic power and profound message Zephaniah imparts for us today.

The prophet lived in a period of turbulent change in his country. Good King Josiah had ascended the throne and reform was brewing. Upon discovering the law book in the temple, Josiah quickly instituted a sweeping reform that effectively purged Judah and what was left of northern Israel of corrupt worship (2 Kings 23:1–25). Only one other king had ever attempted to institute a reform of such proportions—Hezekiah, almost a century earlier. However, his efforts met with only limited success (2 Kings 18:3–7). Zephaniah must have lived in the early part of Josiah's reign (604–609 B.C.), since the prophet makes no particular reference to Josiah's far-reaching reform. Nevertheless, much of his language seems to set the occasion for religious reform, even anticipating it. Whether the prophet was alive to see the fruition of his message is uncertain.

ZEPHANIAH'S PEDIGREE
AND PURPOSE
Zephaniah 1:1

> 1:1 The word of the LORD that came to Zephaniah son of Cushi son of Gedaliah son of Amariah son of Hezekiah, in the days of King Josiah son of Amon of Judah.

The first verse, as with opening verses of most prophetic books, identifies the prophet, the historical background, and the source of his message. Zephaniah has a message to impart and it is unequivocally from God. The prophet did not search it out; rather, the word came to him. Yet Zephaniah is not an anonymous nobody or empty vessel. This first verse makes clear that he came from a particular family, bearing a particular lineage.

Compared to most other introductions to prophetic books, the genealogical information provided in this opening verse is unusually detailed, suggesting that Zephaniah came from a prominent background. Though most of the names are not identifiable, the last one mentioned is strikingly familiar. The prophet is likely a direct descendant of King Hezekiah (2 Kings 18–20), who ruled from approximately 715–687 B.C. Consequently, this prophet was no outcast character who came out of nowhere to condemn and judge. Far from it, Zephaniah was most probably a royal cousin of Josiah, who himself was a great-grandson of Hezekiah. At any rate, Zephaniah's prophetic career and Josiah's reign coincided. As previously mentioned, this was a time in which the winds of change were blowing. When he was no more than eighteen years old, Josiah instituted a religious reform that purged all pagan worship practice from the land, as far north as Bethel and Samaria (2 Kings 23:1–25). Zephaniah's prophecy helped set the stage.

COSMIC JUDGMENT
Zephaniah 1:2–6

> 1:2 I will utterly sweep away everything
> from the face of the earth, says the LORD.
> 3 I will sweep away humans and animals;
> I will sweep away the birds of the air
> and the fish of the sea.
> I will make the wicked stumble.
> I will cut off humanity

from the face of the earth, says the LORD.
⁴ I will stretch out my hand against Judah,
  and against all the inhabitants of Jerusalem;
and I will cut off from this place every remnant of Baal
  and the name of the idolatrous priests;
⁵ those who bow down on the roofs
  to the host of the heavens;
those who bow down and swear to the LORD,
  but also swear by Milcom;
⁶ those who have turned back from following the LORD,
  who have not sought the LORD or inquired of him.

Zephaniah's message begins on the jarring note of universal judgment: Everything is to be swept away, utterly destroyed. Not even the birds and the fish will escape such judgment. It is as if God wanted to start over with an entirely clean slate, to go back to the drawing board and begin again. Such indeed was the case much earlier. The story of the flood (Genesis 6—8) begins with a state of affairs that is so hopeless that nothing can be done except to begin anew. Wickedness and violence so permeated God's creation that it "grieved him to his heart" (Gen. 6:6, 11–13). The story of Noah is the story of a fresh beginning. As the flood set the stage for proper worship with Noah's sacrifice (Gen. 8:20–21), Zephaniah finds the corruption of worship resulting in the world's demise in judgment. Such prophetic judgment, however, exceeds the severity of the flood in that, now, even the fish of the sea have come under divine judgment! The means by which God is to effect such devastation is of little importance to the prophet; all that matters is that the whole of creation must suffer judgment, and for good reason.

That reason comes in verses 4–6. As the focus of divine judgment becomes more narrow, the reason behind the prophet's words of doom begins to emerge. With Judah and Jerusalem as the primary objects of God's wrath (v. 4), Zephaniah issues his complaint against strange practices that are foreign to authentic worship. God's people are worshiping not only the Lord God of Israel but also the pagan gods Baal and Milcom! Baal was the god of the Canaanites, with whom the Lord expressly forbade the Israelites to make a covenant. Milcom was the deity of the Ammonites, one of Israel's many neighboring countries. Not only these gods but also the heavenly deities such as the sun, moon, and the stars were part of the ever-expanding religious repertoire of God's people. To Zephaniah they were all idols, abominations that flew in the face of the first commandment, "You shall have no others gods before me" (Exod. 20:3; Deut. 5:7).

True worship is *exclusive* worship of God. For Zephaniah there is no middle ground. Zephaniah's indictment against his people is loud and clear: All attempts to integrate into Israel's worship other objects of adoration are doomed to failure, for they abrogate the exclusive allegiance God demands. The Lord is a "jealous" God (Exod. 20:5; 34:14) who passionately cares for people with undying love while expecting the same measure of zealous faithfulness in return. Zephaniah warns that those who delude themselves into thinking that certain foreign practices are compatible with true worship have in effect "turned back from following the Lord" (v. 6). Worship of God cannot be shared with other objects of adoration, be it other "gods," money, family, or oneself. As God chose a particular people to be a blessing to the whole human family (Gen. 12:3), so God expects reciprocity in worship and praise. For Zephaniah the fierceness of God's judgment is firmly rooted within the expanse of God's relentless love, a love that ultimately moves beyond judgment without bypassing it. Love without accountability is an impotent, cheap love. The kind of love that works through judgment is a powerful, visceral love that makes all things irrevocably new.

THE DAY OF DISTRESS
Zephaniah 1:7–18

> 1:7 Be silent before the Lord GOD!
>   For the day of the LORD is at hand;
> the LORD has prepared a sacrifice,
>   he has consecrated his guests.
> 8 And on the day of the Lord's sacrifice,
> I will punish the officials and the king's sons
>   and all who dress themselves in foreign attire.
> 9 On that day I will punish
>   all who leap over the threshold,
> who fill their master's house
>   with violence and fraud.
>
> 10 On that day, says the LORD,
>   a cry will be heard from the Fish Gate,
> a wail from the Second Quarter,
>   a loud crash from the hills.
> 11 The inhabitants of the Mortar wail,
>   for all the traders have perished;
>   all who weigh out silver are cut off.

12 At that time I will search Jerusalem with lamps,
    and I will punish the people
who rest complacently on their dregs,
    those who say in their hearts,
"The LORD will not do good,
    nor will he do harm."
13 Their wealth shall be plundered,
    and their houses laid waste. Though they build houses,
    they shall not inhabit them;
though they plant vineyards,
    they shall not drink wine from them.
14 The great day of the LORD is near,
    near and hastening fast;
the sound of the day of the LORD is bitter,
    the warrior cries aloud there.
15 That day will be a day of wrath,
    a day of distress and anguish,
a day of ruin and devastation,
    a day of darkness and gloom,
a day of clouds and thick darkness,
16 a day of trumpet blast and battle cry
against the fortified cities
    and against the lofty battlements.

17 I will bring such distress upon people
    that they shall walk like the blind;
    because they have sinned against the LORD,
their blood shall be poured out like dust,
    and their flesh like dung.
18 Neither their silver nor their gold
    will be able to save them
    on the day of the Lord's wrath;
in the fire of his passion
    the whole earth shall be consumed;
for a full, a terrible end
    he will make of all the inhabitants of the earth.

Having issued his indictment (vv. 4–6), Zephaniah specifies how divine judgment will take place. The prophet uses the traditional designation of the "day of the Lord," a time that was considered by many Israelites to designate the day God would deliver Israel from its enemies, a day of light and hope (cf. Amos 5:18–20). But as with other prophets, such as Amos, Ezekiel (30:1–4), and Joel (2:1–2), Zephaniah quickly dispels all false hopes attached to this dreaded day. Not unlike Amos's "day of darkness," the day of the Lord for Zephaniah marks the culmination of God's punishment. Indeed, the day begins in awed silence with a sacrifice. The command for silence before God anticipates the in-breaking of something new and dangerous (Hab. 2:20; Zech. 2:13). A sacrifice is about to be held. The prophet intentionally refrains from specifying who is invited and what is to be sacrificed. Many a Judean would have doubtlessly thought that the prophet was referring to Israel's enemies as the sacrificial victims. To the contrary, and much to the chagrin of his listeners, Zephaniah makes the dangerously disturbing claim that it is the royal administration who will be the object of God's sacrifice. Along with them, those who wear foreign attire, "leap over the threshold," and fill their houses with "violence and fraud," will also receive judgment.

Zephaniah's prophetic punch is akin to Isaiah's song of the vineyard (Isa. 5:1–7) and Nathan's oracle to David (2 Sam. 12:1–14) in that the hearers' interpretation is suddenly turned upside down at the end of the prophet's message. Zephaniah's audience no doubt welcomed the prophet's words, thinking that he was announcing God's deliverance from their enemies. However, it quickly became clear that they themselves were deemed the enemy by the prophet. Many of them "leapt over the threshold," a common superstitious practice rooted in the belief that evil spirits congregated at the doorways of buildings, especially temples (see 1 Sam. 5:5). Many wore some form of foreign attire, particularly people of means who bought wares from foreign merchants. For Zephaniah, wearing fashionable attire was another sign of assimilating the practices of pagan foreigners. The clothes make the worshiper, Zephaniah reasons.

The list of judgments goes on in verses 10–13. Zephaniah refers to different places in Jerusalem that were, presumably, centers of commerce and affluence: the Fish Gate, located in the north wall of Jerusalem, was perhaps the entrance to the fish market in Jerusalem; the Second Quarter was a residential district populated by affluent citizens that was located on the western hill overlooking the temple; and the Mortar was probably the lower area, later known as the Tyropoeon or Central valley. It separated the Second Quarter from the temple mount, and most likely was the place where merchants conducted their business. Along with these geographical locales, the prophet lists business people, the complacently affluent, and large estate owners as especially deserving of God's wrath. Their wealth will be plundered, their property ruined. Searching them out with lamps, God will spare no wealthy citizen. Why? Because the wealthy find God completely impotent and indifferent (v. 12). To them God does nei-

ther harm nor good—in short, nothing. Such a pronouncement is tantamount to contradicting God's very nature. As Deuteronomy warns,

> Do not say to yourself, "My power and the might of my own hand have got-
> ten me this wealth." But remember the LORD your God, for it is he who
> gives you power to get wealth, so that he may confirm his covenant that he
> swore to your ancestors, as he is doing today. (Deut. 8:17–18)

Wealth is a gift to be used wisely on behalf of others. For Zephaniah,
the wealthy's attitude about God only betrays an intractably self-serving
independence. They have accrued their wealth by their own wits; they
consider themselves self-made. The value of rugged individualism and
self-initiative espoused by the wealthy is, however, no virtue; it is an illusion, a puffed-up self-image that only expands as one's possessions grow.
Soon the bubble will burst, the prophet warns. The wealthy will no longer
benefit from their amassed possessions. Their complacent, self-assured attitude is rooted in a self-delusion that only makes a mockery of God.
Zephaniah's pronouncement against the wealthy strikes at the very heart
of the biblical message: Human beings cannot save themselves, whatever
the means (see v. 18; Gen. 11:1–9). It is a message that will become
painfully clear on the day of wrath.

Like an approaching army, the day of the Lord is imminent (vv. 14–16).
Zephaniah employs the language of battle and storm to describe this fate-
ful time. The Lord is the divine warrior who commands the heavenly
hosts to wage war against the fortified cities and lofty battlements of Judah. Devastation will be total. Zephaniah takes up images of life and turns
them into images of decay and death (v. 17). The whole earth will be consumed by "the fire of his passion" (v. 18). As noted above, God's love is a
passionate love that is fierce and unrelenting both in mercy and in judgment. The prophet ends his first chapter as he began it, in universal judgment. Not by flood but by fire will God's judgment be accomplished. In
the ancient Near East, destruction by conflagration was most always the
final act used by the successfully invading army to devastate the enemy utterly, a fate that Jerusalem itself suffered on two occasions in biblical times
(587 B.C. and 70 A.D.) Zephaniah envisions such an invasion on a cosmic
scale. Fortunately, however, this day of dread is not the end of the matter;
rather, it sets the stage for something no less earth shattering: the renewal
and transformation of God's people (3:9–20).

How God moves from exercising judgment to bringing about restoration is told in the intervening passages.

REPENTANCE AND HOPE
Zephaniah 2:1–3

2:1 Gather together, gather,
O shameless nation,
2 before you are driven away
like the drifting chaff,
before there comes upon you
the fierce anger of the LORD,
before there comes upon you
the day of the LORD's wrath.
3 Seek the LORD, all you humble of the land,
who do his commands;
seek righteousness, seek humility;
perhaps you may be hidden
on the day of the LORD's wrath.

These three verses comprise the link between judgment and hope. One would think that after having heard the pronouncement of God's judgment so vividly conveyed in the first chapter, all that is left to do is to wait in fear and trembling for the execution. Far from it! Against all odds, the prophet issues a call to action, encouraging his people to turn from their ways. All is not lost. Zephaniah musters his people, but not to fight against the inevitable onslaught of divine judgment, as if it were an invading army to be resisted. Zephaniah's "call to arms" is a call to repent, to seek earnestly three things: righteousness, humility, and God (cf. 1:6). The prophet's pronouncement echoes Micah's famous line: "What does the Lord require of you, but to do justice, and to love kindness, and to walk humbly with your God?" (Mic. 6:8). The virtue of humility runs counter to the attitude of the wealthy expressed in 1:12. Righteousness is a corporate virtue that denotes just order (Amos 5:24), the fruit of seeking the Lord. Zephaniah's command is equivalent to that of Jesus: "Strive first for the kingdom of God and his righteousness, and all these things will be given to you as well" (Matt. 6:33). To seek righteousness is to incorporate and reflect the pattern of the divinely ordained order, God's kingdom. Like Jesus, Zephaniah does not command his people to build the kingdom of God, as if it could be done brick by brick. To the contrary, the prophet calls us to model through our action what God will eventually bring about for the world. It is an ethic of anticipation.

Within the scope of divine judgment, the result of repentant behavior is, according to the prophet, a big "perhaps" (2:3). Zephaniah offers no guarantees, but that is entirely in keeping with the profile of humility. The "perhaps" is, of course, entirely up to God, rather than human contrivance. Deliverance is effected solely by God's initiative. From the prophet's point of view, the most that can be said is "perhaps." Amos said something similar over a century earlier: "Hate evil and love good, and establish justice in the gate; *it may be* that the Lord, the God of hosts, will be gracious to the remnant of Joseph" (Amos 5:15). Zephaniah is a bit more blunt (2:3). Like refugees fleeing to the hills to hide out in caves before the divine wave of terror, the most Zephaniah can wish for his people is escape from God's judgment (see Isa. 2:19–21).

On closer scrutiny, the prophet's language is charged with irony. Although Zephaniah can only suggest the possibility of escaping God's wrath, he specifically calls his people to seek God in humility. There is nothing hidden or fearful about serving God. Seeking God and God's righteousness corporately opens up the possibility of divine blessing and just order. Zephaniah's words are certainly no less true today. We are all found worthy of God's judgment, but that is no cause to wail and lament our deserved fate. Rather, such a realization is the beginning point toward serving God earnestly and joyously. By taking upon himself God's judgment against us, Christ completes the movement that Zephaniah saw for his own people, turning judgment into blessing and sanctification. Zephaniah saw far beyond the modest prospect of escaping from God's wrath to glimpse the new life that was in store for God's people.

JUDGMENT AGAINST ISRAEL'S ENEMIES
Zephaniah 2:4–15

> 2:4 **For Gaza shall be deserted,**
>   **and Ashkelon shall become a desolation;**
> **Ashdod's people shall be driven out at noon,**
>   **and Ekron shall be uprooted.**
> 5 **Ah, inhabitants of the seacoast,**
>   **you nation of the Cherethites!**
> **The word of the LORD is against you,**
>   **O Canaan, land of the Philistines;**
>   **and I will destroy you until no inhabitant is left.**
> 6 **And you, O seacoast, shall be pastures,**
>   **meadows for shepherds,**
>   **and folds for flocks.**

7 The seacoast shall become the possession
    of the remnant of the house of Judah,
    on which they shall pasture,
and in the houses of Ashkelon
    they shall lie down at evening.
For the LORD their God will be mindful of them
    and restore their fortunes.

8 I have heard the taunts of Moab
    and the revilings of the Ammonites,
how they have taunted my people
    and made boasts against their territory.
9 Therefore, as I live, says the LORD of hosts,
    the God of Israel,
Moab shall become like Sodom,
    and the Ammonites like Gomorrah,
a land possessed by nettles and salt pits,
    and a waste forever.
The remnant of my people shall plunder them,
    and the survivors of my nation shall possess them.
10 This shall be their lot in return for their pride,
    because they scoffed and boasted
    against the people of the LORD of hosts.
11 The LORD will be terrible against them;
    he will shrivel all the gods of the earth,
and to him shall bow down,
    each in its place,
    all the coasts and islands of the nations.

12 You also, O Ethiopians,
    shall be killed by my sword.

13 And he will stretch out his hand against the north,
    and destroy Assyria;
and he will make Nineveh a desolation,
    a dry waste like the desert.
14 Herds shall lie down in it,
    every wild animal;
the desert owl and the screech owl
    shall lodge on its capitals;
the owl shall hoot at the window,
    the raven croak on the threshold;
    for its cedar work will be laid bare.

15 Is this the exultant city
   that lived secure,
that said to itself,
   "I am, and there is no one else"?
What a desolation it has become,
   a lair for wild animals!
Everyone who passes by it
   hisses and shakes the fist.

This section of Zephaniah's prophecy demonstrates in scathing detail the universal scope of God's judgment. God's people do not stand alone in judgment, although they do stand a chance of escape (v. 3). Israel's enemies, however, don't stand a chance. The wave of God's terrible judgment begins with the cities of Philistia (vv. 4–7), Israel's ancient enemy located on the Mediterranean coast west of Israel, then moves to Moab and Ammon (vv. 8–11), countries east of the Jordan. From there, divine judgment falls upon two superpowers of the ancient Near East, Ethiopia (v. 12) and Assyria (vv. 13–15), whose renowned capital Nineveh is destined for destruction for its false sense of security and pride. Indeed, the city's self-pronouncement in verse 15 is tantamount to self-deification. (See the book of Nahum for a comparable indictment of the city. For an entirely different estimation of Nineveh, see the book of Jonah.) Only the "coasts and islands of the nations" are spared (v. 11). They are the distant islands that have not heard of the Lord but will come to know God's sovereignty (Isa. 66:19).

For those countries regarded as Israel's enemies, Zephaniah's language is dire: Their lands will be made desolate like Sodom and Gomorrah (v. 9); their gods will wither away to nothing (v. 11); and their cities will become a haven for wild animals. All signs of urban culture will be erased. What were once centers of civilization have reverted to pastures and wilderness. But there is something more: Zephaniah's prophecy makes it clear that what is left of Philistia, Moab, and Ammon, shall become a possession of the "remnant" of God's people (vv. 7, 9). The seacoast will become a pasture for the flocks and herds of Judean shepherds (vv. 6, 7). Like the meek inheriting the earth (Matt. 5:5), the prophet grants not only survival but also supremacy to the humble portion (literally, "what is left") of his people. What actually is this remnant? This question is answered in the next chapter. But Zephaniah already drops the first hint by referring to a future restoration of the fortunes of Judah (v. 7).

THE PURIFYING WORK
OF JUDGMENT
Zephaniah 3:1–13

3:1 Ah, soiled, defiled,
      oppressing city!
2 It has listened to no voice;
      it has accepted no correction.
It has not trusted in the LORD;
      it has not drawn near to its God.

3 The officials within it
      are roaring lions;
its judges are evening wolves
      that leave nothing until the morning.
4 Its prophets are reckless,
      faithless persons;
its priests have profaned what is sacred,
      they have done violence to the law.
5 The LORD within it is righteous;
      he does no wrong.
Every morning he renders his judgment,
      each dawn without fail;
      but the unjust knows no shame.

6 I have cut off nations;
      their battlements are in ruins;
I have laid waste their streets
      so that no one walks in them;
their cities have been made desolate,
      without people, without inhabitants.
7 I said, "Surely the city will fear me,
      it will accept correction;
it will not lose sight
      of all that I have brought upon it."
But they were the more eager
      to make all their deeds corrupt.
8 Therefore wait for me, says the LORD,
      for the day when I arise as a witness.
For my decision is to gather nations,
      to assemble kingdoms,
to pour out upon them my indignation,
      all the heat of my anger;

for in the fire of my passion
   all the earth shall be consumed.
9 At that time I will change my speech of the peoples
   to a pure speech,
that all of them may call on the name of the LORD
   and serve him with one accord.
10 From beyond the rivers of Ethiopia
   my suppliants, my scattered ones,
   shall bring my offering.

11 On that day you shall not be put to shame
   because of all the deeds by which you have rebelled against me;
for then I will remove from your midst
   your proudly exultant ones,
and you shall no longer be haughty
   in my holy mountain.
12 For I will leave in the midst of you
   a people humble and lowly.
They shall seek refuge in the name of the LORD—
13 the remnant of Israel;
they shall do no wrong
   and utter no lies,
nor shall a deceitful tongue
   be found in their mouths.
Then they will pasture and lie down,
   and no one shall make them afraid.

The focus of the final chapter returns to Jerusalem, the polluted city. Zephaniah begins with a list of indictments. Refusing to acknowledge God, Jerusalem has become disobedient, undisciplined, and untrustworthy. Particular culpability is assigned to particular classes. Civil servants and judges are likened to predatory animals that devour justice (v. 3). Prophets and priests have undermined their vocations. It was the priest's job to keep separate the domains of the profane and the sacred as well as to teach the law (Lev. 10:10; Ezek. 44:21–23). The prophet's job was to utter God's words and call God's people back to a life of justice and faith. Zephaniah condemns his prophetic colleagues for deceiving God's people through false prophecies.

In stark contrast to Jerusalem's rampant corruption, God remains within the city, rendering judgment despite it all (v. 5). One would expect God to have abandoned Jerusalem long before things got so bad. The idea of God dwelling in the midst of the city goes back to the ancient priestly notion of God's very presence or name abiding in the temple (Lev. 26:11; Deut. 12:5). As a result of God's abiding presence, divine judgment is executed daily.

The daily rising of the sun had deep theological significance for the ancient Hebrews. It signified God's deliverance (Psalm 46:5) as well as divine judgment (read Psalm 19 in its entirety). Indeed, in God's address to Job, the dawn is portrayed as taking hold of the "skirts of the earth" to shake out the wicked (Job 38:12–13). Following the chaos of night, the morning sun is the sign of God's restoration of the creative order, as surely as the rainbow is the sign that God will no longer allow chaos to destroy the land (Gen. 9:8–17). And yet chaos still persists. Zephaniah refers to the persistence of the unjust who "know no shame." Consequently, justice must be rendered on a daily basis to prevent the world from being overrun by wickedness. Untainted by corruption and undaunted by the enormity of the challenge to maintain some semblance of social order (see v. 7), God remains in the city, polluted as it is. God's continued presence demonstrates an unwavering resolve to maintain convenantal solidarity with the people at all costs. With Christ, the cost is death. In Christ, even death is rendered powerless to separate us from God (Rom. 8:37–39; 1 Cor. 15:54–57).

God begins to speak directly in verse 6, declaring fulfillment of Zephaniah's prophecies against the nations in 2:4–15. The destruction of Israel's enemies serves to demonstrate not the liberation of God's people but the severity of God's dreadful punishment of Jerusalem. God expects Jerusalem to repent and fear God (cf. Prov. 1:7; 9:10), thereby averting a destruction similar to that of the nations (cf. 2:3). Yet Jerusalem just doesn't get it. One can feel the pain of God's disappointment over the people's eager willingness to pursue corrupt deeds (3:7). So God has one piece of advice left: Wait for the day of destruction when the earth will be consumed by the fire of God's passion or jealousy (see 1:18).

This fire comes, however, not only to destroy but to refine and transform. After the cosmic conflagration, whoever is left will invoke God's name with pure speech, not with the perverted speech of idolatrous worship and the double-speak of treachery. No longer will God's people "swear by Milcom" (1:5), or the wealthy denounce God's ability to act, or Nineveh arrogantly proclaim its supremacy (2:15). All will humbly serve the supreme God, even those scattered to the farthest reaches of the civilized world.

The transformation continues with God's own people. The Lord proclaims that Jerusalem's punishment will be rescinded (v. 11). God's people are acquitted, the sentence is commuted, despite the serious nature of their rebellious deeds (see v. 15). God will remove their guilt by removing the cause, namely those who are exultant and haughty (cf. 2:15). The prideful arrogance that seems so endemic to urban centers, including Jerusalem, will be purged, and what will be left is not so much a city as it is God's "holy mountain," the mountain upon which God dwells (see v. 5). Jerusalem had forgotten that it was a city in residence in God's land, not a monument to human achievement and pride. Only the humble and lowly will be left, a remnant that seeks refuge not in possessions or in themselves but in God (see Psalm 118:8). Moreover, no lies or deceit will be found upon their lips, their speech having been purified (v. 9). Like God, they shall do no wrong (v. 5). Like sheep under the protection of the Good Shepherd, they shall live in absolute security. Zephaniah lifts up the pastoral image to convey the ideal of peace (cf. 2:6–7), similar to the serene picture painted in the opening verses of Psalm 23: "He makes me lie down in green pastures; he leads me beside still waters; he restores my soul. He leads me in the right paths for his name's sake" (vv. 2–3).

SONG OF JOY
Zephaniah 3:14–20

> 3:14 **Sing aloud, O daughter Zion;**
>   **shout, O Israel!**
> **Rejoice and exult with all your heart,**
>   **O daughter Jerusalem!**
> ¹⁵ **The LORD has taken away the judgments against you,**
>   **he has turned away your enemies.**
> **The king of Israel, the LORD, is in your midst;**
>   **you shall fear disaster no more.**
> ¹⁶ **On that day it shall be said to Jerusalem:**
> **Do not fear, O Zion;**
>   **do not let your hands grow weak.**
> ¹⁷ **The LORD, your God, is in your midst,**
>   **a warrior who gives victory;**
> **he will rejoice over you with gladness,**
>   **he will renew you in his love;**
> **he will exult over you with loud singing**
> ¹⁸ **as on a day of festival.**
> **I will remove disaster from you,**
>   **so that you will not bear reproach for it.**

¹⁹ I will deal with all your oppressors
   at that time.
And I will save the lame
   and gather the outcast,
and I will change their shame into praise
   and renown in all the earth.
²⁰ At that time I will bring you home,
   at the time when I gather you;
for I will make you renowned and praised
   among all the peoples of the earth,
when I restore your fortunes
   before your eyes, says the LORD.

Zephaniah's book appropriately ends with a call to sing with joy, and who wouldn't after such a message of hope and salvation? The prophet addresses his people with special terms of endearment, "daughter Zion" and "daughter Jerusalem." The name Zion sometimes refers to the holy mountain upon which the temple was located (cf. v. 11). In our context, Zion is identical with the city of Jerusalem and its people. The prophet twice intones the refrain that the Lord is "in your midst" (vv. 15, 17). God has not given up on Jerusalem or given its inhabitants over to utter judgment. To the contrary, God continues to abide with them, transforming them as part of a new order. The righteousness that was once only God's (v. 5) has now circumscribed the entire city. The reign of judgment and fear is over, but that doesn't mean that all is done. Far from it, there is much yet to be done, the prophet declares (v. 16). The age of renewal has begun, and there is no place for idle hands. There is joyful work to be done. Even the physically challenged, who were traditionally barred from the temple (Lev. 21:6–23; Deut. 23:1; 2 Sam. 5:8), have a central place in this new Jerusalem (3:19). Their "shame" is turned into praise, as is that of all the people. One thinks of Jesus' triumphal entry into Jerusalem: He first purges the temple of the money changers and then cures the blind and the lame within it (Matt. 21:12–14). God the shepherd will bring everyone home restored. Nothing is self-made here. As the fulfillment and end of judgment, restoration is wrought entirely by God's merciful initiative.

This song of praise marks the final word of God's "judgment" against Jerusalem, a word that fulfills as well as reverses the judgment of destruction conveyed in chapter 1. All things have been overturned and renewed. God is no longer the destructive warrior (1:10–16) but now is the vigilant deliverer. God's relentless hunt through the dark alleyways of Jerusalem to punish the complacent (1:12) has turned into a far-reaching search to the ends of the earth to gather up the dispossessed and bring them home. After judgment, the prophet says, there is one thing that will be in hot pursuit, doggedly crossing time and space, ruthless in its quest, and from which there will be no escape: God's blessing of healing and restoration. The journey of Zephaniah is the journey from judgment to blessing and hope. His message ends with an address to all who will listen (v. 20), to all who have experienced the pain of alienation from others and from God.

We also await the time when we will be brought to our true home, God's kingdom, and united with all the families of the earth, past, present, and future, to give God praise and glory. As the psalmist proclaims after a harrowing journey through the darkest of valleys and having reached his destination, "I shall dwell in the house of the Lord my whole life long" (Psalm 23:6). Home is a destination as well as a direction. God is our home, and homesick is what we are. The invitation to be "home free" is given in Christ's own prophetic announcement: "The time is fulfilled, and the kingdom of God has come near; repent, and believe in the good news" (Mark 1:15).

Haggai

Introduction

The book of Haggai delivers a bold message in a time of indifference and despair. The prophet's words are meant to call people to action when all hands had become idle and all hearts had given up. Haggai saw his people languishing in resignation and despair; his message was a sharp wake-up call before it was too late.

The book attributed to Haggai the prophet covers only a narrow slice of his life, less than four months between August and December, 520 B.C. Yet this was an eventful time. Since 539 B.C., after the defeat of Babylon, Persia had reigned as the superpower of the fertile crescent. One year later, the Persian emperor Cyrus released the Jewish exiles who began to return to Palestine only to find their homeland devastated. Through the leadership of Sheshbazzar, who was appointed by Cyrus to return the holy vessels of the temple, work on the temple began immediately (Ezra 5:14–16). Nevertheless, due to limited resources and spirited opposition, restoration of the temple never got off the ground. Some years later in 520 B.C., the Persian king Darius I ascended the throne, sparking widespread insurrections throughout the empire.

The year 520 B.C. was an important one for post-exilic prophets like Haggai and his colleague Zechariah (Ezra 5:1, 6:14), who began to prophesy soon after this tense period of international turmoil. Haggai calls for a new beginning in building the temple as the way to restore the fledgling community. The temple was finally completed in 516 or 515 B.C. Whether Haggai lived to witness this, we do not know.

Since no genealogical information about him is recorded in Scripture, we know little about the life of this prophet. However, the name *Haggai* is derived from a Hebrew verb that means "to make a pilgrimage" or "hold a festival." Given the fact that Jerusalem was throughout ancient (and modern history) a center for pilgrims and holy festivals, Haggai's name clearly resonates with his message. His message is divided into five major sections: 1:1–11; 1:12–15; 2:1–9; 2:10–19; 2:20–23, which are all arranged chronologically.

WHAT TIME IS IT?
A CALL TO ACTION
Haggai 1:1–11

> 1:1 **In the second year of King Darius, in the sixth month, on the first day of the month, the word of the LORD came by the prophet Haggai to Zerubbabel son of Shealtiel, governor of Judah, and to Joshua son of Jehozadak, the high priest:** 2 **Thus says the LORD of hosts: These people say the time has not yet come to rebuild the LORD's house.** 3 **Then the word of the LORD came by the prophet Haggai, saying:** 4 **Is it a time for you yourselves to live in your paneled houses, while this house lies in ruins?** 5 **Now therefore thus says the LORD of hosts: Consider how you have fared.** 6 **You have sown much, and harvested little; you eat, but you never have enough; you drink, but you never have your fill; you clothe yourselves, but no one is warm; and you that earn wages earn wages to put them into a bag with holes.**
>
> 7 **Thus says the LORD of hosts: Consider how you have fared.** 8 **Go up to the hills and bring wood and build the house, so that I may take pleasure in it and be honored, says the LORD.** 9 **You have looked for much, and, lo, it came to little; and when you brought it home, I blew it away. Why? says the LORD of hosts. Because my house lies in ruins, while all of you hurry off to your own houses.** 10 **Therefore the heavens above you have withheld the dew, and the earth has withheld its produce.** 11 **And I have called for a drought on the land and the hills, on the grain, the new wine, the oil, on what the soil produces, on human beings and animals, and on all their labors.**

The introduction to the book dates Haggai's first prophetic message as August 29, 520 B.C. Whereas the earlier prophets were consistently dated with respect to Israelite kings who ruled at the time of their prophecies (for example, Isa. 1:1; Jer. 1:1–3; Mic. 1:1), Haggai, who prophesied after the exile, must be dated in relation to a *foreign* king, Darius I (the Great) of Persia, since the Judean monarchy ended with the exile. By default, then, the prophetic word is given an international context.

The prophet is introduced as the one through whom the word of the Lord is transmitted. He receives God's word and passes it on to Zerubbabel, governor of Judah, and Joshua, the high priest. The Persian emperor Darius, now two years into his reign, appointed Zerubbabel, the grandson of the exiled king Jehoiachin, (2 Kings 25:27–30; 1 Chron 3:17–19), as the new governor over Judah. Zerubbabel's colleague, Joshua, whose father Jehozadak was a priest among the exiles in Babylon (1 Chron. 6:15) has the distinction of being the first to bear the title "high priest" (see Zech. 3:1–10). Together, Zerubbabel and Joshua represent the seats of civil and religious authority in the struggling post-exilic community of Judah. It is to the top leaders of the community that Haggai's prophetic message is addressed.

Haggai speaks out in a period of social conflict. The issue of contention is not so much *whether* the temple is to be rebuilt but *when*. The people find that the time is not ripe for building (v. 2). Who these people are is unclear, although the context suggests that they are the ones who live in "paneled houses," hence, the more affluent members of Jerusalem (v. 4). "These people" feel that any call to action is premature. Haggai, however, thinks otherwise, and the prophetic word emerges within the arena of divided opinions.

Haggai first accuses them of living in prosperity while the temple remains in ruins. "Paneled houses" refers to interior paneling, such as what the temple once had (1 Kings 7:7), evidence of well-furnished homes. The accusation is thick with irony: Paneling that was perhaps intended to be used for the temple is being used to furnish homes. Moreover, Haggai's question recalls David's own concern about living in a palace of cedar while God resided only in a tent (2 Sam. 7:2). Like David, Haggai sets in sharp relief the contrast between the people's homes and God's house, a contrast rooted in an indifference toward anything that reaches beyond mere selfish concern for individual prosperity. As Haggai points out, however, such prosperity is an illusion. In a series of stern observations, the prophet describes the impoverished conditions that plague the community: insufficient food staples, clothing, and capital, as well as scorching drought. Life is still one of harsh subsistence, despite individual signs to the contrary.

Haggai is quick to identify the root cause of such social malaise as the failure to build the temple while the people remain secure in their own houses (v. 9). He describes the people "hurrying off" to their homes. Concern for the larger community is nowhere in evidence. Like impregnable enclaves, households have become barriers rather than foundations for community life. The walls of hearth and home have become cloistered and closed while the community decays. Political theorist and ethicist James Q. Wilson cites a recent study of a southern Italian village whose extreme poverty is directly attributable to an unwillingness to cooperate beyond the families' material interests. Without a sense of community that calls people to look and work beyond their own familial concerns, miserable conditions will always prevail. What Haggai's audience does not realize is that family security is by no means guaranteed by turning within and taking refuge in one's home, cut off from the challenges of the larger community. Even when wages are rightfully earned and brought home, they are blown away (v. 9)! Home security is nothing but a facade when the community lies in shambles, whether from rampant crime, economic problems, or ecological disaster.

For Haggai, failure to restore the temple is a stark testimony to apathy at its basest level, an entrenched indifference so pervasive that it has provoked God to judgment: God withholds both produce of the land and life-giving water from the heavens (vv. 10–11). Yet this present time of judgment can pass, if the people simply let it. God, through Haggai, gives a simple command to remedy the situation: Go and build! (v. 8). It is not so much that Haggai has an obsession for temple building (an "edifice complex!"), as it is that he is concerned about the restoration of the community as a whole and for God's glory. For the prophet, the restored temple is the sign and seal of the restored people of God, restored in worship as well as in blessing.

The prophet would no doubt differ with those who today would claim that the church is not a building but the people, as if the people had nowhere to orient themselves. On the other hand, Haggai would also not claim that the church is just a building. The church requires a tangible, public center within the religious landscape of the worshiping community that, like spokes in a wheel, reaches outward to the very edges of the community. Proper worship requires both a building and the people! That is why Haggai's command to build the temple is all inclusive. Such an effort requires a concerted and cooperative venture of the community from top to bottom, for the very means by which the temple is built holds the key to the community's malaise. The *whole* community must claim ownership in such a crucial endeavor if it hopes to be restored. By building the temple, the community is rebuilt and due honor is given to God (v. 8). It is often said that without vision the people perish, but, as Haggai would remind us, if no one is ready to roll up his or her sleeves and get to work, the same fate holds.

THE TIME IS NOW:
THE RESPONSE OF THE PEOPLE
Haggai 1:12–15a

> 1:12 **Then Zerubbabel son of Shealtiel, and Joshua son of Jehozadak, the high priest, with all the remnant of the people, obeyed the voice of the LORD their God, and the words of the prophet Haggai, as the LORD their God had**

sent him; and the people feared the LORD. [13] **Then Haggai, the messenger of the LORD, spoke to the people with the LORD's message, saying, I am with you, says the LORD.** [14] **And the LORD stirred up the spirit of Zerubbabel son of Shealtiel, governor of Judah, and the spirit of Joshua son of Jehozadak, the high priest, and the spirit of all the remnant of the people; and they came and worked on the house of the LORD of hosts, their God,** [15] **on the twenty-fourth day of the month, in the sixth month.**

The response of the people, including their two leaders Zerubbabel, the governor, and Joshua, the high priest, is wholehearted. The "remnant of the people" refers to what is left of the Judean community after the exile, namely those who have remained in the land as well as those who have returned to it from Babylonia. Quickly responding to Haggai's words, they obey and fear the Lord. It is rare for the words of the prophet *not* to find intractable resistance (for example, 2 Chron. 36:15–16; Matt. 23:30–32). Remarkably, however, Haggai's words are received with utmost seriousness. The people fear God as a result, perhaps apprehensive about what might be in store.

Yet God dispels all fears with the simple words: "I am with you" (v. 13). Now that the people are unified in a common cause, God declares solidarity with the people (see Isa. 41:10; 43:5). God intends to stand by and accompany the remnant, empowering them for action. Indeed, with such words of reassurance the people are "stirred up" to act. They become renewed in hope and vision and thus are able to begin work on the temple. Such language recalls the description of the first phase in the construction of the wilderness tabernacle: "And they came, everyone whose heart was stirred, and everyone whose spirit was willing" (Exod. 35:21). The work began on September 21, 520 B.C. Successfully countering the idleness of despair, Haggai has imparted a hope that assures as well as convicts God's people of a better, glorious future.

In her classic book *The Death and Life of Great American Cities*, Jane Jacobs talks about necessity of what she calls "social capital" for any urban community—that intangible reservoir of human trust, coordination, cooperation, and mutual benefit that maintains a community and makes life easier. An ample supply of social capital enables people to pool resources, communicate directly, negotiate effectively, and collectively celebrate rewards. From it, the pronoun "I" can blossom into the pronoun "we." Haggai would remind us that the church, like ancient Israel, finds the storehouse of its "social capital" in worship. Without common worship and service to God, turning back upon ourselves to find only our solitary selves is inevitable. For the prophet, the stakes could not have been higher for his community. The stakes are just as high for the church today.

THE FUTURE SPLENDOR
OF THE TEMPLE
Haggai 1:15b–2:9

1:15b In the second year of King Darius, 2:1 in the seventh month, on the twenty-first day of the month, the word of the LORD came by the prophet Haggai, saying: 2 Speak now to Zerubbabel son of Shealtiel, governor of Judah, and to Joshua son of Jehozadak, the high priest, and to the remnant of the people, and say, 3 Who is left among you that saw this house in its former glory? How does it look to you now? Is it not in your sight as nothing? 4 Yet now take courage, O Zerubbabel, says the LORD; take courage, O Joshua, son of Jehozadak, the high priest; take courage, all you people of the land, says the LORD; work, for I am with you, says the LORD of hosts, 5 according to the promise that I made you when you came out of Egypt. My spirit abides among you; do not fear. 6 For thus says the LORD of hosts: Once again, in a little while, I will shake the heavens and the earth and the sea and the dry land; 7 and I will shake all the nations, so that the treasure of all nations shall come, and I will fill this house with splendor, says the LORD of hosts. 8 The silver is mine, and the gold is mine, says the LORD of hosts. 9 The latter splendor of this house shall be greater than the former, says the LORD of hosts; and in this place I will give prosperity, says the LORD of hosts.

Haggai's second message from God comes on October 17, 520 B.C., almost a month after work on the temple had begun (1:15). The twenty-first day of the seventh month of the Jewish calendar places Haggai's message at the end of the feast of booths (Lev. 23:33–36), a festival in which people from far off gathered in Jerusalem. The recipients of the prophetic word are identical to the parties listed in 1:12, namely the community with its leaders. Evidently not much progress had been made since Haggai's last prophetic address.

With three questions, Haggai sets in high relief the contrast between the former glory of the temple and its present state, which he describes "as nothing." Sixty-seven years have elapsed now since the destruction of the temple. One cannot imagine very many still alive who would have beheld the Solomonic temple's "former glory." Yet traditions about its splendor were no doubt fresh in the people's minds. The remnant of the people had heard about the temple from their elders. The temple had been the material witness to what bound the covenant people together. Now the temple ruins serve as a poignant symbol of the dispersed and despairing community, a struggling remnant beginning the monumental task of restoration.

Haggai encourages the people, including their leaders, to take heart. The prophet addresses a situation in which some people feel that the current work on the present temple cannot result in a temple that will measure up to the former one. What could muster the meager resources of a discouraged community to exceed the temple's former splendor? Repeating what he said in 1:13, Haggai offers an answer that is powerfully simple: The Lord is with the people (2:4); hence, with God all things are possible. Divine solidarity with the community began in the Exodus event, Haggai reminds them. God's abiding presence as a pillar of cloud by day and a pillar of fire by night led them to safety (Exod. 13:21–22; 14:19–20). As it was in the Exodus, so it is also in the present. God's spirit casts out all fear, for God has promised to accompany the people against all odds. As God liberated their ancestors from Pharaoh and his army, God will now deliver the community from the enemies of apathy, despair, and fear.

God's empowering presence within the community has international and cosmic ramifications (vv. 6–7). The cosmos and the nations will be shaken for Israel's sake (see Zech. 1:14–17). The shaking of the foundations is a dramatic testimony that God is acting, not in judgment, but on behalf of God's people. In the process, the nations' wealth will be sifted out for the temple. Silver and gold are designated for the temple, and declared to be the Lord's. Haggai perhaps is recalling that such "investment" also played a major role in the Exodus. As the Israelites once "plundered the Egyptians" of silver and gold before escaping (Exod. 11:2–3; 12:35–36), the people will now collect from the international superpowers costly tribute for the temple. The temple will in turn become a source of prosperity for the community.

In short, Haggai's second message is meant to inspire confidence and new vision for a people who can see only futility. With God, small beginnings are the signs of great things (cf. Zech. 4:10).

DESECRATION AMONG THE RUINS
Haggai 2:10–14

2:10 On the twenty-fourth day of the ninth month, in the second year of Darius, the word of the LORD came by the prophet Haggai, saying: 11 Thus says the LORD of hosts: Ask the priests for a ruling: 12 If one carries consecrated meat in the fold of one's garment, and with the fold touches bread, or stew, or wine, or oil, or any kind of food, does it become holy? The priests answered, "No." [13] Then Haggai said, "If one who is unclean by contact with a dead body touches any of these, does it become unclean?" The priests answered, "Yes, it becomes unclean." [14] Haggai then said, So is it with this people, and with this nation before me, says the LORD; and so with every work of their hands; and what they offer there is unclean.

Haggai's third prophetic address comes on the day the foundation of the temple is laid (2:18), December 18, 520 B.C., two months after his second address (1:15b). Instead of addressing Zerubbabel, Joshua, or the people, Haggai is commanded to address the priests in the form of an inquiry. He asks the priests to "make a ruling." One of the functions of the priests was to instruct the people on matters pertaining to the holy and profane, to the clean and unclean (Lev. 10:10–11). The issue that Haggai raises is whether holiness is contagious. Indeed, part of the priests' job was to establish effective boundaries between these separate categories. It was paramount, for instance, that the holy, such as the temple altar, not come into contact with the unclean. Consecrated meat was by definition holy, since it was meat dedicated in sacrifice to God as, for instance, in the sin offering (Lev. 6:26–27). Haggai asks if contact with holy meat makes other food holy, to which the priests respond negatively.

Haggai follows up with another question, this time concerning the state of uncleanness, the antithesis of holiness. Unlike holiness, uncleanness can contaminate. Like a disease it can be contagious. Touching a corpse renders a person unclean for seven days, according to priestly teaching (Num. 19:11–13). Similarly, the people, the "work of their hands," and what they offer have become contaminated, according to Haggai. The emphasis falls upon what the people bring to offer, that is, their agricultural produce. The source of their contamination is not mentioned, but it can be inferred from the context. It is, in fact, the temple in its ruined, desecrated state. Ever since it was destroyed in 587 B.C., the temple lay in a state of defilement or uncleanness (Lam. 1:8–9a; 4:14–15; Ezekiel 8). Throughout the exile, the temple was a lifeless shell, even though those who remained in the land still worshiped and offered sacrifices among its ruins. Haggai claims, however, that such practice has not only been ineffectual but has also rendered the people impure. Worshiping in a desecrated sanctuary unavoidably desecrates the worshiper.

Haggai's point is that without proper worship, whatever work is done in the name of the Lord is doomed to failure. Indeed, work and worship are inseparably tied, for to worship God means to serve God, earnestly and joyously. If it is not done to God's glory, Haggai implies, then it is not worth doing at all.

THAT WAS THEN;
THIS IS NOW
Haggai 2:15–19

2:15 **But now, consider what will come to pass from this day on. Before a stone was placed upon a stone in the Lord's temple,** [16] **how did you fare? When one came to a heap of twenty measures, there were but ten; when one came to the winevat to draw fifty measures, there were but twenty.** [17] **I struck you and all the products of your toil with blight and mildew and hail; yet you did not return to me, says the LORD.** [18] **Consider from this day on, from the twenty-fourth day of the ninth month. Since the day that the foundation of the LORD's temple was laid, consider:** [19] **Is there any seed left in the barn? Do the vine, the fig tree, the pomegranate, and the olive tree still yield nothing? From this day on I will bless you.**

The people now stand at a turning point. With the laying of the temple's foundation, there is no going back to a past filled with judgment and despair (cf. Ezra 3:10–11; Zech. 4:9). No longer will the people defile themselves in worship and exist in misery. Haggai draws a stark contrast between the lamentable reality of the past, which impinges upon the present, and the blessings of the future, which lie just around the corner. The past is depicted by a lack of agricultural produce: One can only find half of the stored grain and less than half of the wine. The products of one's toil are disappearing, not unlike the shrinking wages described in 1:6b. The law of diminishing returns carries the day. Moreover, agricultural diseases and harsh weather (hail) have depleted the crops (v. 17). God is the expressed agent behind such calamities, whose purpose is to bring about repentance (cf. Amos 4:9), but without success. Despite the people's history of failure, abundance will replace lack, and blessing will supersede punishment. This day of all days, for Haggai, serves as the turning point around which everything will change, since the temple, with its foundation now in place, has become once again the center of holiness that will generate abundant blessings.

However, such blessings come slowly and must be anticipated with patience and perceived with the eyes of faith. There is some seed left in the barn, and the fruit trees are beginning to bear (v. 19). This is not the thunder showers of blessing, but the natural, simple signs of new life. From the olive tree comes precious oil essential for cooking and lighting. From the pomegranate, a prized delicacy, comes wine and leather dye. The fig, the first fruit mentioned in the Bible (Gen. 2:7), provides the ingredient for sweet cakes and wine. Flourishing and beginning to bear, these three fruit trees, however undramatic, point to a new era of plenitude. Small and gradual at first, blessing follows the completion of the temple's foundation, a turning point for the new community. Haggai depicts this event as the axis upon which defilement is displaced by holiness, and judgment gradually makes way for grace. The era of blessing comes at first in only small doses. A bud here, a fig there, a good night's sleep, a loving hug; they are all signs of renewal. They point beyond judgment and despair to a new era of grace and renewal, a new age that begins when people look beyond their own selfish concerns toward the God who yearns to reestablish the ties that bind one another in love and service.

THE WORLD ON ITS HEAD:
THE CONSUMMATION OF HISTORY
Haggai 2:20–23

2:20 The word of the LORD came a second time to Haggai on the twenty-fourth day of the month: 21 Speak to Zerubbabel, governor of Judah, saying, I am about to shake the heavens and the earth, 22 and to overthrow the throne of kingdoms; I am about to destroy the strength of the kingdoms of the nations, and overthrow the chariots and their riders; and the horses and their riders shall fall, every one by the sword of a comrade. 23 On that day, says the LORD of hosts, I will take you, O Zerubbabel my servant, son of Shealtiel, says the LORD, and make you like a signet ring; for I have chosen you, says the LORD of hosts.

Haggai's final words come on the day of his previous message (2:10–19) to the priests (v. 11). This time, however, Haggai addresses Zerubbabel, the governor. And what a speech it is! The language recalls 2:6 and announces that the world with all of its mighty nations will be turned inside out. Whereas the cosmic shake-up in 2:6 meant wealth for the temple, this quake spells disaster for all oppressive military powers (2:22). As the Egyptian army was destroyed at the crossing of the Red Sea (Exod. 15:1–10), now the superpowers of the Near East will be rendered powerless, their weapons and warriors erased. In their place, a new order of peace will prevail, and a new balance of power will emerge: Zerubbabel, God's servant, will become "like a signet ring" (v. 23). This ring alludes to a prophecy given by the earlier prophet Jeremiah, wherein the ring is equated with kingship (Jer. 22:24), the ring of God's right hand. Zerubbabel is designated God's earthly representative and royal servant. Being of Davidic stock, Zerubbabel is to assume preeminent royal status at some future point in time, for God has chosen him. Haggai's prophecy thus ends on the full establishment of a new community that has far-reaching, even international, consequences. The book of Haggai began with the reign of a foreign king (1:1) and ends with the anticipation of a new kingdom whose power is not lodged in military might but in the might of mercy.

In his own way, Haggai anticipates the reign of Jesus Christ. Like Zerubbabel, the person of Christ ushers in a new era in which the principalities and powers of this world are doomed to destruction and the seeds of new life for God's people and, indeed, the world are sown. With Christ as the living cornerstone (1 Pet. 2:4–8), the foundation is laid for a new community and a new era of hope and blessing. Though we may not see it, the blessings of God are present and prevailing against all things that attempt to constrain the bounty of love. Haggai reminds us that by taking part in the unfolding drama of grace, we will be able to see all the more clearly with the eyes of faith the consummation of that drama, when all things will be reconciled to God and Christ will reign supreme.

Zechariah

Introduction

As a whole, the book of Zechariah is about resilient hope amid the faith community's struggle to rediscover its identity as God's people. As the penultimate book of the Twelve Minor Prophets, Zechariah is actually a composite work that can be divided into two parts, chapters 1—8 and 9—14, which are frequently designated as First and Second Zechariah by scholars.

The first eight chapters consist of a number of visions and speeches that are reported to have occurred within a short period of time, roughly two-and-a-half years (August 20, 520 to December 7, 518 B.C.). Visions were not unusual for prophets, but the particular form in which they are reported in Zechariah marks a new development of this prophetic phenomenon, a development that began with the prophet Amos over two centuries earlier (Amos 7:1–9; 8:1–3; 9:1–4). Like his colleague Haggai, the prophet of chapters 1—8 stressed the necessity of rebuilding the temple in order to inaugurate a new age of blessing and order. However, while Haggai's message addressed the immediacy of the situation, Zechariah placed his message within the larger, sweeping history of God's saving grace and judgment.

Little can be said about the person and life of Zechariah. Zechariah is mentioned in Nehemiah 12:16 as having come from a priestly family. According to a tradition that diverges from Zechariah 1:1 and 7, Zechariah was the *son*, rather than grandson, of Iddo (Ezra 5:1; 6:14). In addition, Matthew 23:35 makes mention of Zechariah's martyrdom, though this may be the result of a confusion with an entirely different Zechariah mentioned in 2 Chronicles 24:20–22. Thus, all that can be said for certain is that Zechariah had priestly roots.

Lacking the vision accounts of the first eight chapters, chapters 9—14 of Zechariah ("Second Zechariah") consist of various prophetic speeches that derive from different hands. (Matthew 27:9–10, for example, attributes authorship of Zechariah 11:12–13 to Jeremiah!). Devoting much attention to the end times, these chapters attest to increasing disillusionment with the direction the faith community has taken. The more strident tone of these final chapters reflects the work of authors who are increasingly marginalized in Judahite society, perhaps as much as a century after the prophet Zechariah himself. Although their historical background remains elusive, these chapters have helped shape the Gospel accounts of Jesus' ministry and death, as well as provided one of the most powerful portrayals of the new age of peace in all of biblical literature.

THE HISTORY OF PROPHECY:
FROM ANGER TO REPENTANCE
Zechariah 1:1–6

> 1:1 In the eighth month, in the second year of Darius, the word of the LORD came to the prophet Zechariah son of Berechiah son of Iddo, saying: 2 The LORD was very angry with your ancestors. 3 Therefore say to them, Thus says the LORD of hosts: Return to me, says the LORD of hosts, and I will return to you, says the LORD of hosts. 4 Do not be like your ancestors, to whom the former prophets proclaimed, "Thus says the LORD of hosts, Return from your evil ways and from your evil deeds." But they did not hear or heed me, says the LORD. 5 Your ancestors, where are they? And the prophets, do they live forever? 6 But my words and my statutes, which I commanded my servants the prophets, did they not overtake your ancestors? So they repented and said, "The LORD of hosts has dealt with us according to our ways and deeds, just as he planned to do."

Zechariah's message is introduced with a historical note that situates his prophecy in the year 520 B.C., sometime between October and November, around the same time as the prophet Haggai. King Darius I ascended the throne of the Persian empire in 522 B.C., sparking widespread revolts and dissension throughout the Persian empire as well as igniting prophetic fervor to renew efforts toward reconstructing the temple (see also Haggai). It was soon after this tense period of international turmoil that Zechariah (and Haggai) began to prophesy. The meaning of Zechariah's name is "The Lord has remembered," a name that can be taken to suggest new promise for a people dispersed by exile in Babylonia.

Appropriate to his name, the prophet recalls for his audience the history of the prophetic word with the previous generations of his people. There is a movement from divine anger (v. 2), prompted by the rejection of the prophetic message (v. 4b; see 7:11–14), to punishment and final repentance (v. 6). Of note is the striking way Zechariah describes divine punishment as God's words and statutes having "overtaken" the people. Such language recalls the covenant curses of Deuteronomy (Deut. 28:15), whose power is set in motion when God's people flagrantly disobey the commandments. Similarly, Deuteronomy speaks of certain blessings "overtaking" Israel when God's people abide by the covenant (Deut. 28:2). Such language suggests that what we do unleashes a kind of power, a moral efficacy, that affects us as well as others for good or for worse. To use another analogy, good works are contagious, but so is evil, which brings down upon itself punishment. For Zechariah, the intended result of divine punishment is confession and acknowledgment of the Lord's just ways (v. 6).

This is not a "dead" history of the ancient past that Zechariah recounts. It serves, rather, as necessary background for the prophet's pronouncements to his contemporaries. Like the message of his predecessors, Zechariah's message rings out loud and clear: Repentance ("returning") is necessary for bringing about reconciliation with God (v. 3). In order to return to God, one must also turn *from* something (v. 4; see also Jer. 18:11; 25:5; 35:15). That is to say, a fundamental reorientation toward God is required. Zechariah hopes that the present generation is not doomed to repeat its ancestral history by failing to heed the call to repentance. Although the Lord was angry with their ancestors, this anger need not continue (see Isa. 57:16), since a new generation is now in place (v. 5). The time is ripe for a new beginning. Even the prophets of old suffered the same fate as those who did not heed God's words. The opportunity now avails itself to break the seemingly endless cycle of sin and prophetic doom of the past.

Yet if the past is forgotten, the present generation is condemned to repeat it. In learning from the past, the current generation that hears Zechariah stands at the threshold of a new beginning, a new era of redemption, for which past generations have set the stage. Zechariah recounts the history of prophecy, judgment, and repentance as a fitting preface to the following visions. Though they may strike one as odd and fantastic, Zechariah's visions do not stand in opposition but in continuity with the redemptive ways of God throughout history.

ZECHARIAH'S FIRST VISION:
COMPASSION AND COMPLACENCY
Zechariah 1:7–17

1:7 On the twenty-fourth day of the eleventh month, the month of Shebat, in the second year of Darius, the word of the LORD came to the prophet Zechariah son of Berechiah son of Iddo; and Zechariah said, 8 In the night I saw a man riding on a red horse! He was standing among the myrtle trees in the glen; and behind him were red, sorrel, and white horses. 9 Then I said, "What are these, my lord?" The angel who talked with me said to me, "I will show you what they are." 10 So the man who was standing among the myrtle trees answered, "They are those whom the LORD has sent to patrol the earth." 11 Then they spoke to the angel of the LORD who was standing among the myrtle trees, "We have patrolled the earth, and lo, the whole earth remains at peace." 12 Then the angel of the LORD said, "O LORD of hosts, how long will you withhold mercy from Jerusalem and the cities of Judah, with which you have been angry these seventy years?" 13 Then the LORD replied with gracious and comforting words to the angel who talked with me. 14 So the angel who talked with me said to me, Proclaim this message: Thus says the LORD of hosts: I am very jealous for Jerusalem and for Zion. 15 And I am extremely angry with the nations that are at ease; for while I was only a little angry, they made the disaster worse. 16 Therefore, thus says the LORD, I have returned to Jerusalem with compassion; my house shall be built in it, says the LORD of hosts, and the measuring line shall be stretched out over Jerusalem. 17 Proclaim further: Thus says the LORD of hosts: My cities shall again overflow with prosperity; the LORD will again comfort Zion and again choose Jerusalem.

Zechariah's first vision is dated to February 15, 519 B.C. It is introduced in a similar manner to Zechariah's speech in 1:1, but in fuller detail. Common to both historical notes is the deliberate reference to the foreign king Darius. Divine activity is given an international context. In addition, both verses 1 and 7 refer to what follows as the Lord's *word*. The divine word can have not only auditory but visual dimensions. Indeed, common to most of Zechariah's visions is movement from perception to understanding. In most cases, Zechariah must engage in dialogue with an angelic figure in order to discern the vision and its import. A prominent function of this angel, who appears in all of Zechariah's visions, is to disclose the meaning of the mystery. The angel's mission is to lead Zechariah toward clarity of vision. The process of gaining clarity is perhaps not unlike Mark's account of the healing of the blind man at Bethsaida: At first the blind man could only see people as walking trees; but after another healing act of Jesus, the man could see "everything clearly" (Mark 8:25). Similarly, Zechariah sees things at first dimly but upon inquiry his visions become clarified. The prophet does not hesitate even to ask "dumb" questions before the angelic messenger. Though rich in visual imagery, the visions are ultimately understood through corresponding words of explanation (for example, 1:14–17, 21). The prophet's visions are filled with dramatic events and words with which the prophet himself has active engagement.

Like the prophet, we too need the help of others—pastors, counselors, spouses, friends—to understand experiences that either point beyond ourselves or plumb the depths of our being, whether in agony or in joy. In helping us make sense of our experiences, they are acting as angels in our midst. Indeed, the key to understanding can very well lie with someone else who knows us better than we know ourselves. Frequently a simple word from a friend in faith can shed new light, indeed new revelation, on experiences that perplex us. Just as Zechariah was no passive recipient of visions, we must engage with others within the community of faith to understand more fully who we are and what we are to do as Christians. Zechariah's visions were *interactive* by nature. The prophet gained insight and clarity in what he saw before him. Through others, we can see what is needed to be seen, not through rose-colored spectacles or restrictive blinders, but through the eyes of faith, discerning with ever greater clarity how God is at work in us and in our world. There are still angels in our midst!

Zechariah's first night vision is no exception. The prophet sees a man mounted on a red horse with other horses, presumably also with riders, behind him. The reference to myrtle suggests luxuriant growth associated perhaps with the garden of Eden. The colors mentioned are typical of horses in biblical times. In conversation with an angel or divine messenger, Zechariah learns that these horses are charged by God to patrol the earth (1:10). They have roamed throughout the land and report that all is well and at peace. This, however, does not satisfy the angel, who cries out before God over the seemingly interminable duration—seventy insufferable years—of misery and exile. The angel's sharp complaint in 1:12 echoes the language of the psalmic laments (see Psalms 6:3; 13:2; 79:5). The angel's pointed question does not stem from curiosity, but finds its home in a legitimate and poignant complaint to God, a protest intended to convey the message "enough is enough!" This angelic complainant seeks a dramatic and irreversible change in the current state of affairs by charging God to disturb the status quo. The angel's complaint centers directly on Judah's fate, which has languished over too many years.

The period of seventy years is a conventional number—much like the often-used number "forty" in scripture—that can be applied to various periods of time (cf. Jer. 20:10; 25:1). In this case, the angel refers to the duration of time from the destruction of the Jerusalem temple in 587 B.C., up to the time of Zechariah's first vision, sixty-eight years to be exact. The devastation wrought upon Jerusalem by the hands of the Babylonians is cast in terms of divine action, of withholding mercy. Nevertheless, it is not God's nature to withhold mercy for too long. God can no more permanently withhold compassion than a person can hold his or her own breath. Compassion constrained is compassion ready to explode in zealous mercy. The initial words of mercy are held in private intimacy: The Lord's response to the angel's lament is described as one of grace and comfort. The conversation is private, but it is quickly made public to Zechariah when the angel turns to readdress the prophet, no doubt with a smile. Zechariah is given the responsibility of proclaiming this celestial conversation to all, an announcement of the Lord's zealous love for Jerusalem.

It is an explosive announcement. God's "jealousy" for Israel is not simply a deeply felt emotion, but a zealous resolve translated into action on behalf of Israel (see Joel 2:18). God's partiality toward Jerusalem is about to be demonstrated. The era of divine withholding is coming to an end. God was once angry with Israel (1:2), but now such anger is transferred to those nations that remain accountable for and in control of Israel's degraded and impoverished state. God indicts the nations for having exceeded the punishment exacted by God for the community, and thereby turning it into evil (1:15). No one nation is identified for condemnation, in contrast to a similar message in Isaiah 54:7–8, which specifically indicts Babylon for having gone too far in carrying out the Lord's punishment against Israel. It is rather the general state of ease and indifference among the nations in the face of Israel's continued degradation that is set in relief. This kind of peace is an unjust peace. To attain true and lasting peace, God's compassion cannot avoid disturbing the world's complacency. If not all peace is good, then the converse is also true: not all discord is bad. Without struggle and conflict, there is no progress, whether it is the struggle for civil rights at home or for human rights abroad.

Zechariah's first night vision concludes with the pronouncement that the Lord has returned to Jerusalem (v. 16), fulfilling the contingent promise of reconciliation made in verse 2. The rebuilding of the temple ("my house") is the tangible witness to God's return. The house of the Lord was regarded as a dwelling place for God or God's name (2 Sam. 7:13; 1 Kings 8:12–13, 27–30). Hand in hand with the rebuilding of the temple is the city's restoration: The carpenter's measuring line is to be stretched over Jerusalem (cf. Isa. 44:13; Jer. 31:38–39) to begin God's program of urban renewal. And like expanding ripples in a pond, the result of Jerusalem's restoration means abundant prosperity for *all* of God's cities (1:17). This widening circle of blessing is specifically rooted in God's election of Zion/Jerusalem. Such language is well attested elsewhere in connection with the choice of David and his dynasty (for example, Deut. 12:1–28; 1 Kings 8:44, 48; 11:13, 32; Psalms 78:68–70; 132:13). The time is at hand for Jerusalem's *re*election, as it were, an election for consolation (see Isa. 40:1). The surprising impact of this message for a despairing people is no less dramatic than the first words of Jesus, as recorded by the earliest Gospel (Mark 1:15). Zechariah's first nocturnal vision is good news through and through.

ZECHARIAH'S SECOND VISION:
THE FOUR HORNS
Zechariah 1:18–21

> 1:18 **And I looked up and saw four horns.** [19] **I asked the angel who talked with me, "What are these?" And he answered me, "These are the horns that have scattered Judah, Israel, and Jerusalem."** [20] **Then the LORD showed me four blacksmiths.** [21] **And I asked, "What are they coming to do?" He answered, "These are the horns that scattered Judah, so that no head could be raised; but these have come to terrify them, to strike down the horns of the nations that lifted up their horns against the land of Judah to scatter its people."**

Zechariah's second vision is remarkably brief compared to his first. As in the first vision, Zechariah must inquire about what he sees (1:19), in this case four horns and four blacksmiths. There is no clue in the text as to whether these horns are of an animal or of helmets. It is tempting to think that Zechariah discerns the projected corners of the standard four-horned altar. In any case, the messenger/angel interprets the horns politically (cf. Deut. 33:17; Jer. 48:25; Dan. 7:7–8). They are the nations that have dispersed Judah, Israel, and Jerusalem (see 1:21). As in Zechariah 1:15, no particular nations are identified in this vision. What is more significant is the number four, which represents totality in the same sense as the metaphorical expression "the four corners of the earth" (cf. 2:6). Although one can readily identify those nations that contributed to Israel's and Judah's demise (for example, Assyria in 721 B.C.; Babylonia in 587 B.C.), the "four horns" in Zechariah's vision more likely serve to signify the totality of international powers that have sought the destruction of God's people throughout Israel's history.

Yet that is not all to Zechariah's vision. Four blacksmiths, or perhaps more generally, artisans, appear. The Hebrew word can refer to metalworkers as well as those who work with stone (for example, Exod. 28:11). Again, Zechariah must inquire of their significance. The artisans have come to destroy the "horns of the nations." As with the horns, it is impossible to identify the artisans, but they are likely divine agents of some sort not unlike the horse riders of the first vision. What is crucial is the pronouncement that the constricting web of power that has nearly squeezed the life out of God's people is about to be shredded. No longer will the nations remain at ease in their oppressive policies (1:15); they will be overturned so that Judah may no longer suffer under their yoke.

ZECHARIAH'S THIRD VISION:
THE PROTECTIVE WALL OF FIRE
Zechariah 2:1–5

> 2:1 I looked up and saw a man with a measuring line in his hand. ² Then I asked, "Where are you going?" He answered me, "To measure Jerusalem, to see what is its width and what is its length." ³ Then the angel who talked with me came forward, and another angel came forward to meet him, ⁴ and said to him, "Run, say to that young man: Jerusalem shall be inhabited like villages without walls, because of the multitude of people and animals in it. ⁵ For I will be a wall of fire all around it, says the LORD, and I will be the glory within it."

Though the shortest of the visions, Zechariah's third vision is nonetheless filled with movement and dialogue. As usual, the prophet sees someone and poses a question. This time, however, the question is not posed to his interpreting messenger but to the actual object of his vision, namely a human figure carrying something. The prophet's question avoids the typical issue of identity and broaches the purpose, specifically the destination, of this character's action. In fact, what catches the prophet's attention is not the person *per se* but what is dangling from the person's hand, a measuring line. The Hebrew term for *measuring line* in this passage (different in 1:16) refers specifically to the parceling out of land (Deut. 32:9; Amos 7:17; Mic. 2:5), particularly in connection with Israel's "inheritance" (cf. Zech. 2:12). This measuring line marks, as in 1:16, the beginning of Jerusalem's restoration.

Abruptly another angel/messenger adds, quite urgently, a new message: Jerusalem will support a multitude of people and animals, but *without* walls. The abundance of both people and animals suggests great prosperity. The "young man" in 2:4 refers to the first character mentioned in the vision, who has gone off to fulfill his task. This new message suggests that measuring the dimensions of Jerusalem is no longer necessary. The city walls lie in ruins, but no matter. Even if they stood fully erect, they would not be able to contain the dramatic rise in the city's population. Ezekiel is the only other prophet who speaks of the physical dimensions of the restored Jerusalem (Ezek. 48:15). Zechariah, however, foresees Jerusalem as an unwalled settlement. Will Jerusalem, then, be defenseless? No, for Jerusalem will be protected directly by God with a wall of fire.

Fire is frequently the vehicle of divine presence in scripture (for example, Exod. 3:2–4; 13:21–22). A wall of fire signifies a radically new form of protection, the result of God's indwelling presence. Not just limited to the temple, God's glory will be infused everywhere about the city, from its center to its outskirts. Described as glory from within and fire from without, God's presence restores Jerusalem to what it was meant to be, a *holy* refuge, an impregnable sanctuary (cf. Ezek. 43:1–5; Psalm 46:1). Such a fire dismantles the walls of fear; all human defenses are rendered useless. Zechariah's vision of the protective wall of fire dramatically describes God's protective presence, a presence that burns with the pathos of love for God's people.

THE PEOPLE'S RESPONSE:
FLIGHT, SONG, AND SILENCE
Zechariah 2:6–13

2:6 Up, up! Flee from the land of the north, says the LORD; for I have spread you abroad like the four winds of heaven, says the LORD. 7 Up! Escape to Zion, you that live with daughter Babylon. 8 For thus said the LORD of hosts (after his glory sent me) regarding the nations that plundered you: Truly, one who touches you touches the apple of my eye. 9 See now, I am going to raise my hand against them, and they shall become plunder for their own slaves. Then you will know that the LORD of hosts has sent me. 10 Sing and rejoice, O daughter Zion! For lo, I will come and dwell in your midst, says the LORD. 11 Many nations shall join themselves to the LORD on that day, and shall be my people; and I will dwell in your midst. And you shall know that the LORD of hosts has sent me to you. 12 The LORD will inherit Judah as his portion in the holy land, and will again choose Jerusalem.

[13] **Be silent, all people, before the LORD; for he has roused himself from his holy dwelling.**

Immediately following upon the heels of his third vision, Zechariah continues the theme of the holy sanctuary that concluded his third vision (2:5), but adds a unique twist. Speaking on behalf of God, Zechariah begins with an urgent call to God's people in exile to flee and return to Zion. The "land of the north" is a formulaic expression that refers to the land of Israel's enemies. Here, it refers to Babylon (2:7), whose army historically had to march from the north, through Syria, in order to attack Jerusalem (Jer. 6:22; 10:22). So it was also from the north that the exiles were to return (Jer. 3:18; 16:15). Zechariah's call is a call not to escape from an invading enemy but to free oneself from a land of bondage, a land that is about to be subjugated by God's judgment. The reason for such urgency is rooted in God's intensely personal relationship with Judah: The exiles are likened to the apple of God's eye. This term of endearment suggests that Judah is as close to God as, figuratively speaking, the pupil of God's eye, one of the most sensitive parts of the body. The metaphorical language graphically illustrates that any violation of Judah is a personal violation of God that demands retribution. Even a light "touch" against Judah warrants the raising of God's hand, which is ready to strike back with full force.

Dietrich Bonhoeffer, the German theologian and pastor who was martyred by the Nazis only days before Germany surrendered to the allies, found this reference to the apple of God's eye urgently relevant during the Crystal Night pogrom, that infamous night in 1938 that began the annihilation of the Jews. Bonhoeffer realized that what was set in motion on that night was nothing short of a direct assault upon God. With the angels and the psalmists, Bonhoeffer lamented "O God, how long?" (Zech. 1:12; Psalm 74:10–11), to which he was led to ask, "O God, how long can I stand by and simply watch?" (Miller, "Dietrich Bonhoeffer and the Psalms," 281–82).

For the fledgling community, the outcome of God's endearing love for Israel is a complete reversal of fortune: The slaves, that is, those in exile, shall plunder their masters. The language echoes the account of the Exodus (Exod. 12:35–36). Zechariah proclaims, in effect, a new Exodus. As Miriam and the Israelites sang a victory song after having crossed the Red Sea, God commands daughter Zion to sing a new song. The address to Zion as "daughter" is not uncommon (cf. 2:7). This term of endearment often appears in proclamations of good news (for example, Isa. 12:6; 52:2;

62:11; Mic. 4:8; Zech. 3:14–15; 9:9). The occasion for such jubilation is God's homecoming. As in Isaiah 52, the return of the exiles is paralleled with the return to God's habitation, Zion. It is a reunion of the most joyous kind, and not simply between God and Judah. Zechariah's prophecy is truly international in scope: "Many nations" shall join in and become the one people of God (cf. 8:20–23). In the past the foreign nations had rallied against Zion (Psalms 2:1–3; 83:2–8), but on that future day God's sovereignty will cut across all ethnic and national lines (cf. Isa. 56:3–8; Jer. 50:5). Zechariah's vision anticipates the imminent consummation of history when once again Judah will be God's favored portion and Jerusalem/Zion will be chosen as God's dwelling place.

In only two other places in scripture other than verse 12 is God described as *inheriting* anything (Exod. 24:9; Psalm 82:8). Much more common are references to Judah or Israel inheriting the land (for example, Exod. 23:30; 32:13). In addition, the reference to "holy land" is unique to the Old Testament, although it becomes a common designation in later Jewish literature. With such unconventional language, the prophet demonstrates that God's ties to Judah and the land are inviolably secure. Never again will God's special claim upon the land and its people be challenged, much less annulled. The language of inheritance and choice recalls as well as intensifies the language of promise one finds in the stories of Israel's sojourn from Egypt to the promised land (cf. Deuteronomy 12). Long ago, God chose Jerusalem, and now God chooses it again.

While there is a time to sing and rejoice before God, there is also a time to refrain (2:13). Zechariah's prophecy ends on a commanding note of awe-struck silence (see also Hab. 2:20 and Zeph. 1:7). The scope of Zechariah's address is universal: All peoples are to be reverently silent before the Almighty, for God has "roused himself from his holy dwelling" in heaven, poised to act on behalf of his people. God's movement toward the people is about to be completed: God is about to come home to reclaim them. Zechariah does not tell us precisely where God has been, but he does tell us where God's people have been—in exile, subjected to the whims of worldly powers and principalities. Now, however, God's indwelling presence will be far from benign. Zechariah vividly ends his prophetic message with a declaration of impending action. Things are about to change dramatically for Israel. As God's movement toward Israel is achieved, so also is Israel's movement toward God: They are now "before the Lord." Whereas Zechariah's exhortation began with an urgent call for the people to rouse themselves and flee from the present land of bondage (2:6), it ends with a call for hushed silence as God moves to respond on their behalf. Zechariah's final command is a command to gasp and catch one's breath in anticipation of what is about to transpire. The waiting is over; God is poised for action (see 1:12–17).

ZECHARIAH'S FOURTH VISION:
THE HIGH PRIEST JOSHUA
Zechariah 3:1–10

> 3:1 Then he showed me the high priest Joshua standing before the angel of the LORD, and Satan standing at his right hand to accuse him. [2] And the LORD said to Satan, "The LORD rebuke you, O Satan! The LORD who has chosen Jerusalem rebuke you! Is not this man a brand plucked from the fire?" [3] Now Joshua was dressed with filthy clothes as he stood before the angel. [4] The angel said to those who were standing before him, "Take off his filthy clothes." And to him he said, "See, I have taken your guilt away from you, and I will clothe you with festal apparel." [5] And I said, "Let them put a clean turban on his head." So they put a clean turban on his head and clothed him with the apparel; and the angel of the LORD was standing by.
>
> [6] Then the angel of the LORD assured Joshua, saying [7] "Thus says the LORD of hosts: If you will walk in my ways and keep my requirements, then you shall rule my house and have charge of my courts, and I will give you the right of access among those who are standing here. [8] Now listen, Joshua, high priest, you and your colleagues who sit before you! For they are an omen of things to come: I am going to bring my servant the Branch. [9] For on the stone that I have set before Joshua, on a single stone with seven facets, I will engrave its inscription, says the LORD of hosts, and I will remove the guilt of this land in a single day. [10] On that day, says the LORD of hosts, you shall invite each other to come under your vine and fig tree."

Zechariah's fourth vision begins abruptly without the typical opening "I looked up and saw . . . ." Zechariah's command for silence in 2:13 sets the scene for what is to follow, namely the acquittal or restitution of the high priest Joshua. God has "roused himself" to exonerate Joshua in a dramatic courtroomlike confrontation. Two new characters are introduced. As to the identity of Joshua, Haggai and Ezra-Nehemiah tell us that the high priest was the son of Jehozadak, the son of Seraiah, the chief priest during the destruction of Jerusalem in 587 B.C. Joshua, whose father was taken into exile, was raised in Babylon before returning to Jerusalem with Zerubbabel (1 Chron. 6:15). Joshua is consistently labeled high priest, an office that achieved prominence after the exile. The other character, Satan, plays the role of prosecuting attorney, with God standing at Joshua's defense.

The Hebrew word for *Satan* always contains the definite article ("*the* satan"), indicating that the word is a title rather than a proper name, which means the accuser or adversary. And that is precisely what "the satan" does—accuse. In Job 1:6–12, "the satan" takes on a similar role and is regarded as a bona fide member of God's heavenly council. It is only in later Jewish and Christian tradition that this enigmatic figure is treated as a fallen angel and rebel against God. In the Old Testament, the only thing damnable about the satan is that he does his work presenting "damning" evidence against individuals.

The scene opens with the Lord's rebuttal to "the satan's" case. The case against Joshua is not actually presented, but allegations are flying, to which God responds with a twofold rebuke directed at Joshua's accuser. God's only defense of Joshua is cast in the form of a rhetorical question. Joshua is likened to a burned piece of wood yanked from the fire, hinting perhaps of some ordeal that Joshua has suffered. The same expression is found in Amos 4:11, in which the fire-brand signifies the aftermath of devastating judgment. Here, however, the expression represents an act of grace on behalf of Joshua. God delivers Joshua in the nick of time from some calamity. Such imagery also accounts for his filthy apparel, which in and of itself could signify some form of self-incurred guilt. However, God's rebuttal affirms Joshua's innocence. His clothes simply suffer from the effects of fire.

The command to remove Joshua's clothes is tantamount to an act of exoneration or restoration: Joshua is to be given new apparel. In the Old Testament view of priesthood, clothes made the priest. Exodus 28 meticulously describes Aaron's sacred vestments, which pertained to the various functions of the priest. Consequently, a priest wearing "filthy clothes" marked nothing less than a violation or desecration of the priestly office, specifically an act of contamination that infringed upon the priest's holiness. In addition, the high priest had to undergo ritual changes in clothing in order to cleanse the people of their sins and thereby maintain fellowship with God, as during the day of atonement (Leviticus 16). And so the high priest Joshua must receive a change in clothes in order for him to remain and function as high priest. Through no fault of his own, Joshua is in a state of ritual uncleanness, perhaps due to his having lived in a foreign land. In any case, Joshua is in need of purification, and Zechariah himself suggests that a clean turban be placed on Joshua's head. Analogous to the king's crown, the turban was an indispensable part of the high priest's vestments in that it signified the priest's indispensable function of bearing the guilt of the people (Exod. 28:37–38; Lev. 16). In short, the new vestments, particularly the new turban, enables Joshua to function in the role of the high priest.

What follows is a divine charge that lists both responsibilities and privileges, including access into the divine realm (v. 7). God's house and courts evidently refer to the temple complex. What is remarkable is that Joshua is singled out to be charged with judicial responsibilities that are usually assumed by an entire class of priests (cf. Deuteronomy 17 and Ezekiel 44). Such responsibilities are now given to the high priest himself. Further, the way in which the charge is cast comes close to investing Joshua with some degree of *royal* authority over the temple, a precedent that is not surprising given the absence of an Israelite king during this period after the exile. Judah's political situation allows for the high priest to begin to take on certain royal privileges over the temple, the most far reaching of which is access to the divine council. "Those who are standing here" are the members of the heavenly council, including the prominent angel of the Lord. Joshua is promised access to this august gathering, a privilege that has traditionally been assumed by certain prophets (cf. 1 Kings 22; Isaiah 6; Jer. 23:18). By this charge, Joshua assumes both royal and prophetic-like authority, in addition to his authority as high priest.

Along with Joshua, another central character is introduced. While declaring that Joshua's colleagues, those who have returned from exile, anticipate Judah's reconstitution as a community, the angel heralds the coming of the "Branch," a Davidic heir to the throne. This metaphor of plant growth traditionally symbolizes the image of a beneficent monarch (cf. Isa. 11:1; Jer. 23:5). For the prophet, the identity of this Messianic figure was none other than Zerubbabel, the returned Davidic heir (Hag. 2:23). In context, the renewal of the high priest's office and the advent of Zerubbabel are the two factors that are to reconstitute the community of God's people. How they function together is not yet made clear, since focus on Zerubbabel is brief and reverts back on Joshua as well as on the "stone," whose identity is shrouded in greater mystery. Most probably, the "stone" is a veiled reference to the golden rosette that is to be fastened on the front of the chief priest's turban with the engraving "Holy to the Lord," which in Hebrew can be spelled with seven letters or "facets" (Exod. 28:36). For Zechariah, however, the engraving is not to be done by human hands but by the Lord of hosts. Such action will thereby cleanse the land from all guilt as well as invite abundant prosperity and peace (Mic. 4:4).

In short, Zechariah's fourth vision makes clear how the developing community will be restored. It begins with the restored status of a certain individual, Joshua, and concludes with the entire restored community.

With the high priest cleansed, and consequently the people's guilt removed, the community can thereby recapture the security and prosperity it once enjoyed under Solomon (see 1 Kings 4:25). The author of the book of Hebrews similarly describes Christ as the great high priest, who "did not glorify himself in becoming a high priest, but was appointed by [God]" and who "learned obedience through what he suffered" (Heb. 5:5, 8). As Joshua's new status ushered in a new age for the struggling community, Christ's work as high priest is "the source of eternal salvation for all who obey him" (Heb. 5:9).

ZECHARIAH'S FIFTH VISION:
THE LAMPSTAND AND OLIVE TREES
Zechariah 4:1–14

4:1 The angel who talked with me came again, and wakened me, as one is wakened from sleep. 2 He said to me, "What do you see?" And I said, "I see a lampstand all of gold, with a bowl on the top of it; there are seven lamps on it, with seven lips on each of the lamps that are on the top of it. 3 And by it there are two olive trees, one on the right of the bowl and the other on its left." 4 I said to the angel who talked with me, "What are these, my lord?" 5 Then the angel who talked with me answered me, "Do you not know what these are?" I said, "No, my lord." 6 He said to me, "This is the word of the LORD to Zerubbabel: Not by might, nor by power, but by my spirit, says the LORD of hosts. 7 What are you, O great mountain? Before Zerubbabel you shall become a plain; and he shall bring out the top stone amid shouts of 'Grace, grace to it!' "

8 Moreover the word of the LORD came to me, saying, 9 "The hands of Zerubbabel have laid the foundation of this house; his hands shall also complete it. Then you will know that the LORD of hosts has sent me to you. 10 For whoever has despised the day of small things shall rejoice, and shall see the plummet in the hand of Zerubbabel.

"These seven are the eyes of the LORD, which range through the whole earth." 11 Then I said to him, "What are these two olive trees on the right and the left of the lampstand?" 12 And a second time I said to him, "What are these two branches of the olive trees, which pour out the oil through the two golden pipes?" 13 He said to me, "Do you not know what these are?" I said, "No, my lord." 14 Then he said, "These are the two anointed ones who stand by the Lord of the whole earth."

The fifth vision constitutes nothing less than the centerpiece of Zechariah's message. It is set apart from the other vision reports at the outset with the statement that the prophet was "awakened" by the angel. Not to imply that Zechariah had been dozing off, this introductory verse provides a glimpse into the mystery of prophetic psychology. Zechariah receives the vision at a heightened level of awareness, as if he had been asleep all along. There is no mention of anything the prophet does in preparation to evoke such enlightenment; it is rather the angel who intervenes to "awaken" him. Zechariah's "awakening" suggests that the backdrop to this vision is one of utter darkness, in the middle of the night, as it were, a time of potentially horrific proportions. What the prophet sees in the foreground, in contrast, is the warm glow of light. The effect is jarring. As Zechariah is wincing from the bright images of light, he hears the angel prod him about what he can see.

What the prophet sees is an elaborate lampstand of pure gold that has a bowl on its top as well as seven lights and seven pinched lips to hold the wicks (not forty-nine!). Archaeologists have so far discovered at least two lampstands in Palestine that resemble the features Zechariah describes, that is, an oil basin supported by a base with seven pinched indentations along the rim of the bowl to serve as separate lamps. Such a picture is quite different from the description of the lampstand found in Exodus 25:31–40, which more closely resembles the Jewish menorah of seven branches.

Also present are the two olive trees, flanking each side of the bowl. Despite the visual clarity with which he perceives the image, Zechariah still feels compelled to inquire about its significance. The angel, however, counters with a question, a reprimand of sorts, to which the prophet can only confess his ignorance. What follows after verse 5 is an abrupt shift in subjects, for without any reference to the lampstand or olive trees the angel begins to pontificate on Zerubbabel.

Zerubbabel is given an effusive endorsement that begins with a proclamation regarding the divine source of his status: Through God's spirit alone, in contrast to human strength, is Zerubbabel empowered. Although human strength and power are rejected, God's spirit can evoke a new power as well as inspire imagination and skill. One need only recall the master architect Bezalel, who is filled with God's spirit, making him eminently skillful and ingenious for constructing the tabernacle (Exod. 31:30). Now God's spirit is invested in Zerubbabel. Before him the great mountain is leveled. That mountain is no doubt the massive ruins of the former temple complex that must be cleared from the temple mount. To be sure, the leveling of the temple mount was no mean feat, given the meager resources of the impoverished community (see Haggai). Yahweh's spirit is irrevocably on the side of Zerubbabel, making everything as level ground, free of obstacles (cf. Isa. 40:4). Nothing can prevent Zerubbabel from fulfilling the task at hand—the construction of the temple. What Zerubbabel is about to do, no human can do alone without divine help.

In light of what we know about how the people of the ancient Near East built temples, the "top stone" in 4:7 probably refers to a stone, perhaps the cornerstone, of the former temple that was to be used as the first stone for the new temple. The placement of the stone was accompanied by great ceremony. As in Haggai, the building of the new temple was to usher in nothing less than a new age of blessing (cf. Hag. 2:15–19). In Zechariah's vision, the ceremony is accompanied with appropriate shouts of joy, invoking God's favor.

Zechariah's oracle makes clear that the royal figure Zerubbabel will not only set the construction in motion by laying the foundation, but will also be the one to cut the ribbon, as it were, when the temple is completed. All this is confirmation of Zechariah's prophetic mission (9b) and a sign of great things to come, in stark contrast to the present reality of "small things," of frustrated goals and lack of direction. With Zerubbabel the Davidic prince at the helm, reality is ripe with promise. With Zerubbabel as its builder, the new temple becomes the harbinger of a new reality. His "plummet" most probably refers to a piece of precious metal that was to be deposited in the walls of the new structure. To see the plummet in Zerubbabel's hand is to witness first hand the completion of the temple. With the evocative images of the foundation stone and the plummet, the alpha and omega of temple construction, as it were, Zechariah's prophecy powerfully conveys the passionate hope for a new temple and consequently of a new, fully restored community.

In the middle of verse 10, the voice of the angelic host intervenes to finally explain the lampstand vision. The seven lamps are likened to the seven eyes of the Lord that range throughout the earth, echoing perhaps the function of the different colored horses that patrol the earth in 1:11. God's all-seeing, all-knowing gaze is a common theme in scripture that frequently denotes God's beneficence as well as judgment (2 Chron. 16:9; Job 36:7; Psalm 38:18; Prov. 15:3; Ezra 5:5). Through God's constant sight, all creation is sustained; when God's countenance is hidden, life simply ceases (Psalm 104:29). It is no accident that the number seven for the seven days of creation is a prominent structural feature of this lampstand. Divinely created light (Gen. 1:3), indeed the light that makes perception itself possible, is indispensable to the maintenance of creation. In Zechariah's case, it is the survival of the community that is at stake.

As for the significance of the two olive trees, the prophet must ask twice before receiving an answer. Zechariah's second question, however, is cast differently from the first in that it focuses specifically on the two branches of golden conduits that pour out oil from the olive trees to the lamps. There is, thus, a material link between the lampstand and the trees. These two branches represent the "two anointed ones" (literally, "sons of oil"), Joshua and Zechariah. The particular Hebrew word here denotes fresh, unprocessed oil, as opposed to the traditional oil of anointment, whose detailed recipe can be found in Exodus 30:22–33.

New oil represents a fresh beginning; consequently, leadership for the community is structured in a new way. Equal and symmetric in their relationship to each other, these two figures stand by God's side in a doubled form of messiahship. Rather than the old order of royal dominance over the priesthood, a new model of governance has emerged: Royal and priestly figures are set on the same footing. Moreover, there is a relationship of interdependence between the trees or branches and the lampstand. By itself, oil does nothing. Yet the lamps need the oil from the olive trees in order to provide light. On the other hand, the trees need the light generated by the lamps to flourish. It is God, thus, who empowers and sustains both priest and prince.

Zechariah's vision provides a blueprint for the new community that is characterized by a balance of leadership and authority, a polity of *shared* leadership that weaves together the sacred and the secular. Zechariah envisions a community of mutually shared responsibilities between God and human beings. The Lord's work is by nature a shared endeavor, for God has chosen not to do it alone. By becoming flesh in Jesus Christ, God's work with and for human beings is brought to an entirely new level. As Christ shared and emptied out his life with us in death, we are called to devote our lives in shared ministry as living sacrifices to the One who gave us life.

ZECHARIAH'S SIXTH VISION:
THE FLYING SCROLL
Zechariah 5:1–4

5:1 **Again I looked up and saw a flying scroll.** 2 **And he said to me, "What do you see?" I answered, "I see a flying scroll; its length is twenty cubits, and its width ten cubits."** 3 **Then he said to me, "This is the curse that goes out over the face of the whole land; for everyone who steals shall be cut off according to the writing on one side, and everyone who swears falsely shall**

be cut off according to the writing on the other side. [4] I have sent it out, says the LORD of hosts, and it shall enter the house of the thief, and the house of anyone who swears falsely by my name; and it shall abide in that house and consume it, both timber and stones."

Whereas all previous visions have been of weal and blessing, Zechariah's vision of the flying scroll introduces the harsh note of judgment and accountability. This vision ensures that along with restoration comes serious responsibility. One cannot exist without the other.

The symbol of the scroll is apt, for it attests to the power of the written word. For Ezekiel and the author of Revelation, the scroll was the basis for the prophetic commission and message, which was to be absorbed by eating (Ezek. 2:8–3:3; Rev. 10:9–11). Zechariah's scroll, however, is not meant to be consumed but to consume (5:4)! It is described as a "curse" that roams throughout the land, searching out those who steal and utter false oaths (5:3). The dimensions of this unrolled scroll are immense, approximately thirty by fifteen feet. The Dead Sea scroll of Isaiah, by comparison, is more than twenty-four feet long, but only less than a foot wide. What is unusual about Zechariah's scroll is that it is disproportionately half as long as it is wide, not to mention, of course, that it flies.

The identification of the scroll as a curse echoes the language of the covenant, the treaty between God and Israel established at Sinai and explicated in the book of Deuteronomy. Deuteronomy 28 and 29 are replete with curses against those who violate the stipulations contained in the covenant, which begins with the Ten Commandments (Deut. 5:6–21). The curses are specifically described as written down (Deut. 29:20–21). In Hebrew thought, curses had an efficacy or power of their own that afflicted the guilty party (Num. 5:21–28; cf. Zech. 1:6). A flying scroll, thus, is an apt symbol of the power of the curse set in motion against those who have flagrantly violated the covenant.

Zechariah's vision highlights two covenant violations in particular: swearing falsely by God's name, the third commandment (Exod. 20:7, see also Lev. 19:12), and stealing, the eighth commandment (Exod. 20:15). Together, these two infractions represent crimes against God, on the one hand, and crimes against humanity, on the other. Theft was, to be sure, a serious crime in the early exilic community, since the issue of rightful land ownership was critical in the restoration of Judah and Jerusalem. False swearing or lying under oath as in the case of perjury constituted a flagrant violation of judicial proceedings. Noteworthy is the fact that the punishment exacted is one in which the violator's property, in particular the home, is thoroughly destroyed (5:4). In short, Zechariah's flying scroll ensures that the new community remain subject to the normative traditions of Israel's ancient covenant. There is no blessing without responsible and faithful conduct; law and gospel are inseparable.

ZECHARIAH'S SEVENTH VISION:
A BASKET FOR BABYLON
Zechariah 5:5–11

> 5:5 Then the angel who talked with me came forward and said to me, "Look up and see what this is that is coming out." ⁶ I said, "What is it?" He said, "This is a basket coming out." And he said, "This is their iniquity in all the land." ⁷ Then a leaden cover was lifted, and there was a woman sitting in the basket! ⁸ And he said, "This is Wickedness." So he thrust her back into the basket, and pressed the leaden weight down on its mouth. ⁹ Then I looked up and saw two women coming forward. The wind was in their wings; they had wings like the wings of a stork, and they lifted up the basket between earth and sky. ¹⁰ Then I said to the angel who talked with me, "Where are they taking the basket?" ¹¹ He said to me, "To the land of Shinar, to build a house for it; and when this is prepared, they will set the basket down there on its base."

The seventh vision is no less bizarre than the previous one. Indeed, Zechariah cannot make out the image initially and must inquire about its nature. The patient angel explains that it is a "basket," but not any ordinary basket. The Hebrew term is quite specific: It is a basket that holds an *ephah*, a unit of dry measure for grain and flour that approximates two thirds of a bushel. The container is identified as "iniquity" (v. 6). Whose iniquity? In the fourth vision, God promised to remove such iniquity ("guilt") from the land (3:9). Clearly, it is the sin of the whole community.

The feminine image used to convey the contents of the basket is no doubt troublesome to modern readers. Wickedness is personified as a woman. She is discovered once the lid is lifted, but is hastily thrust back into the basket, perhaps for fear she would escape. (In reality, an *ephah* basket is much too small for any adult). Such an image is not especially flattering to women. In the history of biblical interpretation, it must be readily admitted that many commentators have incorrectly singled out Eve as bringing about the fall, thereby disparaging the woman as the source of sin and evil (see 1 Tim. 2:13–14). The biblical story of creation in Genesis 2—3, however, makes it quite clear that *both* Adam and Eve are inexcusably culpable. The particular imagery of the container and the woman figure in our passage recalls the popular Greek myth of Pandora's box, which tells of a certain woman who unwittingly releases all evil into the world by opening a mysterious container. The symbolic image Zechariah perceives, however, is not so important as its significance, namely that wickedness is contained and removed. In fact, the basket is moved by two other women who are cast in the role of angelic beings that move between the earthly and heavenly realms.

The purpose of the vision comes at the end with the prophet's question concerning where the basket will end up. Its destination is Shinar, its future home. Shinar is another name for Mesopotamia (Gen. 10:10; 11:2). It provides, for example, the geographical setting for the "tower of Babel" story of Genesis 11. Shinar can refer more specifically to Babylon, the place of exile (Isa. 11:11). Wickedness sent to Babylon thus completes the removal of iniquity that began with Joshua's exercise of his priestly office in the fourth vision (3:1–10). The removal of guilt from the land of Judah sets in motion the opposite and equal reaction of imputing guilt upon the land of Babylon.

This basket symbolizes no ordinary house. Indeed, it is a temple (the Hebrew word for house frequently designates the temple). In such a temple, iniquity and wickedness will be venerated. Babylon's "house" is in effect the very antithesis of the new Jerusalem temple (the house of the Lord)! Despite its strange imagery, this vision dramatically portrays the effect Israel's restoration will have on the nation that once plundered and exiled its people. Israel's purification, which is to culminate in the establishment of a new temple and priesthood, will in turn bring about Babylon's contamination, which, absurdly enough, will be venerated.

ZECHARIAH'S EIGHTH VISION: THE FOUR CHARIOTS
Zechariah 6:1–8

6:1 **And again I looked up and saw four chariots coming out from between two mountains—mountains of bronze.** 2 **The first chariot had red horses, the second chariot black horses,** 3 **the third chariot white horses, and the fourth chariot dappled gray horses.** 4 **Then I said to the angel who talked with me, "What are these, my lord?"** 5 **The angel answered me, "These are the four winds of heaven going out, after presenting themselves before the LORD of all the earth.** 6 **The chariot with the black horses goes toward the north country, the white ones go toward the west country, and the dappled ones** go toward the south country." 7 When the steeds came out, they were impatient to get off and patrol the earth. And he said, "Go, patrol the earth." So they patrolled the earth. 8 Then he cried out to me, "Lo, those who go toward the north country have set my spirit at rest in the north country."

Between the bronze mountains come four chariots, drawn by different colored horses. Their mission is identical to that of the horses found in the first vision, namely to "patrol the earth" (cf. 1:10–11). The two bronze mountains, nowhere else mentioned in scripture, likely mark off the boundary between heaven and earth. The image of the chariot represents the presence of God (Hab. 3:8). Indeed, a common title for God was "rider of the clouds" (Psalm 68:4). As the four winds, the chariots are commanded to scatter in all directions (cf. Jer. 4:13). The winds were traditionally conceived as messengers of God (Psalm 104:4).

Since it is not mentioned in the list of directions (6:6), the first chariot, with red or bay horses, is the one, presumably, to fly eastward. Yet it is the second chariot (with black horses), which heads towards the north, that gains the spotlight. It is through the black horses that God's spirit is set at rest. The land that lay to the north, which included the land of Shinar (5:11), was traditionally regarded as the land of the enemy by Israel. To claim that God's spirit is at rest in the north is tantamount to claiming that the superpowers that have plagued Israel throughout its history have been subjugated once and for all. Echoes of Genesis are deliberate. God's spirit rested at the end of creation (Gen. 1:2; 2:1–3); now such rest marks the culmination of Israel's restoration. The earth has now received its sabbath rest from the warring conflicts and injustices wrought by the nations against God's people.

This vision is the last in a series of eight visions and it stands in continuity with the first. Together, the first and last visions form a sort of theological envelope. The patrol of the chariots commanded in the last vision in effect responds to the initial complaint given in the first vision (1:12). True peace has finally been achieved, not the kind that simply glosses over injustice (1:15), but one that sets the stage for Zion to be comforted (1:17). Now the nuts-and-bolts task of restoring God's community can begin.

THE CROWNING OF JOSHUA
Zechariah 6:9–15

6:9 The word of the LORD came to me: 10 Collect silver and gold from the exiles—from Heldai, Tobijah, and Jedaiah—who have arrived from Babylon; and go the same day to the house of Josiah son of Zephaniah. 11 Take the silver and gold and make a crown, and set it on the head of the high priest Joshua son of Jehozadak; [12] say to him: Thus says the LORD of hosts: Here is a man whose name is Branch: for he shall branch out in his place, and he shall build the temple of the LORD. [13] It is he that shall build the temple of the LORD; he shall bear royal honor, and shall sit and rule on his throne. There shall be a priest by his throne, with peaceful understanding between the two of them. [14] And the crown shall be in the care of Heldai, Tobijah, Jedaiah, and Josiah son of Zephaniah, as a memorial in the temple of the LORD.

[15] Those who are far off shall come and help to build the temple of the LORD; and you shall know that the LORD of hosts has sent me to you. This will happen if you diligently obey the voice of the LORD your God.

With the series of visions completed, what follows is a series of prophetic speeches. Henceforth, Zechariah assumes the role of prophetic messenger who speaks on behalf of God. As with his previous speeches (cf. 1:1–6; 2:6–13; 4:6–10a), the following messages are decidedly this-worldly in nature, providing a counterbalance to his cosmic visions of the transcendent realm. The prophet's delivery in 6:9–15 is no exception. It begins with a specific command to action, to gather from certain exiles the necessary materials to fashion a crown. The donors of the gold and silver are also given charge of the crown (6:14). As for one who is to wear this crown, the text identifies the high priest Joshua, who is to be called "Branch" (6:12), the title for a future Davidic ruler (see Jer. 23:5). The title is a play on words: Joshua will "branch out" or flourish and thereby build the temple. The same play on words can be found in Jeremiah 33:15.

In Zechariah 3 the name "Branch" was ascribed to someone other than Joshua (3:8), namely, Zerubbabel, who is elsewhere described as the one to lay the foundation of the temple (4:7–9). In the present passage, however, Zerubbabel is enigmatically missing. Joshua, rather, is the recipient of the crown and effusive praise. The pronouncement in 6:13 recalls the convenantal promise in 2 Samuel 7:13, which solemnly designates David's son and successor as temple builder. Such language is now applied to Joshua. Zechariah's message clearly presupposes a different social situation from the one in which Zerubbabel was regarded as the sole heir to the Davidic throne and builder of the temple (4:6–10a). Zerubbabel has vanished from the scene. Given the social turmoil of the times, perhaps it is no surprise that there is no historical explanation for his absence.

What is more remarkable is that Zechariah's prophecy has been effectively adapted to a new situation. Joshua is now the one to assume heightened status, but even so, such honor is not to be exclusively received. A priest shall also be at his side, working in mutual cooperation in a bicameral form of government (Hag. 1:1–15). Shared power and cooperation, "peaceful understanding," characterize the leadership of the new community (6:13; cf. 4:14). Indeed, in such a manner is the entire exilic community (those who "are far off") to contribute to the temple's construction (6:15). This ethos of mutual cooperation is concretely modeled by the actions of the three exiles who donated their resources and met in the house of Josiah to fashion a crown. As the tabernacle in the wilderness was the product of an inclusive effort of the community (see Exodus 35—36), so it is hoped for the new temple. As in 4:9, Zechariah boldly stakes his reputation as one sent by God on its successful completion.

TO FAST OR TO FEAST
Zechariah 7:1–7

> 7:1 **In the fourth year of King Darius, the word of the LORD came to Zechariah on the fourth day of the ninth month, which is Chislev.** 2 **Now the people of Bethel had sent Sharezer and Regem-melech and their men, to entreat the favor of the LORD,** 3 **and to ask the priests of the house of the LORD of hosts and the prophets, "Should I mourn and practice abstinence in the fifth month, as I have done for so many years?"** 4 **Then the word of the LORD of hosts came to me:** 5 **Say to all the people of the land and the priests: When you fasted and lamented in the fifth month and in the seventh, for these seventy years, was it for me that you fasted?** 6 **And when you eat and when you drink, do you not eat and drink only for yourselves?** 7 **Were not these the words that the LORD proclaimed by the former prophets, when Jerusalem was inhabited and in prosperity, along with the towns around it, and when the Negeb and the Shephelah were inhabited?**

Zechariah's "word from the Lord" comes on December 7, 518 B.C., about two years after Zechariah's prophecies began (1:1), and almost a year since receiving his first vision (1:7). A delegation is sent from Bethel that urgently seeks guidance from the temple administration on maintaining a rite of lamentation "in the fifth month." Although the temple was not completed until March 12, 515 B.C. (see Ezra 6:15), temple personnel were already in place, comprising both priests and prophets (7:3), of which Zechariah was one. The fifth month (Jewish name Ab) was set aside to commemorate the temple's destruction in August, 587 B.C., when Nebuchadrezzar's troops stormed Jerusalem. The question from the Bethel delegation is a leading one (2 Kings 25:8–9; see also Jer. 52:12–13). To cease from fasting and lamenting would inaugurate a new chapter in the way the community would discern God's presence. With temple restoration well underway, the question of Sharezer and Regem-melech was more than appropriate. Their question marks the beginning of the end to mourning, the end of commemorating that interminable period of suffering and the beginning of a new reality of grace and restoration. Their question is posed at the threshold of grace, through which old habits of worship are transformed and where the rite of bitter lamentation is displaced by songs of joy and praise.

While inquiry is being made to the temple administration, Zechariah receives word from God. Reference is made to the approximately seventy-year duration of the exile (see 1:12), during which periods of official lamentation and fasting were conducted in both the fifth and seventh months (July/August and September/October, respectively). Presumably, the seventh month commemorated the death of Gedaliah, the Babylonian appointed governor (2 Kings 25:25; Jer. 41:1–3). Zechariah's message from God fundamentally questions the purpose of fasting. Is it for God's *benefit* that fasting is to be practiced or for the benefit of those who participate in such rituals? Since eating and drinking are done in the self-interest of the people, so also fasting in times of mourning focuses on the life of the community and not on God. A similar observation was made by Jesus regarding another form of worship: "The sabbath was made for humankind and not humankind for the sabbath" (Mark 2:27). Fasting was frequently practiced as a way of petitioning God during times of lamentation (2 Sam. 12:15–23; Jer. 14:12). However, by associating fasting with its opposite, feasting, Zechariah strips away all theological expectations associated with this rite but without denying its human significance. Ritual is relativized: It can sustain a people in the midst of crisis, but it can neither define nor transform a people's relationship with their God. (For a different view of fasting, see Joel 2:12–13.)

Zechariah finds his support from the earlier prophets. During a time when peace, prosperity, and population were in abundance, Zechariah claims, his predecessors were critical of Israel's public piety (for example, Isa. 1:16–17; Amos 5:14–15). In short, Zechariah does not respond to the query by pronouncing that lamenting is over and joy has begun. Rather, he circumvents the issue by suggesting that public lamentation has accomplished nothing in terms of defining God's relationship with Israel during the exile: It did not sway God one way or the other. Rather, in the face of the new reality impinging upon the old, fasting remains at best superfluous. More will be said about this form of public piety that is to embrace the new.

THE MESSAGE OF THE
FORMER PROPHETS: JUSTICE
Zechariah 7:8–14

> 7:8 The word of the LORD came to Zechariah, saying: ⁹ Thus says the LORD
> of hosts: Render true judgments, show kindness and mercy to one another;
> ¹⁰ do not oppress the widow, the orphan, the alien, or the poor; and do not
> devise evil in your hearts against one another. ¹¹ But they refused to listen,
> and turned a stubborn shoulder, and stopped their ears in order not to hear.
> ¹² They made their hearts adamant in order not to hear the law and the
> words that the LORD of hosts had sent by his spirit through the former
> prophets. Therefore great wrath came from the LORD of hosts. ¹³ Just as,
> when I called, they would not hear, so, when they called, I would not hear,
> says the LORD of hosts, ¹⁴ and I scattered them with a whirlwind among all
> the nations that they had not known. Thus the land they left was desolate,
> so that no one went to and fro, and a pleasant land was made desolate.

The prophet's response to the delegation from Bethel does not end with the
two rhetorical questions presented in the previous passage. Zechariah's answer continues and is shown to stand in strong continuity with the prophets
of old. This part of Zechariah's message begins in classical prophetic style
("thus says the Lord") and follows with the fundamental normative practices of the covenant community. Defending the rights of the widow, orphan, alien or sojourner, and the poor—those most vulnerable in society—
is the yardstick by which the convenantal community is to be measured; it
is the clarion call of both the prophets and the sages for justice (see Deut.
14:29; 24:19–21; Prov. 22:22–23; 23:10–11; Isa. 1:16–17; Jer. 22:3; 7:5—6;
Amos 5:14–15; 21–24). A just society is what Zechariah recalls from the
prophets of old, who were inspired by the very spirit of God. Yet the people, Zechariah is quick to point out, historically rejected outright their message. The stubborn shoulder, closed ears, adamant hearts (literally, "hearts
of emery") graphically describe the resistant posture the people assumed
against God's law and words. And God's response was to react in kind:
"When I called, they would not hear, so, when they called, I would not hear"
(v. 13; cf. Prov. 1:28; Jer. 11:11; Ezek. 8:18). God's refusal to attend to the
people's cries resulted in exile and devastation of the land. What was once
pleasant and fertile had become barren and inhospitable.

Within the larger context of Zechariah's hope-filled message this passage strikes a dissonant chord, but it simply serves as a retrospective backdrop. That was then, but something new is now unfolding. God's wrath
has come to an end; mercy is no longer withheld (1:12). God has heard
the cries of those in exile. The desolate land is about to fructify; the dead,

dry bones of a once vibrant community are about to be given new flesh (Ezek. 37:1–13).

THE PROFILE OF RESTORATION
Zechariah 8:1–8

8:1 **The word of the LORD of hosts came to me, saying:** 2 **Thus says the LORD of hosts: I am jealous for Zion with great jealousy, and I am jealous for her with great wrath.** 3 **Thus says the LORD: I will return to Zion, and will dwell in the midst of Jerusalem; Jerusalem shall be called the faithful city, and the mountain of the LORD of hosts shall be called the holy mountain.** 4 **Thus says the LORD of hosts: Old men and old women shall again sit in the streets of Jerusalem, each with staff in hand because of their great age.** 5 **And the streets of the city shall be full of boys and girls playing in its streets.** 6 **Thus says the LORD of hosts: Even though it seems impossible to the remnant of this people in these days, should it also seem impossible to me, says the LORD of hosts?** 7 **Thus says the LORD of hosts: I will save my people from the east country and from the west country;** 8 **and I will bring them to live in Jerusalem. They shall be my people and I will be their God, in faithfulness and in righteousness.**

This chapter focuses entirely on how restoration is to take shape. The profile of restoration begins in divine passion or pathos. God's jealousy (or better translated "zeal") for Zion is demonstrated both in grace and in wrath. This is a marvelous testimony to divine providence (see also 8:14–15)! Divine anger is not the result of arbitrary rage, but rather is rooted in passionate concern. Zechariah has already identified the reason behind the wrathful side of God's zeal for Zion as being the people's obduracy (7:11–12). Now, however, God's zeal becomes manifest in gracious restoration. The language of 8:3 echoes that of 1:16: "I have returned to Jerusalem with compassion; my house shall be built in it." God's return will recapture Jerusalem's former integrity and status as a center of worship. Jerusalem will once again be called the faithful city, and Zion will be called the holy mountain. God's restorative grace casts a net of protection and prosperity upon the struggling community, wherein all, particularly the aged and the very young, shall sit and rest out in the open (see Isa. 65:20), in contrast to the former days described in 8:10. The beleaguered community is now a veritable playground!

It is significant that the most riveting image of urban renewal Zechariah has to offer is one that does not focus upon a robust economy or booming industry, but rather draws from the themes of play and rest, perhaps the two most indispensable elements that define quality of life. Indeed, what is a person's life without play and leisure except a cog in the wheel of work? Ecclesiastes, for all of its despair and pessimism, finds that the peaceful enjoyment of simple things makes life worth living (for example, Eccl. 2:24–25; 3:12–13; 5:18–19). According to Genesis, the culmination of creation was on the seventh day, the day of rest (Gen. 2:1–3). The picture of security and leisure is so vividly depicted in Zechariah that even God admits that such urban renewal may *seem* next to impossible for the covenant people to accept (8:6). But nothing is too marvelous for God (Gen. 18:14; Jer. 32:17, 27). The realm of possibility for such a dramatic reversal of suffering becomes all the more certain in God's solemn declaration in verses 7–8. Salvation is defined as a return to Jerusalem from the exile, and there God will once again be the people's and the people will be God's own. This statement of mutuality in verse 8 recalls the covenant formula that sums up the binding relationship between God and the people (Jer. 7:23; 24:7; 31:33; 32:38).

EXHORTATION FOR RESTORATION
Zechariah 8:9–17

8:9 Thus says the LORD of hosts: Let your hands be strong—you that have recently been hearing these words from the mouths of the prophets who were present when the foundation was laid for the rebuilding of the temple, the house of the LORD of hosts. 10 For before those days there were no wages for people or for animals, nor was there any safety from the foe for those who went out or came in, and I set them all against one another. 11 But now I will not deal with the remnant of this people as in the former days, says the LORD of hosts. 12 For there shall be a sowing of peace; the vine shall yield its fruit, the ground shall give its produce, and the skies shall give their dew; and I will cause the remnant of this people to possess all these things. 13 Just as you have been a cursing among the nations, O house of Judah and house of Israel, so I will save you and you shall be a blessing. Do not be afraid, but let your hands be strong. 14 For thus says the LORD of hosts: Just as I purposed to bring disaster upon you, when your ancestors provoked me to wrath, and I did not relent, says the LORD of hosts, 15 so again I have purposed in these days to do good to Jerusalem and to the house of Judah; do not be afraid. 16 These are the things that you shall do: Speak the truth to one another, render in your gates judgments that are true and make for peace, 17 do not devise evil in your hearts against one another, and love no false oath; for all these are things that I hate, says the LORD.

Following the promise and profile of restoration is an exhortation of encouragement that frames the first section (vv. 9, 13). The promise of restoration is by nature an empowering prospect. With such a vision clearly within one's sight, the work can begin. The community has received the words from the prophets, including Haggai and Zechariah, who have witnessed the founding of the new temple (4:8–10), the official beginning of restoration. In the same way that the prophet declares that Zerubbabel's hands shall complete the temple, Zechariah urges the hands of the community to partake in building the new Jerusalem. The former days were marked by abject poverty and rampant violence. The books of Nehemiah and Ezra paint a grim social picture that is rife with political conflict and economic hardship during the time of restoration (Ezra 4—5; Nehemiah 4—5).

Nevertheless, the former days have run their course, according to Zechariah. A sowing of peace or well-being ("shalom") shall blanket the land, yielding bountiful produce and prosperity. No longer a curse among the nations (Jer. 25:18; 29:18; Mic. 6:16), Judah and Israel will experience nothing short of full regeneration. And there is no turning back, for such blessing is part and parcel of God's plan (v. 15). Yet even amidst blessing there is much work to be done. Zechariah details the way "strong hands" are to be put to work (8:13), namely to work for truth, justice, and peace (vv. 16–17). These cardinal virtues of the covenant community (see also 7:9–10; 8:19b) are set in opposition to devising evil and swearing falsely, vices that can threaten to collapse any community at its foundation. Though a new era of rest and security has arrived (8:4–5), Zechariah exhorts his people to come and labor on.

Zechariah reminds us of the fact that service to God never really ends, either in this life or in the next, when God will wipe away every tear. Nevertheless, this is not something to lament. Like the elders who surround God's throne in heaven to "worship him day and night" (Rev. 7:15), the work of God's people is to labor joyously for God's glory.

THE SEASONS OF UNIVERSAL JOY
Zechariah 8:18–23

8:18 **The word of the LORD of hosts came to me, saying:** [19] **Thus says the LORD of hosts: The fast of the fourth month, and the fast of the fifth, and the fast of the seventh, and the fast of the tenth, shall be seasons of joy and gladness, and cheerful festivals for the house of Judah: therefore love truth and peace.**

²⁰ Thus says the LORD of hosts: Peoples shall yet come, the inhabitants of many cities; ²¹ the inhabitants of one city shall go to another, saying, "Come, let us go to entreat the favor of the LORD, and to seek the LORD of hosts; I myself am going." ²² Many peoples and strong nations shall come to seek the LORD of hosts in Jerusalem, and to entreat the favor of the LORD. ²³ Thus says the LORD of hosts: In those days ten men from nations of every language shall take hold of a Jew, grasping his garment and saying, "Let us go with you, for we have heard that God is with you."

Zechariah's own prophecies end with an effusion of joy. The somber fasts mentioned in 7:3, 5, along with two others, will be replaced with "cheerful festivals." Such occasions had traditionally commemorated events in the destruction of Jerusalem by Nebuchadrezzar (2 Kings 25:1–4); now they shall look forward to a new era of peace and prosperity. The transition from mourning to rejoicing provides a new foundation for a community ethic founded upon truth and peace (v. 19b). In a spirit of joy the people of God are commanded to embody truth and peace within the life of the community.

In the spirit of celebration the international community will be well represented in Jerusalem. The vision of universal harmony that Zechariah paints in 8:20–23 has its roots in other prophetic visions of the peaceable kingdom (Isa. 2:2–4; 11:6–9; 60:1–3; 66:18–21; Mic. 4:3), as well as in God's blessing to Abram to be a blessing for "all the families of the earth" (Gen. 12:1–3). Inhabitants of one city will invite those of another to join them in pilgrimage to the new temple in Jerusalem in order to "entreat the favor of the Lord" (v. 22). Now even Gentiles (non-Jews) can proclaim, "I was glad when they said to me, 'Let us go to the house of the Lord!' " (Psalm 122:1). Gentiles will join themselves to Jews on their way to Jerusalem. Indeed, such a pilgrimage has the power to engender a new community among pilgrims of various backgrounds. The shared experiences of a common journey can bond people of very different walks of life, nationalities, ethnic backgrounds, and native languages into a cohesive whole. Such was the journey of faith as Zechariah saw it; such is the journey for the Church today.

GOD'S APPROACH TO JERUSALEM
Zechariah 9:1–8

9:1 The word of the LORD is against the land of Hadrach
and will rest upon Damascus.

For to the LORD belongs the capital of Aram,
    as do all the tribes of Israel;
2 Hamath also, which borders on it,
    Tyre and Sidon, though they are very wise.
3 Tyre has built itself a rampart,
    and heaped up silver like dust,
    and gold like the dirt of the streets.
4 But now, the Lord will strip it of its possessions
    and hurl its wealth into the sea,
    and it shall be devoured by fire.

5 Ashkelon shall see it and be afraid;
    Gaza too, and shall writhe in anguish;
    Ekron also, because it hopes are withered.
The king shall perish from Gaza;
    Ashkelon shall be uninhabited;
6 a mongrel people shall settle in Ashdod,
    and I will make an end of the pride of Philistia.
7 I will take away its blood from its mouth,
    and its abominations from between its teeth;
    it too shall be a remnant for our God;
    it shall be like a clan in Judah,
    and Ekron shall be like the Jebusites.
8 Then I will encamp at my house as a guard,
    so that no one shall march to and fro;
    no oppressor shall again overrun them,
    for now I have seen with my own eyes.

This prophetic passage is introduced as an "oracle," a special kind of prophetic message that is usually of judgmental nature (cf. Zech. 12:1; Jer. 23:33–40; Mal. 1:1). It begins with a list of Israel's enemies. God's word is a message leveled first of all against the kingdom of Aram, otherwise known as Syria. The "land of Hadrach" (v. 1) refers to an Aramean city-state in northern Syria on the Orontes river, south of Hamath and north of Damascus. Damascus, the capital of Syria, does not escape mention, along with Hamath and the Phoenician cities of Tyre and Sidon, along the Lebanese coast. Why are all these foreign kingdoms singled out? Because God's sovereign word is not confined to Israel's boundaries. The foreign nations also belong to the Lord (v. 1), contrary to their own bloated self-estimations (for example, Sidon and Tyre; Ezekiel 28).

God comes to reclaim the whole land. Justice will be restored because nothing stands outside the bounds of God's kingdom; all kingdoms, no matter how powerful, are subject to God, even Philistia, Israel's hated enemy. Comprising Ashkelon, Gaza, Ekron, and Ashdod, the land of the Philistines is subject to special punishment, presumably because of past atrocities committed against Israel. The reference to the remnant of Philistia in verse 7 is no complement. Remnant literally refers to whoever remains after divinely wrought devastation (cf. Isa. 1:9; Amos 1:8). The examples of Judah, which was defeated by the Babylonians in 587 B.C., and the Jebusites of Jerusalem, who were vanquished by the conquering David (2 Sam. 5:6–10), are good cases in point. Nevertheless, there is a positive side to which our passage alludes: Philistia will be a remnant *for* our God" (v. 7). Rather than at odds with God and with God's people, the remnant of Philistia will be devoted to God, like "the clan of Judah." Devastation leads to devotion. Even the Philistines will be included in the family of Israel.

Approaching from the north, along the coast from Syria to Phoenicia to Philistia, God comes to encamp at the now completed temple, "my house." God's presence ensures that Jerusalem enjoys complete security. The divine warrior has set up camp to ward off any who would threaten the well-being of God's people. God has returned to behold and sustain a people on the verge of complete destruction. God reclaims them as the "apple of my eye" (Zech. 2:12). God has come back to stay.

GOD'S REIGN OF PEACE
Zechariah 9:9–13

> 9:9 **Rejoice greatly, O daughter Zion!**
>   **Shout aloud, O daughter Jerusalem!**
> **Lo, your king comes to you;**
>   **triumphant and victorious is he,**
> **humble and riding on a donkey,**
>   **on a colt, the foal of a donkey.**
> 10 **He will cut off the chariot from Ephraim**
>   **and the war horse from Jerusalem;**
> **and the battle bow shall be cut off,**
>   **and he shall command peace to the nations;**
> **his dominion shall be from sea to sea,**
>   **and from the River to the ends of the earth.**
>
> 11 **As for you also, because of the blood of my covenant with you,**
>   **I will set your prisoners free from the waterless pit.**

12 **Return to your stronghold, O prisoners of hope;**
   today I declare that I will restore to you double.
13 **For I have bent Judah as my bow;**
   I have made Ephraim its arrow.
I will arouse your sons, O Zion,
   against your sons, O Greece,
   and wield you like a warrior's sword.

God's return to Jerusalem elicits songs of praise from the inhabitants. Zion and Jerusalem—synonymous names—are addressed and personified as daughters. "Daughter" is a term of endearment used frequently in the context of deliverance (see Zech. 2:10; Isa. 12:6; 52:2; Mic. 4:8; Zeph. 3:14–15). Like Miriam at the banks of the Red Sea (Exod. 15:20–21), the daughters of Judah respond with cadences of joy, attesting to God's victory. God as victorious king has finally arrived. Yet the divine warrior approaches the city not with an iron fist to wreak punishment, as in the case of Israel's enemies (vv. 1–7), but in open humility, riding on a donkey rather than on a war horse (see v. 10). God has come to make peace, and the divine manner of approach provides dramatic demonstration. The docile donkey has replaced the war chariot, and an open hand has overcome the battering ram.

The description of God's peaceful approach in verse 9 appears in two Gospel accounts of Jesus' arrival into Jerusalem on Palm Sunday (Matt. 21:5; John 12:15). The account in Matthew, however, depicts Jesus on two animals, a donkey and a colt (Matt. 21:2–5; cf. Mark 11:2–7). Matthew erroneously interpreted Zechariah 9:9 to refer to two distinct animals, not realizing that in this poetic passage "donkey" and "colt" refer to the same beast of burden. In any case, the manner of Jesus' entry into Jerusalem marks a dramatic enactment of this ancient text as Jesus begins to conclude his earthly ministry. Palm Sunday demonstrates that Jesus comes in the power of powerlessness that overcomes the power of power. In his crucifixion and death, Christ vanquishes the power of death, to unleash the power of peace that surpasses all understanding (Phil. 4:7).

In powerlessness God will destroy all instruments of war: chariot, war horse, and battle bow (v. 10; cf. Psalm 46:8–9; Isa. 57:19). The nations are demilitarized by the divine warrior; they will "study war no more" (see Isa. 2:4; Mic. 4:3). God's dominion will be a reign of peace that spreads from the inside out. Like ripples in a pond, peace will radiate from God's people, stretching out to encompass the ends of the earth. The "River" is the mighty Euphrates. Whereas the Mesopotamian superpowers were known to make such claims of universal sovereignty, God's kingdom is one whose reign will know no end, spatially or temporally.

The growing expanse of God's kingdom also has internal implications as well. The prisoners will be set free, restored doubly, no less! God's grace knows no bounds or bonds! The basis of such restoration comes from God's recognition of Israel's covenant, the blood of which ratified the formal relationship between God and the people that was established on Mount Sinai (see Exod. 24:8). The "prisoners of hope" are all those in exile or captivity who are released to return to Jerusalem. Even the prisoners have an integral place in God's reign of peace.

Before peace is fully realized, however, there are some scores to be settled, according to the prophet (v. 13). Both Judah and Ephraim (what is left of the northern kingdom) will be transformed into an invincible war instrument against Greece. This is perhaps the earliest reference to Greece in the Bible (cf. Joel 3:6). Perhaps our passage reflects a certain weariness against the rise of Greek power along the Mediterranean seaboard in the mid-fifth century B.C. or the domination of Hellenistic culture after Alexander the Great's conquest in 323 B.C. Regardless of the historical setting, the text dramatically claims that God's kingdom is one that supersedes all others.

THE DAY OF THE LORD
Zechariah 9:14–17

¹⁴ Then the LORD will appear over them,
and his arrow go forth like lightning;
the Lord GOD will sound the trumpet
and march forth in the whirlwinds of the south.
¹⁵ The LORD of hosts will protect them,
and they shall devour and tread down the slingers;
they shall drink their blood like wine,
and be full like a bowl,
drenched like the corners of the altar.
¹⁶ On that day the LORD their God will save them
for they are the flock of his people;
for like the jewels of a crown
they shall shine on his land.
¹⁷ For what goodness and beauty are his!
Grain shall make the young men flourish,
and new wine the young women.

Though battle is waged, God's people do not directly participate; rather, they serve only to reap the spoils of victory, for it is God and God alone who fights on their behalf. It is God who shoots the arrow, sounds the trumpet, marches forth, protects, and saves "the flock of his people." Those who have persecuted Israel will be defeated, slain as sacrifice (9:15). Chapter 9 ends on a note of restoration. With the Lord as Israel's shepherd, the people are likened to the jewels of a crown. Whose crown is referred to? None other than God's. God comes as king to fight on behalf of Israel and reign in "goodness and beauty," and the people play an indispensable part in reflecting that beauty and goodness. One is reminded of Psalm 133:1: "How very good and pleasant it is when kindred live together in unity!" Peace and prosperity are not abstract, unattainable ideals for the covenant community; they are rather its hallmarks. This vision of hope makes quite clear that the prosperity of God's people is reflected in the condition of its youth: If the youth flourish in the land, then restoration is achieved (v. 17). If the children suffer, then God's people have not embodied the restorative vision God intends. Ancient prophets and modern sociologists alike have demonstrated that the way in which children are raised and treated is a direct caliber of the moral character and fate of the whole community.

THE LORD AS PROVIDER AND SHEPHERD
Zechariah 10:1–2

> 10:1 Ask rain from the LORD
> in the season of the spring rain,
> from the LORD who makes the storm clouds,
>   who gives showers of rain to you,
>   the vegetation in the field to everyone.
> 2 For the teraphim utter nonsense,
>   and the diviners see lies;
> the dreamers tell false dreams,
>   and give empty consolation.
> Therefore the people wander like sheep;
>   they suffer for lack of a shepherd.

Though these two verses appear to talk of different things, there is a deep and enduring connection. The prophet exhorts the people to make their requests directly to God and not to depend on such unreliable intermediaries as the teraphim, diviners, and dreamers. The Bible abhors any attempt to discern God's will other than directly through prayer and supplication. In ancient Israel, the teraphim were statues or amulets used to predict God's will. Diviners had a host of techniques, from examining sheep livers to tracking bird patterns and celestial movements, all in the attempt to determine God's plan for the future. Today, we would call such actions superstitious, despite the fact that astrology is still widely popular today. In addition, the prophet rightly asserts that dreams cannot be relied upon for sure knowledge, although one must recall that Joseph and Daniel had the gift of interpreting some dreams (Genesis 41; Daniel 2). These, however, were more the exception than the rule. Together, all attempts to gain access to God based on human technique are actually twisted attempts to second guess and manipulate God. They simply do not stand up to direct inquiry through prayer and supplication. To rely on anything less than directly approaching God invites only confusion and suffering, a life without direction (10:2).

THE LORD AS
SHEPHERD AND REDEEMER
Zechariah 10:3–12

10:3 My anger is hot against the shepherds,
    and I will punish the leaders;
for the LORD of hosts cares for his flock, the house of Judah,
    and will make them like his proud war horse.
⁴ Out of them shall come the cornerstone,
    out of them the tent peg,
out of them the battle bow,
    out of them every commander.
⁵ Together they shall be like warriors in battle,
    trampling the foe in the mud of the streets;
they shall fight, for the LORD is with them,
    and they shall put to shame the riders on horses.

⁶ I will strengthen the house of Judah,
    and I will save the house of Joseph.
I will bring them back because I have compassion on them,
    and they shall be as though I had not rejected them;
    for I am the LORD their God and I will answer them.
⁷ Then the people of Ephraim shall become like warriors,
    and their hearts shall be glad as with wine.
Their children shall see it and rejoice,
    their hearts shall exult in the LORD.

8 I will signal for them and gather them in,
    for I have redeemed them,
    and they shall be as numerous as they were before.
9 Though I scattered them among the nations,
    yet in far countries they shall remember me,
    and they shall rear their children and return.
10 I will bring them home from the land of Egypt,
    and gather them from Assyria;
I will bring them to the land of Gilead and to Lebanon,
    until there is no room for them.
11 They shall pass through the sea of distress,
    and the waves of the sea shall be struck down,
    and all the depths of the Nile dried up.
The pride of Assyria shall be laid low,
    and the scepter of Egypt shall depart.
12 I will make them strong in the LORD,
    and they shall walk in his name,
                                        says the LORD.

God's role as the shepherding caretaker now turns political in this passage. Not merely a rain provider (v. 1), God metes out punishment against Israel's own leaders. God is the true shepherd that supersedes all other shepherds. The change in imagery in verse 3 is telling. Israel is not simply a frail sheep; the people will become God's war horse, fierce and proud (10:3; see Job 39:19–25). God has empowered them for whatever challenge they will encounter (10:4–5). Salvation and empowerment go hand in hand (10:6a), the two sides of God's beneficence for Israel. The houses of Judah and Joseph (sometimes called Ephraim, as in 10:7) refer to the southern and northern regions (formerly kingdoms) of Israel, respectively. The reconstitution of both houses is a clear testimony that only in unity is there renewed strength and purpose.

God's act of gathering a disparate people attests to God's compassion. Though once scattered, the people themselves provide the possibility for their return through their remembrance (v. 9). For any dispersed people, memory is the foundation of hope. Israel vividly remembered the promises made to their distant ancestors and the ways in which God had acted decisively on their behalf in the past through Abraham, Moses, Miriam, Joshua, Gideon, and Deborah. They retold the stories; indeed, they found their identity through them. Their common heritage was the tie that bound them together, regardless of the distance. Their common tradition was their life blood as a community of faith. What was passed down from one generation to the next enabled them to raise their children wherever they were and keep alive their hope for return. And now that time has arrived. One *can* go home again, but without memory nourished and kept alive, there would be no home to which to return!

Wherever we are, home is meant to be a special place of refuge and fellowship. Home may not be a physical place, especially if one's parents have died. Nevertheless, nurtured in the heart, home never passes away. The prophet knows that his people are homesick and proclaims that the fulfillment of God's plan is to bring the people home. For the ancient Israelite, home meant in part the land in which their ancestors once lived. Christians, as well as Jews, look forward to their true home at the end of history when all the families of the earth will be united.

For the prophet, too, home is far grander than one ever remembered. The references to Gilead (east of the Jordan) and Lebanon as overflow areas (v. 10) make for an expanded home front. Homeward bound through the "sea of distress" echoes the story of the Exodus (v. 11; cf. Exodus 14—15). The peoples, scattered from Egypt to Mesopotamia, will triumph over all attempts to stop them. The superpowers will be divested of their power as God's people will once again walk homeward with God's name upon their lips. Whereas the children of the Exodus had the ark of the covenant to accompany them in their travels through the wilderness, the new generation of exiles from Egypt and Assyria have the name of the Lord, which affords them God's accompanying presence. For the ancient Israelites, God's name was everything, and so also for Christians today, whose prayers are accompanied by the name of Jesus.

THE RAZING OF LEBANON
Zechariah 11:1–3

11:1 **Open your doors, O Lebanon,**
so that fire may devour your cedars!
² **Wail, O cypress, for the cedar has fallen,**
   for the glorious trees are ruined!
Wail, oaks of Bashan,
   for the thick forest has been felled!
³ **Listen, the wail of the shepherds,**
   for their glory is despoiled!
Listen, the roar of the lions,
   for the thickets of the Jordan are destroyed!

In 10:10, Lebanon was prophesied as becoming overpopulated with re-turning Israelites. Now the land is called upon to lament the destruction of its vast and majestic forest in order to make it sustainable for habitation. The cedars, cypress, and the oaks of Bashan (a region east of the Sea of Galilee) are to give their laments in the face of their destruction by an in-creasing population. This passage conveys the negative side of the re-gathering of God's people. In addition, the shepherds lament the loss of their wealth ("glory") in pasturage, while the lions lament the loss of their domain.

Environmental destruction from overpopulation is not condemned by the ancient text. Rather, the leveling of forests, particularly the majestic cedars for which Lebanon was noted, was seen by this ancient prophet as the un-fortunate but natural consequence of the reestablishment of Israel's popula-tion after a long history of depletion and exile. Yet is is significant that this passage gives the voice of pathos to arboreal life. Trees are not mute. For modern readers, the text invites shared lamentation over the destruction of rain forests and the wildlife habitations that runs rampant today.

SHEPHERD AGAINST SHEPHERD
Zechariah 11:4–17

11:4 **Thus said the LORD my God: Be a shepherd of the flock doomed to slaughter. 5 Those who buy them kill them and go unpunished; and those who sell them say, "Blessed be the LORD, for I have become rich"; and their own shepherds have no pity on them. 6 For I will no longer have pity on the inhabitants of the earth, says the LORD. I will cause them, every one, to fall each into the hand of a neighbor, and each into the hand of the king; and they shall devastate the earth, and I will deliver no one from their hand.**

7 So, on behalf of the sheep merchants, I became the shepherd of the flock doomed to slaughter. I took two staffs; one I named Favor, the other I named Unity, and I tended the sheep. 8 In one month I disposed of the three shepherds, for I had become impatient with them, and they also detested me. 9 So I said, "I will not be your shepherd. What is to die, let it die; what is to be destroyed, let it be destroyed; and let those that are left devour the flesh of one another!" 10 I took my staff Favor and broke it, annulling the covenant that I had made with all the peoples. 11 So it was annulled on that day, and the sheep merchants, who were watching me, knew that it was the word of the LORD. 12 I then said to them, "If it seems right to you, give me my wages; but if not, keep them." So they weighed out as my wages thirty shekels of silver. 13 Then the LORD said to me, "Throw it into the treasury"—this lordly price at which I was valued by them. So I took the thirty shekels

of silver and threw them into the treasury in the house of the LORD. [14] Then I broke my second staff Unity, annulling the family ties between Judah and Israel.

[15] Then the LORD said to me: Take once more the implements of a worthless shepherd. [16] For I am now raising up in the land a shepherd who does not care for the perishing, or seek the wandering, or heal the maimed, or nourish the healthy, but devours the flesh of the fat ones, tearing off even their hoofs.

[17] Oh, my worthless shepherd,
     who deserts the flock!
May the sword strike his arm
     and his right eye!
Let his arm be completely withered,
     his right eye utterly blinded!

This passage is one of the most difficult passages in the entire Old Testament, since the language is so vague that it is difficult to tell whether this is an allegory, parable, or actual historical account. Consequently, any interpretation must be made with the broadest of strokes; the details must remain elusive. At the outset, the reader may be puzzled over the fact that this passage follows the prophet's message of restoration for Israel in Zechariah 10 and 11:1–4. This passage about the shepherd of a doomed flock no doubt echoes the earlier situation mentioned in 10:3, namely, of the Lord's anger against the shepherd/leaders of Israel. In short, the prophet recalls the earlier and still present situation of social chaos and corruption that besets the community before God comes to restore it.

The prophet is the appointed shepherd of the doomed flock Israel. In context, the figure of the shepherd denotes a position of prophetic leadership among other leaders. Who the "sheep merchants" are is anyone's guess; perhaps they refer to the temple personnel who have hired the prophet (cf. 11:8). The picture painted of Israel's situation under the shepherd's leadership is one of horrible distress: Israel's own leaders pay no heed. There is constant strife between neighbors, and kings rampage the land.

Why does God permit such a situation to occur? God allows human corruption, beginning with the leaders, to work itself through the entire community, destroying everything in its path. God does not intervene to stop it, but rather impresses all the more the need for future restoration and deliverance amid an inherently corrupt community. And so the prophet is caught up in this tidal wave of social chaos. He himself becomes a leader who in disgust relinquishes his role. Instead of being summoned to provide happy prophecies, the prophet espouses an outlook of "let be what will be." The prophet feels it is futile to try to change the way things are during this period of gloom. Nothing can stop the whirlpool of torment. One must simply wait it out like a fever that must break before healing can begin.

In addition, the prophet breaks his staffs called Favor and Unity, symbolically annulling the covenant that God made with Israel at Mount Sinai as well as severing any semblance of unity between the northern and southern peoples of Israel. Evidently the people, particularly the authorities, were counting upon God's automatic favor to lead them through the crisis. The two symbolic actions of the prophet, however, show that divine favor can never be taken for granted.

In between these two extreme actions is the brief account of payment given to the prophet by the "sheep merchants" for services rendered. Such a sum of money is identical to what was due a slave owner when an ox gored a slave (Exod. 21:32), not an inconsequential sum. Prophets, like priests, were professionals, and our author is no exception (see Amos 7:12). The prophet, however, exhibits a peculiar apathy for being paid (11:12–13), and for good reason. With thirty shekels carefully weighed out, he is instructed by God to throw them in the temple treasury. No particular reason is given, but one can surmise that this symbolic act is meant to illustrate that corruption has struck even the temple, the heart of Israel's religious life. Clearly this theme is picked up in the account of Judas' betrayal of Jesus (Matt. 26:14–16; 27:3–10). Paid thirty shekels by the chief priests, Judas realizes his guilt, throws the money in the temple, and hangs himself. Both events dramatically illustrate the extent to which the religious and political authorities can become steeped in wrongdoing. The prophet finds himself used as a pawn for another's ulterior motives. Yet by allowing himself to be hired, as God had commanded, he exposes deceit to its core.

The second message from God continues the slide into social chaos (v. 15). God proclaims that a new shepherd will arise, one whose actions are completely at odds with his prescribed role. Simply put, he is an anti-shepherd, one bent on destroying the flock rather than sustaining it. He will desert the flock. The passage ends with a curse raised against this shepherd, an invective so terrible that it mirrors the vicious treatment to which the shepherd had subjected his flock (v. 17). The bad shepherd ends up treated in the same manner as he treated his flock.

THE EMPOWERMENT OF JERUSALEM
Zechariah 12:1–9

12:1 **The word of the LORD concerning Israel: Thus says the LORD, who stretched out the heavens and founded the earth and formed the human spirit within:** 2 **See, I am about to make Jerusalem a cup of reeling for all the surrounding peoples; it will be against Judah also in the siege against Jerusalem.** 3 **On that day I will make Jerusalem a heavy stone for all the peoples; all who lift it shall grievously hurt themselves. And all the nations of the earth shall come together against it.** 4 **On that day, says the LORD, I will strike every horse with panic, and its rider with madness. But on the house of Judah I will keep a watchful eye, when I strike every horse of the peoples with blindness.** 5 **Then the clans of Judah shall say to themselves, "The inhabitants of Jerusalem have strength through the LORD of hosts, their God."**

6 **On that day I will make the clans of Judah like a blazing pot on a pile of wood, like a flaming torch among sheaves; and they shall devour to the right and to the left all the surrounding peoples, while Jerusalem shall again be inhabited in its place, in Jerusalem.**

7 **And the LORD will give victory to the tents of Judah first, that the glory of the house of David and the glory of the inhabitants of Jerusalem may not be exalted over that of Judah.** 8 **On that day the LORD will shield the inhabitants of Jerusalem so that the feeblest among them on that day shall be like David, and the house of David shall be like God, like the angel of the LORD, at their head.** 9 **And on that day I will seek to destroy all the nations that come against Jerusalem.**

Chapters 12—14 constitute a new prophetic message, introduced as a new "oracle" (see 9:1). From here on out, the focus of the book of Zechariah is on the day of God's victory on behalf of Jerusalem, a day that ushers in a new age and new creation. It is only appropriate, then, that the Lord is introduced as Creator in verse 1. The image of God "stretching out" the heavens is likened to setting up a tent in Psalm 104:2b. The sequential order of heaven, earth, and human beings is also followed in the creation account in Genesis 1. The "human spirit" is the animating force that occasions life, breathed into human beings (Gen. 2:7). This language of creation prefaces the day of judgment and deliverance that is to follow, the effect of which is a return to the glorious time of creation. As we will see later, restoration and creation, consummation and genesis, merge together with history itself coming full circle (see 14:6–11).

In this final drama, God as Creator enters history by vindicating Jerusalem before the nations. As a symbol of divine judgment and wrath, the cup is a common image in biblical literature (see Psalms 11:6; 78:5; Isa.

51:17; Jer. 25:15, 28; Hab. 2:16). The "cup of reeling" suggests a cup whose contents are so strong that all who partake are sent into a state of deadly intoxication. In Jeremiah 25:15–31, the nations who take such a cup are depicted getting drunk, vomiting, and falling to their doom. Such a drink was to be avoided at all costs!

What is disturbing in this passage is that Judah is also included with the nations that are to suffer God's judgment to the vindication of Jerusalem (v. 2b; see also v. 7). Evidently at some point in history after the exile, there was inner conflict between Jerusalem, Judah's capital, and the general populace living in the area surrounding the city. Though it is hard, with what little we know, to place this situation historically, it is naive to think that communities of faith are somehow immune to damaging conflict from within, like the church fights and schisms of today. However, this issue of inner conflict is not developed in the passage, except to quote the Judahites for praising the newly founded strength of Jerusalem (v. 5). Elsewhere, the relationship between Jerusalem and Judah remains on solid ground.

At any rate, Jerusalem and Judah are described in a variety of metaphors: a boulder (v. 3), a blazing pot, and a flaming torch (v. 6). Despite the odds, the Lord will rescue Jerusalem and send all the foreign armies into flight (see Psalm 2). The Lord will give Jerusalem strength (v. 5); the city will once again be inhabited (v. 6; see 10:9–10). Jerusalem's newly found strength is dramatically depicted in a series of similes: the weakest will be like David, the youngest of the sons of Jesse, and the house (that is, lineage) of David will be like God (v. 8). The language is no accident. The house of David was divinely sanctioned during the reign of Israel's most famous and beloved king. God promised David that his dynasty in Jerusalem would be permanent (2 Sam. 7:16).

The prophet recalls this language of promise when he describes Jerusalem's glorified fulfillment. In the new age, Jerusalem's leadership will be at one with its God. The reference to the "angel of the Lord" anticipates Malachi (Mal. 2:7, 3:1). An angel was generally a divine being that appeared in human form as a messenger to human beings. There are occasional passages, however, in which the term angel could apply to human beings (for example, Judg. 2:1; 2 Sam. 14:17; Mal. 3:1). In addition, allusion is made to the "angel of God" who led the people of the Exodus, guiding them by day and by night (Exod. 13:21; 14:19). Accordingly, the House of David will lead God's people from misery into freedom. Jerusalem's vindication is matched by a new kind of leadership that reflects the very character of God: passionately protective and abounding in justice and mercy.

A DAY OF MOURNING
Zechariah 12:10–14

12:10 And I will pour out a spirit of compassion and supplication on the house of David and the inhabitants of Jerusalem, so that, when they look on the one whom they have pierced, they shall mourn for him, as one mourns for an only child, and weep bitterly over him, as one weeps over a firstborn. 11 On that day the mourning in Jerusalem will be as great as the mourning for Hadad-rimmon in the plain of Megiddo. 12 The land shall mourn, each family by it-self; the family of the house of David by itself, and their wives by themselves; the family of the house of Nathan by itself, and their wives by themselves; 13 the family of the house of Levi by itself, and their wives by themselves; the family of the Shimeites by itself, and their wives by themselves; 14 and all the families that are left, each by itself, and their wives by themselves.

On the day of vindication and victory there is also a day of mourning. It begins with an outpouring of "compassion and supplication," as well as grief. This is the calm *after* the storm, after the complete reversal of the horrific conflicts described in the previous passages. As a result, both the royal family ("house of David") and the people of Jerusalem are to exhibit great remorse over a particularly reprehensible deed, namely an act of violence against someone of their own (12:10). The historical identity of the victim has been the source of much speculation among ancient and modern interpreters. The Hebrew text leaves the identity unspecified. Perhaps it is a prophet who had a hand in writing some of these passages. At any rate, the open-ended nature of this text has invited reinterpretation by New Testament writers. John 19:37 cites this text in connection with Christ's crucifixion (see also Rev. 1:7). Both Jesus and this unknown victim were innocent figures that were executed because they claimed to speak on behalf of God and preached an unpopular message. Israel's history was frequently marked by deep-seated conflicts between prophets and kings (Matt. 23:37). The prophets Elijah, Jeremiah, Micah of Moreshah (Jer. 26:18), and Uriah ben Shemaiah (Jer. 26:20–23) all suffered persecution by the royal establishment. Some were murdered outright, and Jesus' own execution continued that legacy.

The prophet compares such expression of sorrow to "mourning for Hadad-rimmon in the plain of Megiddo." Though originally the name of a fertility god of Canaan, "Hadad-rimmon" came to be a site of mourning for the good king Josiah, who was killed in conflict with Pharaoh Neco near Megiddo in 609 B.C. (2 Kings 23:28–30; 2 Chron. 35:24–27). Like a parent's grief over the death of a child, such mourning is a sorrow that strikes at the very core of one's being. No greater grief is there. And so all the families associated with Jerusalem's ruling offices, both royal and priestly, are called upon to mourn over the death of this unnamed individual. On Good Friday, the death of Jesus is also commemorated with deep expressions of grief. Both the passion story of Jesus' crucifixion and our passage here suggest that in grief and remorse, there is a complete reordering of one's priorities and values. It is a grief that purges and ultimately renews.

THE PURGING OF JERUSALEM
AND THE END OF PROPHECY
Zechariah 13:1–6

13:1 On that day a fountain shall be opened for the house of David and the inhabitants of Jerusalem, to cleanse them from sin and impurity.
2 On that day, says the LORD of hosts, I will cut off the names of the idols from the land, so that they shall be remembered no more; and also I will remove from the land the prophets and the unclean spirit. 3 And if any prophets appear again, their fathers and mothers who bore them will say to them, "You shall not live, for you speak lies in the name of the LORD"; and their fathers and their mothers who bore them shall pierce them through when they prophesy. 4 On that day the prophets will be ashamed, every one, of their visions when they prophesy; they will not put on a hairy mantle in order to deceive, 5 but each of them will say, "I am no prophet, I am a tiller of the soil; for the land has been my possession since my youth." 6 And if anyone asks them, "What are these wounds on your chest?" the answer will be "The wounds I received in the house of my friends."

With the image of the fountain, Zechariah 13 begins with an evocative description of Jerusalem's restoration, the details of which are to be laid out in the next chapter (cf. 14:8). Such a fountain or river both cleanses and sustains life. The language is not unique. Elsewhere, Jerusalem is frequently envisioned as situated above a perennial stream that flows from its temple (Psalm 46:4; Ezek. 47:1–12; Joel 3:18; Rev. 22:1–2). Indeed, historically the Gihon Spring, located on the eastern embankment of the city, supplied water to the inhabitants, a resource that was important enough for King Hezekiah to construct an underground aqueduct to channel the water into the "Pool of Siloam" (2 Kings 20:20; 2 Chron. 32:30). The image of the fountain is also taken up by Jesus, who compares himself to a life-giving stream (John 4:13–14; 7:37–38). Life and the cleansing or forgiveness of sins are bound up together in the figure of Jesus and are symbolized by the water of baptism.

The following verses describe a particular result of the city being cleansed. A purging of the prophets is foretold. Prophecy evidently had a bad name by this time. Prophets are associated with the "unclean spirit," and their removal from office is compared with the destruction of idols (v. 2). They are accused of deception (vv. 3–4). One gets the impression that Jerusalem has become overrun with such prophets. Throughout Israel's history, these false prophets were a constant source of trouble. In Jeremiah's time, false prophets pronounced peace and easy answers during a time when there was no peace (Jeremiah 28). They were possessed by a "lying spirit" and, consequently, rubber-stamped the whims of kings in times when the true prophets were persecuted (1 Kings 22:13–28). They are frequently associated with apostasy, as in the case of the prophets of Baal in 1 Kings 13:20–40. Ezekiel condemns those prophets who claim to have received God's word but nonetheless prophesy out of their own imagination (Ezek. 13:2–3). Evidently, the problem was so great that "Second Zechariah" (see introduction) called for the end to popular prophesy with the parents killing their own children who claimed to prophesy (v. 3; cf. Deut. 18:20–22). The trademark of the prophetic guild, the hairy mantle (v. 4; 1 Kings 19:13, 19; 2 Kings 2:8, 13; cf. Matt. 3:4), is categorically rejected.

What they prophesied is not said. One can only imagine what the prophets could have been saying, but whatever they said has poisoned the land with a "spirit of impurity." As a result, the prophets are compelled to utter a disclaimer. Quoting directly from Amos 7:14a, these so-called prophets will renounce their office. As Amos made quite clear that he was by trade a "herdsman and a dresser of sycamore trees," these false prophets will return to earning their livelihood by farming. Since prophetic ritual among groups frequently elicited self-flagellation, prophets who renounced their vocation would have to explain their bruises in other ways as an alibi (v. 6). In short, prophecy had generated so much conflict that it was tearing the community apart at the seams. Second Zechariah disassociates himself from the prophets, yet does not give up on his divinely ordained vocation to foretell the fate of the community.

THE SWORD AND THE SHEPHERD
Zechariah 13:7–9

> 13:7 "Awake, O sword, against my shepherd,
>   against the man who is my associate,"
>   says the LORD of hosts.

> Strike the shepherd, that the sheep may be scattered;
>   I will turn my hand against the little ones.
> 8 In the whole land, says the LORD,
>   two-thirds shall be cut off and perish,
>   and one-third shall be left alive.
> 9 And I will put this third into the fire,
>   refine them as one refines silver,
>   and test them as gold is tested.
> They will call on my name,
>   and I will answer them.
> I will say, "They are my people";
>   and they will say, "The LORD is our God."

These striking words continue the themes of conflict and purge so evident in the previous passage. The Lord summons the sword, an instrument of judgment, to mortally wound "my shepherd" and "associate" (cf. 11:15–17), presumably a ruler of Israel (Jer. 23:3; Ezek. 34:5). The resulting blow slays the "shepherd" as well as disperses the community, leaving only a third to survive. God will subsequently transform this remnant into a pure state of faithfulness. The language is drawn from the technology of metallurgy: Metals such as silver are subjected to intense heat in order to melt away the impurities (Isa. 48:10; Jer. 6:27–30; 9:6; Mal. 3:2). Likewise, the survivors will be refined, purified, and tested for their purity. The lasting result is a renewal of the relationship between God and the people: The people are claimed as God's own; the people claim God as their sole object of praise and adoration (v. 9). The quotations are convenantal, conveying an exclusive and intimate relationship (Exod. 6:7; Deut. 26:17–18). In short, the suffering of the leaderless, scattered flock will in the end open the way to a new order and covenant with God.

The picture given in these verses and those before is not a pretty one, full of harsh and painful images: execution, dispersal, purge, and transformation by fire. God's action is discerned amid the violent turns of human history. In such contexts, faith is more a matter of exigency than luxury. On the eve of his death, Jesus quotes from Zechariah 13:7 (Mark 14:27). He foretells that his disciples will desert him, even deny him. Nevertheless, in their failure Jesus assures them that he will be with them. As in the passage from Zechariah, the community of faith will inevitably fail in obedience and even come close to the point of utter dissolution. In the end, however, God's people will be gloriously transformed. With that hope in mind, Second Zechariah is now ready to describe in rich detail the glorious results of this transformation.

THE GLORIOUS RESTORATION
Zechariah 14:1–21

This concluding chapter is the capstone of the entire book of Zechariah. It is the climax of all that the prophet has been building toward: the consummation of history as providentially set by God. This extensive chapter can be divided into five sections, each having its own integrity and message.

The Final Battle
(Zechariah 14:1–5)

> 14:1 **See, a day is coming for the LORD, when the plunder taken from you will be divided in your midst. ² For I will gather all the nations against Jerusalem to battle, and the city shall be taken and the houses looted and the women raped; half the city shall go into exile, but the rest of the people shall not be cut off from the city. ³ Then the LORD will go forth and fight against those nations as when he fights on a day of battle. ⁴ On that day his feet shall stand on the Mount of Olives, which lies before Jerusalem on the east; and the Mount of Olives shall be split in two from east to west by a very wide valley; so that one half of the Mount shall withdraw northward, and the other half southward. ⁵ And you shall flee by the valley of the LORD's mountain, for the valley between the mountains shall reach to Azal; and you shall feel as you fled from the earthquake in the days of King Uzziah of Judah. Then the LORD my God will come, and all the holy ones with him.**

Not surprisingly, the golden rays of restoration are preceded by the storm clouds of destruction (vv. 1–2). The prophet proclaims the plunder of Jerusalem by the nations as well as the exile of half the population (v. 2). Divine victory on the day of battle is initially marked by the defeat of God's chosen people, a theme that is prominent among the earlier prophets (cf. Ezek. 30:1–4; Joel 2:1–2; Amos 5:18–20; Zeph. 1:14–18). The community of faith had become so sinful in the eyes of the prophets that the only recourse was for God to conquer the people. The remnant, however, marks a radical turn of events (cf. 13:8). Jerusalem's capture leads directly to victory over Israel's foes. Only through defeat can true and lasting victory take place. With the people purged, God fights on their behalf, against those very nations that devastated Jerusalem. God is the divine warrior who now fights *for* rather than *against* Israel.

In victory, God will stand upon the Mount of Olives. This is the only place in the Old Testament in which the Mount of Olives is mentioned by name. A ridge situated east of the city, the Mount of Olives is separated from Jerusalem by the Kidron Valley, which forms the city's eastern boundary. It is the place where David wept at the time of Absalom's rebellion (2 Sam. 15:32). Ezekiel has the Mount in mind when he describes God's "glory" resting east of the city (Ezek. 11:23). The Mount of Olives is also the site to which Jesus and his disciples depart following the Passover meal and where Jesus prays in Gethsemane, a grove on the west side of the Mount (Matt. 26:30–46).

The reference to God's "feet" is striking but not unprecedented (v. 4). Micah 1:2–4 and Amos 4:13 depict God walking upon the earth's heights with cataclysmic effect. The symbolic language is intended to display God's intervening power that not only overturns international relations but also transforms the natural order. The crushing weight of God's feet will rend the Mount in two, similar to an earthquake (see Amos 1:1). As a result, a great valley will emerge, enabling God's people to escape from Jerusalem before Israel's enemies are decimated (the place "Azal" is unknown [v. 5]). God's mighty and terrible deeds against the nations are the prelude to Israel's full restoration in the same way as the series of terrible signs and wonders of the Exodus event, the ten plagues, brought about liberation for the Hebrew slaves (Exod. 7:14–12:32; Deut. 6:21–22; cf. Zech. 14:12). As God once parted the Red Sea, God will split the mountains in order to secure Israel's safety.

The Restoration of the Land
(Zechariah 14:6–11)

14:6 **On that day there shall not be either cold or frost. 7 And there shall be continuous day (it is known to the LORD), not day and not night, for at evening time there shall be light.**

8 On that day living waters shall flow out from Jerusalem, half of them to the eastern sea and half of them to the western sea; it shall continue in summer as in winter.

9 And the LORD will become king over all the earth; on that day the LORD will be one and his name one.

10 The whole land shall be turned into a plain from Geba to Rimmon south of Jerusalem. But Jerusalem shall remain aloft on its site from the Gate of Benjamin to the place of the former gate, to the Corner Gate, and from the Tower of Hananel to the king's wine presses. 11 And it shall be inhabited, for never again shall it be doomed to destruction; Jerusalem shall abide in security.

This passage graphically describes the renewal of nature and society. The absence of cold and night as well as the perennial flow of waters ensure unprecedented security and prosperity in the land. No longer interrupted by the chaos of night, the day (literally, "one day") sustains an unending order throughout the land. The new creation is described in relation to the first creation, which was marked by the regular cycle of day and night (Gen. 1:3–5). Moreover, whereas the state of affairs before creation was characterized by complete darkness (Gen. 1:2), this new creation is marked by uninterrupted light. Revelation 22:5 identifies this everlasting light with "the Lord God." Indeed, Psalm 104:1–2 depicts light as an attribute of God. As the very first act of creation (Gen. 1:3), light bears a close association with God. With uninterrupted light, time, as it is known through the regular rhythm of day and night, will cease. One can no longer talk of days and weeks, the order of God's first creation (Gen. 1:1–23). Rather, the light of God will shine even in the darkest recesses of creation and the human heart.

Accompanying perpetual light are the perennial streams of "living waters." Their source is Jerusalem or Zion, the geographical center from which the waters issue forth to both the east and the west, like the river that flows out of the Garden of Eden and divides itself (Gen. 2:10). Psalm 46:4 states, "There is a river whose streams make glad the city of God" (see also Jer. 3:13; Psalm 36:8–9). Such a river is the font of blessing. Already mentioned is the "fountain" that will cleanse all sin in the community (13:1). Fertility, blessing, purity, and life all figure in this evocative image of abundant water flowing from the city of God. The prophets Ezekiel and Joel similarly identify the source with the temple itself (Ezekiel 47; Joel 3:18). Indeed, Ezekiel claims that the water from Jerusalem will even turn the saline waters of the Dead Sea into fresh water, fit for an abundance of fish (Ezek. 47:12). Such is the power of the "living waters." Such also is the power of Christ, the living water, who brings life out of death (John 4:7–15).

With the restoration of the land, the Lord asserts divine sovereignty and "will be one" (v. 9). The language echoes the famous Deuteronomic command known as the Shema, "Hear O Israel: The Lord is our God, the Lord alone" (or "is one"; Deut. 6:4). In both of these passages, the sense is not so much the unity of God, which is assumed, as it is the undivided allegiance and respect to be afforded the Lord on the day of victory and restoration. God will become the *one and only* object of adoration and praise. The Lord's sovereignty extends to all the peoples of the earth. Even the traditional enemies of Israel will in the end bow down and worship the one true God (v. 16).

The focus of the passage then moves from the divine realm to the earthly realm of Jerusalem's geography (vv. 10–11). The town of Geba lies just north of Jerusalem; Rimmon's location, however, is not certain, but evidently lies south of Jerusalem. Together, these locations presumably form the full extent of Jerusalem's environs. The hill country in which Jerusalem is situated will be leveled flat with the exception of the city itself. The Mount of Olives, earlier divided in half (14:4), will also be rendered a plain. Jerusalem shall stand in sharp relief, overlooking the land, a solitary mountain unmatched in height (see Isa. 2:2; Mic. 4:1).

The gates and other landmarks mentioned in verse 10 correspond to the geographical perimeter of the city. The Gate of Benjamin was located somewhere in the northeastern quadrant of the wall surrounding the temple, known today as the Temple Mount. The location of the "former gate" cannot be identified with certainty. The "Corner Gate" presumably lay west of the Temple Mount (2 Kings 14:13; Jer. 31:38; 2 Chron. 26:9). The Tower of Hananel, whose name means "God is gracious," was situated somewhere in the northwest area of the Temple Mount, perhaps the northwest corner itself (Neh. 3:1; 12:39; Jer. 31:38). The last landmark, the king's wine presses, was probably located south, near the King's Garden outside the southern wall of the city (Neh. 3:15). Unfortunately, the precise locations of these architectural landmarks remain elusive, since the city has been repeatedly altered since the days of Second Zechariah, most radically by King Herod during the time of Jesus.

Regardless of the architectural references, however, it is unambiguously clear that this dramatic profile of restoration ends on a note of assurance: Jerusalem will never again be destroyed. With the Lord as supreme king, Jerusalem will forever remain secure. The clash of international conflict will cease; all devices of war will be destroyed (cf. Psalm 46:8–11). The intent of the divine battle described earlier is finally revealed: God's battle is to end all battles.

The Plague (Zechariah 14:12–15)

14:12 **This shall be the plague with which the LORD will strike all the peoples that wage war against Jerusalem: their flesh shall rot while they are still on their feet; their eyes shall rot in their sockets, and their tongues shall rot in their mouths.** 13 **On that day a great panic from the LORD shall fall on them, so that each will seize the hand of a neighbor, and the hand of the one will be raised against the hand of the other;** 14 **even Judah will fight at Jerusalem. And the wealth of all the surrounding nations shall be collected— gold, silver, and garments in great abundance.** 15 **And a plague like this**

plague shall fall on the horses, the mules, the camels, the donkeys, and whatever animals may be in those camps.

This section picks up the events described in 14:3–5 with the calamity that Jerusalem's enemies will suffer. Like the previous verses, this section marks the prelude to restoration. Described is a horrible plague whose outcome is as swift as it is irrevocable against both humans and animals (v. 15). The Hebrews understood the outbreak of pestilence as divine punishment, as some do today, quite erroneously, regarding AIDS. The character of Job, who himself suffered severely from illness but nonetheless retained his integrity, counters such an assumption (Job 2:7–9; 27:1–6). In this passage, however, the plague is unequivocally described as the divine instrument designed to punish the nations that have brutalized Jerusalem. The result is death not only by disease but by violent conflict: Plague provokes panic and the inexorable slide into social chaos, reaching even Judah and Jerusalem (cf. 12:1–9).

The International Remnant
(Zechariah 14:16–19)

14:16 **Then all who survive of the nations that have come against Jerusalem shall go up year after year to worship the King, the LORD of hosts, and to keep the festival of booths.** [17] **If any of the families of the earth do not go up to Jerusalem to worship the King, the LORD of hosts, there will be no rain upon them.** [18] **And if the family of Egypt do not go up and present themselves, then on them shall come the plague that the LORD inflicts on the nations that do not go up to keep the festival of booths.** [19] **Such shall be the punishment of Egypt and the punishment of all the nations that do not go up to keep the festival of booths.**

Like the remnant of Jerusalem described in 13:8–9 and 14:2, there are survivors among the nations. Like the refined remnant of Israel, the nations will finally acknowledge God. Instead of going up against Jerusalem, they will come up in worship and reverence. The prophecies of Second Zechariah end on a strikingly similar note to Zechariah 8:20–23, with a vision of global unity grounded in common worship. And yet for Second Zechariah a warning is still necessary: For those who refuse to acknowledge God as sovereign, there is the threat of drought. Egypt, curiously, is singled out among "the families of the earth" for a different punishment: the continuation of the plague. The reason is due to Egypt's unique climate in the ancient Orient. Egypt's agriculture is based upon the ebb and flow of the Nile rather than on the amount of rainfall. Indeed, whenever famine came to the fertile crescent, immigrants would stream into Egypt, among whom were Abraham, Sarah, and the family of Jacob (Gen. 12:10; 41:52). Moreover, for Egypt to suffer from plague meant to reexperience the judgment of the Exodus.

The kind of worship that the nations are to observe is by no means generic. The prophet specifically identifies the "festival of booths," a special pilgrimage feast of the fall harvest period (Lev. 23:33–36; Deut. 16:13–15; 31:9–31), sometimes called the "festival of ingathering" or "tabernacles" (Exod. 23:16; 34:22). This festival was one among three annual events, including the passover and the festival of weeks or Pentecost, both in the spring. In the Jewish year the festival of booths occurs five days after the Day of Atonement or Yom Kippur.

All three festivals were based upon the yearly agricultural cycle but also had crucial historical and theological significance. The passover festival came to be associated with the Exodus, Pentecost with the imparting of the law on Sinai, and booths with the wilderness wanderings. It is the latter that is singled out for the nations. Celebrating this festival enabled the participants to reenact the wilderness pilgrimage from Egypt to Canaan, the promised land. The booths themselves represented the temporary dwellings or lean-tos in which the Israelites lived during this time of transition. For the prophet, this festival is all inclusive. Ezra's reading of the law to all the people took place during the festival (Neh. 8:14). In short, through this holy, festive occasion, the imperial powers will come to learn and appropriate God's word (cf. Lev. 19:16–25; Isa. 2:2–4; 56:3–8; Mic. 4:1–4).

Sanctifying the Ordinary
(Zechariah 14:20–21)

14:20 **On that day there shall be inscribed on the bells of the horses, "Holy to the LORD." And the cooking pots in the house of the LORD shall be as holy as the bowls in front of the altar; 21 and every cooking pot in Jerusalem and Judah shall be sacred to the LORD of hosts, so that all who sacrifice may come and use them to boil the flesh of the sacrifice. And there shall no longer be traders in the house of the LORD of hosts on that day.**

As the crowning mark of restoration, the prophet proclaims that even the most mundane things will achieve consecrated, holy status, an idea unthinkable in the theological mindset of Israel's priesthood. According to Leviticus, the book of priestly instructions, there were essentially three realms of life: the holy, the clean, and the unclean. The priest's job was to maintain these boundaries for the people. Only God, the temple with its furnishings, and the attendant priests were considered holy. In the new order, however, even the most ordinary things such as cooking pots and horse bells will assume the same status as the holy furnishings of the temple! No longer will sacrifice be conducted within the precincts of the temple; now it can be done anywhere and everywhere. The realm of the holy has become all inclusive. The holy precinct of the temple grounds will embrace the land in its entirety. The boundary between the holy and the profane will be removed (cf. Matt. 27:51).

That does not mean, however, that the demands of holiness are compromised. Second Zechariah ends by proclaiming that "traders" (the same word in Hebrew for "Canaanites") will no longer conduct business within the House of the Lord, a practice that the prophet evidently found reprehensible. The parallel with Christ's ejection of the money changers from the temple resonates with this prophecy (Matt. 21:12–16; Mark 11:15–17; Luke 19:45–46; John 2:13–17).

The concluding message of Zechariah is that God's holiness can be found in the most ordinary of things, even in the day-to-day experience we so often take for granted. One need not look far. As God in Christ took on flesh and dwelt among us, signs of God's sacred grace surround each and everyone of us. Presbyterian minister and theologian Frederich Buechner talks of one holy place that is very dear to him, namely a workshop attached to a barn. The smell of engine oil and wood smoke and the light streaming through the small windows evoke for him a sense of the sacred. A stark homeless shelter for families in Atlanta where I used to volunteer from time to time evokes the sense of the holy for me, more than some sanctuaries in which I've been.

From cooking pots to horse bells, Zechariah looks forward to the day when everything, down to the very least, will be infused with the awe-inspiring sanctity of God. In Christ, whose death overcame the boundary between the sacred and the profane (see Matt. 27:51; Mark 15:38; Luke 23:45), the encroachment of the holy into our lives and world has already begun, "so that God may be all in all" (1 Cor. 15:28).

Malachi

Introduction

As the last book in the collection known as the Twelve Prophets in the Hebrew canon, Malachi is the final book in the Old Testament Christian canon. Whether "Malachi"—the name means "my messenger" or "angel"—is the author's proper name or a title taken from 3:1 cannot be decided with certainty. Lamentably, the author's life is shrouded in obscurity except for what can be inferred from his message. The matters with which Malachi was primarily concerned place him somewhere in the first half of the fifth century B.C., when the issues of the integrity of the priestly office and administrative control over the temple were prominent.

Given the dominant themes of sin, judgment, repentance, and the day of the Lord in the book, Malachi has traditionally been considered a prophet. However, in light of the fact that many standard features of prophetic speech (for example, the introductory formula "Thus says the Lord" and the formal announcement of judgment) are strikingly absent in the book, coupled with Malachi's strong interests in the priesthood and sacrificial system, it is equally plausible that Malachi was a priest who adopted, in part, the language of the prophets. Moreover, the literary style of the book is that of question-and-answer or disputation (1:1–4:3), a form of rhetoric that can be derived from priestly as well as prophetic speech.

Whatever Malachi's vocation precisely may have been, there is no doubt that his book is essentially about the integrity of the priestly office and what it means to serve God in worship and daily life. Malachi aligns himself with a particular priestly circle—the Levitical priesthood (2:4–6)—over and against a rival priesthood that had gained control over the temple after it was rebuilt in 516/515 B.C. While condemning the abuse of priestly power and corrupt worship, Malachi considers himself no less than a reformer, calling both his priestly colleagues and the larger community to renewed fidelity to Yahweh's covenant. Malachi accuses his people of committing worship offenses, entering into mixed marriages, divorcing, and failing to tithe, all violations of God's covenant with Israel.

To be sure, Malachi's message extends far beyond his own historical situation. Though addressing himself specifically to the bitter conflicts of his day (like the "church fights" of today), Malachi was able to apprehend the larger picture of God's redemption for all. Indeed, the New Testament interprets Malachi as pointing straight to the advent of Jesus, particularly as it was announced by John the Baptist (see comments on 4:5). It is no wonder then that Malachi concludes the Old Testament as a preface to the New Testament in the Protestant Christian canon.

THE TITLE
Malachi 1:1

> 1:1 An oracle. The word of the LORD to Israel by Malachi.

Most likely an editorial preface to the prophecies beginning in 1:2, this introductory note affirms that the book is God's word to Israel through Malachi. *Oracle* (literally "burden" in the Hebrew) is a technical term that frequently signifies a prophetic message of a judgmental nature (cf. Nah. 1:1; Zech. 9:1; 12:1; Isa. 13:1; Jer. 23:33–38). The first verse of Malachi introduces the three parties that figure crucially in the message of the book: the Lord, from whom comes the word; Israel, who receives the word; and Malachi, the human, earthen vessel through whom the word is communicated.

GOD'S PREFERENTIAL LOVE
FOR ISRAEL
Malachi 1:2–5

> 1:2 I have loved you, says the LORD. But you say, "How have you loved us?" Is not Esau Jacob's brother? says the LORD. Yet I have loved Jacob ³ but I have hated Esau; I have made his hill country a desolation and his heritage a desert for jackals. ⁴ If Edom says,"We are shattered but we will rebuild the ruins," the LORD of hosts says: They may build, but I will tear down, until they are called the wicked country, the people with whom the LORD is angry forever. ⁵ Your own eyes shall see this, and you shall say, "Great is the LORD beyond the borders of Israel!"

These four verses comprise the first of six messages given by Malachi. Fundamental to Malachi's message is his opening pronouncement of God's word of love toward Israel. Indeed, it constitutes the very foundation to everything Malachi will say in criticism of Israel subsequent to this pronouncement of love.

The Lord's proclamation of love echoes the words of the prophet Hosea in 11:1. Whereas Hosea employs the language of the Exodus to illustrate God's compassion for Israel, Malachi draws from the traditions concerning Isaac's two sons (Gen. 25:19–34; 27:1–45; 32:1–33:20; 36:1–43). Jacob, the younger of the twins, was chosen by God over Esau. The family story of Jacob's reception of his father's blessing to the exclusion of Esau points to the historical establishment of Israel over and against its neighbors, in particular Edom, represented by Jacob's brother (Gen. 36:1–43). Southeast of Palestine, the territory of Edom was a constant source of conflict throughout Israel's turbulent history, ending on a thoroughly sour note: The Edomites were accused of having had a culpable hand in the destruction of Jerusalem (586 B.C.), which the prophet Obadiah described as nothing less than a despicable act of betrayal (Obad. 11–14). By Malachi's time, Edom had been desolated. For Malachi, this was Edom's "just-deserts," clear evidence of God's convenantal love for Jacob (Israel).

Malachi employs the language of love and hatred to set in sharp relief God's preferential kindness toward Israel. In Romans 9:13, Paul quotes Malachi 1:2 to demonstrate God's free elective love and cites Exodus 33:19 in conjunction: "I will have mercy on whom I have mercy, and I will have compassion on whom I have compassion" (Rom. 9:15). Similarly, Malachi stresses the inscrutable nature of God's free love. God's "yes" to Israel involves a "no" to Edom. Israel is the sole object of God's sovereign love. The rationale behind such severe exclusion is never offered by Malachi. Israel does not deserve God's favoritism as surely as Jacob, that cunning character who deceived both his brother and father, did not earn it.

However, it must be noted that Malachi's assertion of God's exclusive love for Israel is made in the midst of an internal dispute between Malachi and the people of Israel, for Malachi's claim of God's preferential love is immediately placed into question once it is uttered (v. 2). Concrete illustration is demanded, to which Malachi offers the example of Edom's demise and reminds Israel of its identity in Jacob. In short, Malachi's dispute is *not* with the Edomites; it is with his own people. Malachi hopes to persuade his people Israel to give due praise and honor to the One who

freely extends mercy with an undying love and whose majesty extends far
beyond territorial boundaries (v. 5).

PRIESTLY MISCONDUCT
Malachi 1:6–14

> 1:6 **A son honors his father, and servants their master. If then I am a father,
> where is the honor due me? And if I am a master, where is the respect due
> me? says the LORD of hosts to you, O priests, who despise my name. You
> say, "How have we despised your name?" 7 By offering polluted food on my
> altar. And you say, "How have we polluted it?" By thinking that the LORD's
> table may be despised. 8 When you offer blind animals in sacrifice, is that
> not wrong? And when you offer those that are lame or sick, is that not
> wrong? Try presenting that to your governor; will he be pleased with you or
> show you favor? says the LORD of hosts. 9 And now implore the favor of God,
> that he may be gracious to us. The fault is yours. Will he show favor to any
> of you? says the LORD of hosts. 10 Oh, that someone among you would shut
> the temple doors, so that you would not kindle fire on my altar in vain! I
> have no pleasure in you, says the LORD of hosts, and I will not accept an of-
> fering from your hands. 11 For from the rising of the sun to its setting my
> name is great among the nations, and in every place incense is offered to my
> name, and a pure offering; for my name is great among the nations, says the
> LORD of hosts. 12 But you profane it when you say that the Lord's table is pol-
> luted, and the food for it may be despised. 13 "What a weariness this is," you
> say, and you sniff at me, says the LORD of hosts. You bring what has been
> taken by violence or is lame or sick, and this you bring as your offering! Shall
> I accept that from your hand? says the LORD. 14 Cursed be the cheat who has
> a male in the flock and vows to give it, and yet sacrifices to the Lord what
> is blemished; for I am a great King, says the LORD of hosts, and my name is
> reverenced among the nations.**

This extensive section is filled with harsh criticism of worship as it was
conducted in Malachi's day. Whereas his first speech addressed all Israel,
Malachi now addresses the priests who conduct the temple sacrifices. The
material in 1:6–14 amounts to an indictment. Then, as we shall see, 2:1–9
issues a judgment against the priests.

The particular issue of contention for Malachi is the purity of worship,
specifically the quality of animals used for sacrifice. Malachi indicts his
colleague priests for offering animals that are blind, lame, sick, and blem-
ished. The Levitical code, by contrast, required sacrifice of a male without blemish from the flock or herd (Lev. 22:20). Anything else was de-

clared unacceptable, even an animal with an "itch" (Lev. 22:22)! The quality of sacrificial animals, however, meant more than simply passing "grade A" inspection. Offering unfit animals was nothing less than a violation of sacred space and an affront to God's holiness. Malachi develops his case by first accusing his colleagues of not showing due honor and respect to God by despising the Lord's name (1:6).

Elsewhere in the Old Testament, despising God is considered to be the inevitable result and offense of violating the sacred norms of worship. For example, in 1 Samuel 2:29–30 there is the account of the abuse of worship committed by Eli's sons, Hophni and Phineas, who both committed sexual misconduct at the entrance to the tent of meeting and ate the choicest parts of the offering to God. Malachi's stress on God's name acknowledges that the priests had everything to do with the Lord's name in worship (Lev. 18:21). The priests ensured that God's name was honored through correct worship. The name of the Lord was as holy as the temple was sacred (Lev. 20:3). Given the fact that they themselves were holy by virtue of their office (Lev. 21:6), the priests had special responsibilities in the use and discharge of the Lord's name, as in the great Aaronic blessing (Num. 6:24–27). That is also why taking the Lord's name in vain was considered a flagrant violation of God's covenant (Exod. 20:7; Deut. 5:11, Lev. 19:12; 24:10–23; Jer. 29:23).

Similar to verse 2, Malachi's audience responds with a series of questions that prompt Malachi to be more specific in his indictment. With great rhetorical flair, Malachi suggests that by carelessly offering polluted food at the Lord's table, the priests show greater deference to their governor, a provincial administrator of the Persian empire, than to the Lord! Furthermore, God condemns the priests for their all too casual attitude toward worship. The priests complain of the tiresome chores of worship. Afflicted with intense boredom, they denigrate the priestly office for their careless lack of interest in their sacred responsibilities. The reference to them "sniffing" at God (1:13) suggests perhaps the weary sighs of arrogant priests who could not care less. By admitting defective sacrifices to the altar, the priests stand accused not simply of carelessly exercising their duties but of adopting an attitude of apathy and arrogance as they carry them out.

Squarely laying the blame on his priestly colleagues, Malachi offers them a way to rectify the situation by exhorting them to implore God's grace. However, he doubts that repentance is possible and bitterly laments over the absolute futility of conducting worship behind the temple doors. God's rejection of their offering seems irrevocable (1:10). In order to highlight the gravity of the offense, Malachi stresses that God's sovereign realm extends far beyond the provincial boundaries of Israel (1:5, 11, 14). God's name is "great among the nations" and "reverenced among the nations." Malachi contrasts the authenticity of worship conducted by dispersed Jews "among the nations," who must live and worship far from the temple, with the impure worship conducted by the temple priests. Beyond the boundaries of the "holy land," God's name is reverently honored, but within the homeland it is profaned, a lamentable situation indeed! Sacral worship is found to be rotten at the very core, within the precincts of the one and only temple of the Lord of hosts.

Malachi addresses a perennial problem that all who minister to others in God's name must face at one time or another: the danger of treating the responsibilities and duties of such a vocation as routine, merely going through the motions of pastoring and serving others. For the prophet, to fall into such a trap profanes the high calling of ministry, plain and simple. The vocation must be taken with utmost care and gravity. It is a serious business that does not dull one's spirit, but rather enlivens it as it is, in turn, enlivened by the Spirit. When the joy of ministry is lost, when the gravity of the office does not probe the depths of one's very being, when the practice of ministry does not elicit a sense of awe-struck excitement and passionate care, then the trap is sprung. The result, as Malachi is quick to point out, is disaffection and despisement of one's calling.

THE FAILURE
OF THE PRIESTHOOD
Malachi 2:1–9

2:1 **And now, O priests, this command is for you.** [2] **If you will not listen, if you will not lay it to heart to give glory to my name, says the LORD of hosts, then I will send the curse on you and I will curse your blessings; indeed I have already cursed them, because you do not lay it to heart.** [3] **I will rebuke your offspring, and spread dung on your faces, the dung of your offerings, and I will put you out of my presence.** [4] **Know, then, that I have sent this command to you, that my covenant with Levi may hold, says the LORD of hosts.** [5] **My covenant with him was a covenant of life and well-being, which I gave him; this called for reverence, and he revered me and stood in awe of my name.** [6] **True instruction was in his mouth, and no wrong was found on his lips. He walked with me in integrity and uprightness, and he turned many from iniquity.** [7] **For the lips of a priest should guard knowledge, and people should seek instruction from his mouth, for he is the messenger of** the LORD of hosts. [8] But you have turned aside from the way; you have caused many to stumble by your instruction; you have corrupted the covenant of Levi, says the LORD of hosts, [9] and so I make you despised and abased before all the people, inasmuch as you have not kept my ways but have shown partiality in your instruction.

Malachi immediately follows his indictment with a "command" from God, cast as a judgment against the priests. Their refusal to give due glory to God's name necessitates the pronouncement of a curse by the prophet/priest, a curse that is specifically leveled against the priestly blessing. Malachi's pronouncement ironically (and quite subversively) alludes to the Aaronic blessing in Numbers 6:24–26. Intended to impart divine favor and well-being upon the people, the benediction was undoubtedly a standard blessing used in the Jerusalem temple at the conclusion of worship. Like the pastor of a church, the priests in ancient Israel had the privilege of giving the blessing. For Malachi, however, God's judgment against the priests twists this solemn blessing into a curse (cf. Num. 6:24 with Mal. 2:2). That the Lord will spread dung on the priests' faces and—literally in the Hebrew—"lift you up to it," is a graphic inversion of the final stanza of the priestly blessing of Yahweh's favor directed toward the people (Num. 6:26). Malachi's judgment regarding the priests' perversion of their office could not be more severe!

Malachi follows up judgment with a portrayal of the ideal priest by appealing to the "covenant of Levi." Levi, the third son of Jacob (Gen. 29:34), became the tribe that was never allocated territory because it was singularly chosen to serve God as priests (Josh. 18:7). Jeremiah 34:21–22 mentions a covenant with Levi and the covenant with Aaron's grandson Phinehas (Num. 25:12), in which God promises an enduring priesthood for his descendants. Such language resembles Malachi's description of the levitical covenant. By tradition Levites were renowned for their zeal for God, having aligned themselves with Moses against their kin after the "golden calf" episode (Exod. 32:25–29; cf. Deut. 33:8–9). Indeed, it was over such loyalty that Moses pronounced the ordination of the sons of Levi "for the service of the Lord" (Exod. 32:29). This tradition serves as background and testimony to the Levites' reverence before God's name.

The covenant to which Malachi refers includes the blessing of life and well-being (cf. Exod. 32:29b), as well as the call for reverence. The teaching role of the Levitical priest echoes the job description of Levitical functions listed in Deuteronomy 33:9b–10, in which the priesthood was regarded as the repository of the knowledge of God. Imparting right instruction or torah (vv. 6, 8) was the essential mark of the priestly office.

According to Malachi, the priest is no less than the "messenger of the Lord of hosts," (see introduction and 3:1), a high calling indeed! In addition to the abuse of sacrificial practice described in 1:7–10, Malachi accuses his colleagues of imparting false instructions, in particular of showing partiality, in strict violation of the covenant.

The vehemence with which Malachi condemns the priests in this section points to hostile relations between rival priesthoods. Malachi squarely sides with—if not identifies himself with—the Levitical priests, who for several centuries were in bitter dispute with a "denomination" of rival priests who also appealed to Levi as a common ancestor in the period after the exile. Beginning with the monarchy, particularly with Josiah's reform (2 Kings 23:8–9), rivalry between these priestly houses only intensified. As such, Malachi's accusations are the product of an "in-house" dispute over the integrity of the priestly office. Yet the fact that Malachi views the controversy as "in-house" and not a full-fledged schism betrays his hope for the unity and renewal of the priesthood (see 2:17–3:5).

UNITY IN MARRIAGE AND GOD
Malachi 2:10–16

> 2:10 **Have we not all one father? Has not one God created us? Why then are we faithless to one another, profaning the covenant of our ancestors?** [11] **Judah has been faithless, and abomination has been committed in Israel and in Jerusalem; for Judah has profaned the sanctuary of the LORD, which he loves, and has married the daughter of a foreign god.** [12] **May the LORD cut off from the tents of Jacob anyone who does this—any to witness or answer, or to bring an offering to the LORD of hosts.** [13] **And this you do as well: You cover the LORD's altar with tears, with weeping and groaning because he no longer regards the offering or accepts it with favor at your hand.** [14] **You ask, "Why does he not?" Because the LORD was a witness between you and the wife of your youth, to whom you have been faithless, though she is your companion and your wife by covenant.** [15] **Did not one God make her? Both flesh and spirit are his. And what does the one God desire? Godly offspring. So look to yourselves, and do not let anyone be faithless to the wife of his youth.** [16] **For I hate divorce, says the LORD, the God of Israel, and covering one's garment with violence, says the LORD of hosts. So take heed to yourselves and do not be faithless.**

After expressing judgment against the priests, Malachi urgently appeals to all Israelites by highlighting their common theological heritage. The key motif that begins and ends this passage is the number one. It is the *one* God who created human beings (v. 10) and demands faithful *unity* in marriage (vv. 14–16). With compelling words, Malachi roots the convenantal sanctity of marriage in the very unity of God. Consequently, to sever the bond of marriage not only violates the marriage covenant (v. 14b) but profanes *the* covenant, the bond of unity between God and Israel, and ultimately fractures the unity of Israel's identity that is uniquely grounded in the Creator.

The crisis to which Malachi is urgently responding is one that threatens to destroy the singular distinctiveness of Israel, namely its identity as a chosen people under pagan domination (that is, Persia). The problem, however, is not simply one of Israelites marrying foreigners. Malachi accuses Israelites of divorcing their spouses "by covenant" *in order to* marry foreigners. To highlight the gravity of the situation, Malachi sets divorce and violence side by side (v. 16). His appeal is based on humane as well as theological grounds. The prophet's stress on unity in marriage strongly echoes the language of Genesis 2:24: Husband and wife are of one flesh in marriage, as ordained in creation. Malachi pushes marital unity further by appealing directly to God's unity. In order to acknowledge God's unity, one must also work for common unity, that is, *community*, whose most intimate and basic form is marriage. By implication, to fracture such a bond of unity is a renunciation of the oneness of God's gracious and commanding nature. Faithlessness to one's spouse constitutes nothing less than a breach in God's solidarity with humankind, a breach that inevitably finds its way to the altar (v. 13).

"WHERE IS
THE GOD OF JUSTICE?"
Malachi 2:17–3:5

2:17 You have wearied the LORD with your words. Yet you say, "How have we wearied him?" By saying, "All who do evil are good in the sight of the LORD, and he delights in them." Or by asking, "Where is the God of justice?"

3:1 See, I am sending my messenger to prepare the way before me, and the Lord whom you seek will suddenly come to his temple. The messenger of the covenant in whom you delight—indeed, he is coming, says the Lord of hosts. 2 But who can endure the day of his coming, and who can stand when he appears?

For he is like a refiner's fire and like fullers' soap; 3 he will sit as a refiner and purifier of silver, and he will purify the descendants of Levi and refine

them like gold and silver, until they present offerings to the LORD in righteousness. ⁴ Then the offering of Judah and Jerusalem will be pleasing to the
LORD as in the days of old and as in former years.

⁵ Then I will draw near to you for judgment; I will be swift to bear witness against the sorcerers, against the adulterers, against those who swear
falsely, against those who oppress the hired workers in their wages, the
widow and the orphan, against those who thrust aside the alien, and do not
fear me, says the LORD of hosts.

This fourth speech of Malachi opens with another indictment. The people, including the priests, are accused of taxing God with their complaints
concerning the lack of divine justice in the world. An inversion of justice,
wherein the wicked prosper, prompts the question of where God is in the
face of moral contradiction. Such questions clearly have precedents in Job
(21:7–16), Jeremiah (12:1), and Habakkuk (1:2, 4, 13). Whereas the laments
of the prophets and psalmists worked toward resolving the problem of human suffering, Malachi finds only entrenched cynicism behind these complaints of the people and priests. Perhaps there is a connection between
the Lord's weariness and the priestly complaint of weariness on the job
(1:13). God is as tired of the people's constant complaints as the priests are
weary from boredom in their responsibilities. Now the priests, along with
the people, subject God to their tiresome complaints about God's governance in the world. The implication is that their complaints are at root insincere. Malachi's previous indictments against the priests and people
nowhere imply that they themselves are suffering. To the contrary, they
are profiting from new sexual liaisons, from lax priestly standards, and
from showing partiality in judgment. To complain of injustice, then, is the
height of hypocrisy!

In the form of a judgment, Malachi answers the question of where God
is by heralding the Lord's coming (3:1). First, a messenger (see 1:1) is to
come to prepare the way. Apart from the appendix in 4:5, the identity of
the messenger remains a mystery. Various commentators have suggested
all of the following: Malachi, an anonymous priest, Ezra, and an "angel."
The messenger is further qualified as one grounded in the covenant,
hence, perhaps a Levitical priest. In any case, the identity of the messenger is not as crucial in relation to the fact that the Lord is coming into the
temple (cf. Isaiah 6).

The refiner's fire and fullers' soap are powerful images in Malachi's
pronouncement of judgment. A fuller was one who bleached and dyed
cloth. The process included washing with lye and cleansing by stomping
(cf. Exod. 19:10; 2 Sam. 19:24). The cloth was then spread out on the

ground to be bleached by the sun. Equal in severity to the fuller's actions, the refiner used a blast oven to melt the metal into a liquid stage before removing the dross. As with refining and bleaching, the objective of such extreme measures on the part of the Lord is to purge and purify the priestly class of Levi, transforming the very character of the one who makes an offering to the Lord.

Judgment continues, however, in ever-expanding circles (v. 5). All of society shall be judged and transformed. The list of sins, ranging from the religious to the social, incorporates the whole of community life, whose center is the temple. The effects of insincere and false worship against which Malachi railed in 1:7–14 have spread over the entire community. Malachi, like his prophetic predecessors, sees worship and justice inseparably bound up together. Worship is not true worship unless it seeks justice for the widow, orphan, and alien (3:5).

THE BLESSINGS OF OBEDIENCE
Malachi 3:6–12

3:6 **For I the LORD do not change; therefore you, O children of Jacob, have not perished.** [7] **Ever since the days of your ancestors you have turned aside from my statutes and have not kept them. Return to me, and I will return to you, says the LORD of hosts. But you say, "How shall we return?"**

[8] **Will anyone rob God? Yet you are robbing me! But you say, "How are we robbing you?" In your tithes and offerings!** [9] **You are cursed with a curse, for you are robbing me—the whole nation of you!** [10] **Bring the full tithe into the storehouse, so that there may be food in my house, and thus put me to the test, says the LORD of hosts; see if I will not open the windows of heaven for you and pour down for you an overflowing blessing.** [11] **I will rebuke the locust for you, so that it will not destroy the produce of your soil; and your vine in the field shall not be barren, says the LORD of hosts.** [12] **Then all nations will count you happy, for you will be a land of delight, says the LORD of hosts.**

The moral force behind Malachi's indictment against the nation is founded upon the Lord's unchangeable character (v. 6). Far from a theological abstraction, divine immutability is cast in terms of its effects: The call to moral integrity and right worship is a call to unwavering constancy in practice. The corollary to God's unchanging nature is the perpetual preservation of Israel (v. 6). The fact that the people have not been consumed for violating the covenant is sufficient testimony to

God's faithfulness and forbearance (cf. Mal. 1:2–5). Similarly, Numbers 23:19 casts God's unchanging nature in terms of the certainty of divinely made promises. For Malachi, God's sustaining grace in no way vitiates the call to faithfulness. Indeed, God makes painfully clear that Israel has consistently turned aside from the divinely established laws and decrees (cf. Jer. 2:4–8). Though Israel will not perish, the people of God are nonetheless called to change in order to effect a reciprocal return between God and the people. Adherence to the law marks nothing less than a radical reorienting of the life and character of the community, a redirection that God promises to meet at least halfway.

In response to the people's question posed in 3:8, Malachi offers a concrete answer: The people must cease robbing God by fully committing their tithes and offerings for what they were intended—the upkeep of the temple. Generally, the tithe designated a tenth part of one's income for sacral purposes. Leviticus 27:30–33 states that all the tithe of the land belongs to God, including all that passes under the herdsman's staff. A different system of tithing is found in Deuteronomy 14:22–29, in which the people are exhorted to give a tithe of their agricultural produce and then eat it in the temple. In every third year, however, the tithe is to be designated for the Levite, the sojourner, the orphan, and the widow. During the time of Ezra and Nehemiah, the tithe was a tax collected at the temple to support the priests and Levites (Neh. 10:37–38; 12:44; 13:5, 12).

To Malachi, refusing to adhere to the tithe was tantamount to robbing God! Echoing 2:2, Malachi levels a curse against the nation but also offers an admonition. Cast almost in the form of a dare, Israel is challenged to test the Lord to determine the extent to which God is able to provide for Israel. God conditionally promises (cf. Hag. 1:9–11; 2:15–19) to bring about the fertility of the land by providing rain and protection from ravaging locusts (literally "devourers"). The tithe thus sets the occasion for the abundance of blessing. On the giving of a mere portion of one's own livelihood rests the livelihood of the whole of the community.

THE BOOK OF REMEMBRANCE
Malachi 3:13–4:3

3:13 **You have spoken harsh words against me, says the LORD. Yet you say, "How have we spoken against you?"** [14] **You have said, "It is vain to serve God. What do we profit by keeping his command or by going about as mourners before the LORD of hosts?** [15] **Now we count the arrogant happy; evildoers not only prosper, but when they put God to the test they escape."**

¹⁶ Then those who revered the LORD spoke with one another. The LORD took note and listened, and a book of remembrance was written before him of those who revered the LORD and thought on his name. ¹⁷ They shall be mine, says the LORD of hosts, my special possession on the day when I act, and I will spare them as parents spare their children who serve them. ¹⁸ Then once more you shall see the difference between the righteous and the wicked, between one who serves God and one who does not serve him.

4:1 See, the day is coming, burning like an oven, when all the arrogant and all evildoers will be stubble; the day that comes shall burn them up, says the LORD of hosts, so that it will leave them neither root nor branch. ² But for you who revere my name the sun of righteousness shall rise, with healing in its wings. You shall go out leaping like calves from the stall. ³ And you shall tread down the wicked, for they will be ashes under the soles of your feet, on the day when I act, says the LORD of hosts.

The last question strikes at the very heart of human indifference toward serving God (cf. 1:13 and 2:17). Moreover, laxity in the exercise of sacrificial responsibilities (1:6–13), showing partiality in instruction (2:9), and withholding God's due in the tithe (3:7–10) are all symptoms of the root problem identified in 3:14–15, namely the false perception of uselessness in serving God. Such futility is confirmed, so argues Malachi's audience, by a reversal of fortune for the wicked: Evildoers prosper and escape divine judgment, whereas, it is implied, the righteous suffer. Why, then, obey God's commandments? What's the point of serving God?

Malachi's answer comes in the form of a brief narrative (3:16): The Lord listens in on the discourse of those who revere the Lord, and then has the "book of remembrance" drawn up for the express purpose of identifying the righteous, the ones who "reflect on God's name." The reference to a written record of the names of the righteous is also attested to in Exodus 32:32–33, Psalm 69:28, Isaiah 4:3; Daniel 12:1, and Revelation 20:12, 15 ("the book of life"). To remember involves more than simply recollecting. Remembering involves active behavior by which a certain outcome is achieved. In this case, it is the selection and sparing of God's special "possession." This term of ownership identifies the people's unique relationship with God among the other peoples and nations (Exod. 19:5; Deut. 7:6; 14:2; 26:18; Psalm 135:4). In Malachi, God's possession includes only those who sincerely serve God—the righteous. Though kept on the shelf for the time being—as it were—the book of remembrance is there to preserve, in the face of present ambiguity and disparity, the distinction between those who serve God and those who refuse to do so. On the day in which God is to act, the book will be opened and its contents revealed and confirmed.

Malachi describes the heat of this day of the Lord as destructive for the wicked but soothing and life-giving for those who revere God's name. The image of the sun with wings is common in ancient Near Eastern, particularly Assyrian, pictures. The rising of the sun ushers in vindication for the righteous and a reestablishment of justice that is nothing short of cosmic in scope (see Job 38:12–13; Psalm 46:5).

THE PAST AS KEY
TO THE FUTURE
Malachi 4:4–6

4:4 **Remember the teaching of my servant Moses, the statutes and ordinances that I commanded him at Horeb for all Israel.**
5 **Lo, I will send you the prophet Elijah before the great and terrible day of the LORD comes.** 6 **He will turn the hearts of parents to their children and the hearts of children to their parents, so that I will not come and strike the land with a curse.**

The last three verses comprise two postscripts or appendices to the book. The first appendix exhorts the reader to remember Moses and his teachings (v. 4); the second, identifies the prophet Elijah as the messenger enigmatically referred to in 3:1. The common ground between these two biblical figures is a mountain. It was at Horeb (Sinai) that Moses received the laws that comprise the covenant (cf. Deut. 5:1–5). The language of this verse (for example, "statutes," "ordinances," "Horeb") points to the essential message contained in the book of Deuteronomy, itself an early work of the Levites. On the plains of Moab where Israel was poised to cross the Jordan and occupy the promised land, Moses exhorted Israel to remember the covenant that the Lord had established with them forty years earlier at Sinai. Similarly, the message of Malachi situates itself at the threshold of a new beginning in which everything will be transformed. To remember means more than simply recalling the past; it means to reenact and follow what has been set in the past in all of its potential for the present and future.

After a glance backwards at the time of Moses, the last two verses look forward to a new age to be ushered in by Elijah, whose feet were also once set on Sinai ("Horeb" in 1 Kings 19:1–18). Why Elijah? Since he was taken up to heaven by chariots with no mention of his death (2 Kings 2:10–12), Elijah could return to earth. Quoting Malachi 3:1, Jesus identifies the prophet Elijah with John the Baptist (Matt. 11:10–15; 17:9–13;

Mark 6:14–15; Luke 1:17). The new age is described as "great and terrible," and yet the final note is one of redemption rather than destruction: Elijah will reconcile parents and their children to each other. The day of the Lord is first and foremost a healing of the wounds within family and community.

It is no accident that the Old Testament begins with a family history full of strife and conflict: Adam's blame of Eve, Cain's murder of Abel, the squabbles between Abraham and Sarah, the rivalry and deception among the later generations. It is out of this conflicted and sordid background that Israel comes into being. Some would say it is the history of a dysfunctional family. It is no coincidence then that the Old Testament ends with Malachi's vision of absolute reconciliation within the family. In the end, the book of Malachi looks forward to that day when peace and unity will break out, beginning with the family.

Works Cited

Jacobs, Jane. *The Death and Life of Great American Cities.* New York: Random House, 1961.

Miller, Patrick D. "Dietrich Bonhoeffer and the Psalms." *The Princeton Seminary Bulletin* 15 (1994): 274–82.

Orwell, George. *1984.* New York: Harcourt, Brace & Co., 1949.

Wilson, James, Q. *The Moral Sense.* New York: Free Press, 1993.

For Further Reading

Obadiah

Allen, Leslie C. *The Books of Joel, Obadiah, Jonah and Micah.* Grand Rapids: Wm. B. Eerdmans Publishing Co., 1976.

Coggins, Richard J., and Re'emi, Paul S. *Nahum, Obadiah, Esther: Israel Among the Nations.* International Theological Commentary. Grand Rapids: Wm. B. Eerdmans Publishing Co., 1985.

Jonah

Fretheim, Terence E. *The Message of Jonah.* Minneapolis: Augsburg Publishing House, 1977.

Limburg, James. *Jonah.* Old Testament Library. Louisville, Ky.: Westminster/John Knox Press, 1993.

Micah

Alfarso, Juan I., O.S.B. *Justice and Loyalty: A Commentary on the Book of Micah.* International Theological Commentary. Grand Rapids: Wm. B. Eerdmans Publishing Co., 1989.

Mays, James L. *Micah.* Old Testament Library. Philadelphia: The Westminster Press, 1976.

Wolff, Hans Walter. *Micah the Prophet.* Translated by R. D. Gehrke. Philadelphia: Fortress Press, 1981.

Nahum

Achtemeier, Elizabeth R. *Nahum-Malachi.* Interpretation. Atlanta: John Knox Press, 1986.

Coggins, Richard J., and Re'emi, Paul S. *Nahum, Obadiah, Esther: Israel Among the Nations.* International Theological Commentary. Grand Rapids: Wm. B. Eerdmans Publishing Co., 1985.

Mason, Rex. *Zephaniah, Habakkuk, Joel.* Old Testament Guides. Sheffield: JSOT Press, 1994.

Roberts, J.J.M. *Nahum, Habakkuk, and Zephaniah.* Old Testament Library. Louisville, Ky.: Westminster/John Knox Press, 1991.

Habakkuk

Achtemeier, Elizabeth R. *Nahum-Malachi.* Interpretation. Atlanta: John Knox Press, 1986.

Mason, Rex. *Zephaniah, Habakkuk, Joel.* Old Testament Guides. Sheffield: JSOT Press, 1994.

Roberts, J.J.M. *Nahum, Habakkuk, and Zephaniah.* Old Testament Library. Louisville, Ky.: Westminster/John Knox Press, 1991.

Zephaniah

Achtemeier, Elizabeth R. *Nahum-Malachi.* Interpretation. Atlanta: John Knox Press, 1986.

Mason, Rex. *Zephaniah, Habakkuk, Joel.* Old Testament Guides. Sheffield: JSOT Press, 1994.

Roberts, J.J.M. *Nahum, Habakkuk, and Zephaniah.* Old Testament Library. Louisville, Ky.: Westminster/John Knox Press, 1991.

Haggai

Achtemeier, Elizabeth R. *Nahum-Malachi.* Interpretation. Atlanta: John Knox Press, 1986.

Jones, Douglas R. *Haggai, Zechariah and Malachi*. London: SCM Press, 1962.
Petersen, David L. *Haggai and Zechariah 1–8*. Old Testament Library. Philadelphia: The Westminster Press, 1984.

Zechariah

Achtemeier, Elizabeth R. *Nahum-Malachi*. Interpretation. Atlanta: John Knox Press, 1986.
Jones, Douglas R. *Haggai, Zechariah and Malachi*. London: SCM Press, 1962.
Petersen, David L. *Haggai and Zechariah 1–8*. Old Testament Library. Philadelphia: The Westminster Press, 1984.
Petersen, David L. *Zechariah 9–14 and Malachi*. Old Testament Library. Louisville, Ky.: Westminster John Knox Press, 1995.

Malachi

Achtemeier, Elizabeth R. *Nahum-Malachi*. Interpretation. Atlanta: John Knox Press, 1986.
Jones, Douglas R. *Haggai, Zechariah and Malachi*. London: SCM Press, 1962.
Petersen, David L. *Zechariah 9–14 and Malachi*. Louisville, Ky.: Westminster John Knox Press, 1995.